ST. FRANCIS
OF ASSISI

ST. FRANCIS
OF ASSISI

WRITINGS FOR A GOSPEL LIFE

Regis J. Armstrong, O.F.M. Cap.

CROSSROAD • NEW YORK

1994

The Crossroad Publishing Company
370 Lexington Avenue, New York, NY 10017

Printed in the United States of America

Library of Congress Cataloging-in-Publication Data

Armstrong, Regis J.
   St. Francis of Assisi : writings for a gospel life / Regis J.
Armstrong.
      p.   cm. — (Crossroad spiritual legacy series)
   Includes bibliographical references.
   ISBN 0-8245-2501-9
   1. Francis, of Assisi, Saint, 1182-1226.   2. Theology—History—
Middle Ages, 600-1500.   3. Catholic Church—Doctrines—History.
I. Francis, of Assisi, Saint, 1182–1226.   Selections.   1994.
II. Armstrong, Regis J.   III. Title.   IV. Series.
BX2179.F64A8   1994
271'.302–dc20   94-847
                                                                  CIP

Contents

Foreword

Writing in the fourth century a North African Christian by the name of Lactantius offered the following definition of virtue. For him, virtue is nothing less than "enduring of evils and labors." How unlike contemporary notions this definition of virtue is and how odd it sounds for us to be told so plainly that the fullness of life can be had only through enduring evils and trials. Yet, despite our inclination to write off Lactantius as an overly pessimistic nay-sayer, we must admit that life does include a large dose of suffering. We can take it well or badly. We can flee it or embrace it, but it will come and find us wherever we hide, and then it will test our mettle. Virtue does involve suffering evils, not simply actualizing ourselves, or conquering our fears, or visualizing success, or learning techniques to cope with stress, or building better "relationships" with members of the opposite sex. There are things in life that simply cannot be so easily manipulated. Situations that don't get better. Unpleasant realities that won't go away. Where do we turn when confronted by them?

We can turn to the externals, to our comforts and our conveniences, to the superficialities of our lives, or we can turn to our depths. Many who have lived before us have learned the hard way that turning to the depths is the way to a fuller life. Their insights have been handed down, often in forms that are now hard to find and harder to read. Their language is archaic. Their morality out of sync with ours. Their clarity, off-putting. Their humility, disconcerting. Yet they are there, waiting quietly to share with us their hard-won wisdom, waiting to dialog with us as we face situations that are different from those they encountered only in the particulars, not in the essences.

Simply put, that is the reason why Crossroad, myself, and a team of well-known scholars and spiritual leaders have joined together to undertake the Spiritual Legacy series. The need for spiritual wisdom is great. Our situation is critical. This then is more than an enterprise in scholarship, more than a literary exercise. It is an effort to convey life.

Certainly the idea of doing editions of the works of spiritual guides from the past is not new. There are a host of books available that do just that. How is the Spiritual Legacy series different?

The uniqueness of this series abides in its content and its style. In content it endeavors to present both texts from the spiritual guide and extensive commentary by a present-day disciple of the sage. It gives the reader the chance to encounter for herself the writings of a spiritual master. Nothing can take the place of that experience. However demanding it might be, whatever efforts it might require, there can be no substitute for it. One, for instance, cannot simply hear a description of the tenth chapter of Augustine's *Confessions*. No commentary, however skilled, can take the place of reading for oneself Augustine's words of unparalleled power: "Late have I loved Thee, O Beauty, so ancient, yet so new!"

While it is true that there is no substitute for encountering the text firsthand, it is also certain that for most people that encounter will be an excursion into a foreign land. Often many centuries and numerous barriers of language, customs, philosophy, and style separate us from the writings of bygone sages. To come to that point where we can understand the horizon of the author, we must be taught something about the historical context, the literary style, and the thought forms of the age, for instance. That is why we have included in this series extensive commentary on the text. That commentary is alternated with the text throughout the books, so that one can be taught, then experience the writings firsthand, over and over as one moves deeper into the text. At that point, the horizon of the reader meets that of the author, aided by the expert guidance of the editor of each book, who suggests not only what the text might mean, but how it might be made part of our lives.

The style of the Spiritual Legacy series is also unique in that it attempts to convey life with a certain degree of sophistication that befits an educated readership. Yet it does not assume that everyone will have a background in the material presented, nor does it purport to offer original or arcane scholarship. The editors' mastery of the texts is in each case complemented by their experience in putting the meaning of the texts into practice and helping others to do so as well. We are trying to present a series of books that will fit somewhere between the scholarly editions that pride themselves on their accuracy and originality and the popular pieces that offer too little substance for the healthy reader.

The series is designed to be used by a broad range of people. For those seekers who wish to journey toward spiritual wholeness as part of a group, the series is ideally suited. The texts presented can be easily divided into sections for discussion by a group meeting, say, on a weekly basis.

For those who are traveling alone, the series is a trustworthy and enjoyable tour book. The direct, simple language of the commentaries frames the memorable words of the classical texts and offers them in an attractive setting for meditation and practical application.

The publisher and editors of the Spiritual Legacy series join me in inviting you to undertake a journey that will take you back to an encounter with ancient wisdom and challenge you to an experience of self-understanding and, at its best, self-transcendence. It is our hope that that experience will help you to grow and to be a source of fresh life for all those around you.

John Farina

Preface

Deceptively simple: such a description aptly applies to the writings of Francis of Assisi. We can read them ever so quickly and mistakenly believe that we have absorbed their riches. Those of us who have attempted to study the relatively few writings of Francis know how they continually surprise and challenge us. Here are the reflections of a simple, down-to-earth, thirteenth-century man who discerned the stirrings of the human heart and whose words resonate deeply to all who read them.

This is not meant to be a scholarly work as much as an introduction to Francis's writings. If it achieves nothing else, it will hopefully encourage its readers to struggle more intensely with Francis's approach to the mystery of God and to realize that, more than anything else, he teaches us a method, a way of discovering, from a lived experience of the gospel, how good God is.

I owe an expression of gratitude to my students from so many parts of the world who have taught me so well. Asians, Latin Americans, Africans, Europeans, North Americans: we have been united in learning the universality of our poverty and of God's love that satisfies it. Yet I owe special debts of thanks to John M. Aexel, who has never hesitated in urging me to express my insights in language as simple and concrete as that of Francis; to John Farina, editor of this series, who patiently prodded and guided me; and, to Crispin Maguire, O.F.M., who, as a true brother, read, criticized, and offered suggestions.

The translation of Francis's writings found in this volume is a new translation by this author. It will appear in *Francis of Assisi: Early Documents*, a thorough, scholarly edition of the saint's writings and biographies soon to be published by New City Press.

As I write, the words of St. Augustine resonate deeply: "I confess then, that I attempted to be one of those who write because they make some progress and who, by means of writing, make further progress."

Introduction

On a dusty Kenyan road a longtime missionary asked me if I knew that the Qur'an claims that everyone is a Muslim at heart. "Of course," he remarked, "St. Augustine maintains that everyone is a Christian at heart. But isn't it also true that everyone is a Franciscan at heart?" I had never heard that sentiment before that moment, but years of teaching Franciscan spirituality throughout the world prompted me to concur. There truly is something about Francis and his vision of God, the human person, society, even the world of creation that has spoken and continues to speak deeply to all of us.

What is so curious about that phenomenon is that most of our knowledge of Francis does not come from his writings but from what others saw in him. Biographies of Francis appeared shortly after his death and kept appearing; in fact, so many were published that in 1266 the friars issued a decree prohibiting any further attempts at writing Francis's biography, but the decree was ignored. People were restless with the portraits of Thomas of Celano and Bonaventure and, in many cases, turned to their imaginations to supply stories or images of the saint to whom they could so easily relate. To this very day, Francis continues to capture our imagination and to absorb our poetic skills. Who was this man? What so inspired him that he has become such a universally beloved saint? Spanish, Danish, Japanese, American — people of all nationalities and cultures have struggled to tell this medieval Italian's story and to communicate what they see as his secret.

For many centuries, only a few of Francis's writings attracted attention. This neglect may have come from a dissatisfaction with the simple, unadorned medieval texts that seem to speak from a distant time and world. Anyone who has had the experience of trying to open up Francis's vision through his writings alone will know how futile the attempt is without referring to his life. The comment of one thirteenth-century observer who tells us that Francis wrote poorly undoubtedly provides an insight into why Francis's writings were neglected for so long. While other religious authors — for example, Dante and Bonaventure, who were both followers of St. Francis — may have challenged by their uplifting, provocative writings, Francis of Assisi spoke more by his life.

In our own age, Francis's writings have been given greater attention. The Second Vatican Council's call to return to the "spirit of the founders" prompted a closer look at the writings. As a result, Francis himself has spoken to us during the past fifteen years as never before. While we still turn to his biographers, we have now examined his writings in a scholarly manner, translated them into a number of languages and dialects, and made them available to an ever-increasing audience. Francis would undoubtedly cringe at the thought that his writings have been computerized and analyzed. This has enabled us to study the patterns of his words and has given us a clearer view of his understanding of the gospel and its way of discipleship. We have examined his writings in the context of the tumultuous society of Assisi and in light of the conciliar and postconciliar period in which he lived and have discovered new insights from Francis himself. What have these writings taught us?

In the first place, Francis unwittingly tells us of his humanity. The first generations of his followers corrected most of his spelling and grammatical mistakes for fear of revealing a less than perfect saint. So his letters, advice, and prayers are undoubtedly more polished than when he wrote them. Yet he still speaks to us in passages and phrases that confuse or mystify us. While his biographers portray Francis as generally speaking forthrightly and clearly, he presents the image of one whose thoughts and insights matured and grew more refined and developed as events and those around him challenged his idealism. His struggle to know what God was asking of him resonates with our own: relentless, at times confusing, and frequently challenging. When we consider that Francis pursued God's will as he made his way through the streets of Assisi and the highways of Italy, France, Spain, and the Middle East, we identify even more with his search. His was not the world of the monastic enclosure in which everything was meant to reflect the wonders of heaven. No, his was the world of the ordinary laborer or of the homeless poor. While the Earlier Rule offers a powerful understanding of the gospel, Francis supplies enough clues that even a very casual reading tells us that its plan of gospel life matured over a period of twelve years. Such a consoling thought — that Francis was, indeed, like those of us who find our gospel idealism continually challenged and sharpened — should prompt us to wonder about his secrets. What were the means he used to grow so profoundly in the spirit of the gospel? Are they limited to someone living in thirteenth-century Italy or so timeless that they are useful for us?

Francis's discovery of a gospel spirituality coincided with his appreciation of two of its most important teachings: the calls to be poor and to recognize our universal human kinship. "This is what I want! This is what I desire with all my heart!" he shouted at hearing Jesus proclaim the gospel as a poor itinerant. Suddenly he did exactly as the gospel demanded: he threw away his cloak, his leather belt, even his sandals and began preaching the wonder of salvation and the promise of peace.

Francis teaches us through his writings that we should look at everything through the prism of poverty. That is undoubtedly his most wonderful contribution to our pursuit of a gospel life. He began, as we should, with an embrace of a material poverty — casting aside whatever his father, Pietro, had provided for his future and then even whatever the church had permitted him as a hermit. Yet that was the beginning of his lifelong journey of poverty. Material poverty enabled him to embark upon a daily stripping away of all that to which he truly clung, his natural talents, his dreams, even his visions for his brothers and sisters. As he looked deeply into his heart, he began letting go of what most of us overlook as part of our appropriations: our anger and hurts, our concern for our good name, even our vices and sins. Poverty, in other words, became the privileged means Francis discovered to ensure a life of true penance, of turning totally to the Lord who so graciously satisfied his every need. It also revealed to him the bond that he shared with his fellow human beings and with all creatures. Who was he after all? Another of God's creatures called to praise and reflect the infinite greatness, power, and goodness that he encountered each day.

The life of poverty, then, is not an end in itself for Francis; it is rather an integral part of our calling as human beings. Poverty, in short, became a means by which Francis deepened his recognition of our fraternity.[1]

That fraternity was clearly one of the outstanding characteristics of Francis's gospel life. Not that others had not accentuated it before him. Christian spirituality certainly sang its praises from the time of Paul. Yet Francis brought the image of Christ our brother ever so forcefully into the spotlight. "Oh how happy and blessed are we to have...such a brother, our Lord Jesus Christ," he proclaimed over and again. It was as if he never fully realized the impact of the Word becoming flesh and living among us. Not only was Francis overwhelmed by this incarnate revelation of God; he also seems challenged by the role this "older" brother plays in showing him how to win the love of their common Father.

Christ taught Francis that we are all related to one another as brothers and sisters. "Only one is your father," he discovered in the Gospels, and he took Jesus at his word. As others were attracted to his message, Francis taught them that simple vision of gospel life.[2] Theirs would be a fraternity. Regardless of living alone in hermitages or as itinerant missionaries, they were related to one another. There would be no hierarchy of superiors and subjects, no pecking order of authority, no class distinctions based on work or ministries. No, only a gathering of those eager to follow the path of Christ. If there were any distinctions, they were based quite simply on Christ's example of loving service. To be a "superior" meant in Francis's mind to be, as Jesus, at the feet of the others.

The simplicity of Francis's gospel vision makes it apparent that he sought direction primarily in God's Word. Not only

---

1. If there is any term that has been "sanctified" in Franciscan vocabulary, it is "fraternity" or "fraternal life." Among all Franciscans, women as well as men, Francis's accent on fraternity is considered — together with poverty — *the* Franciscan charism.

2. Curiously, he never uses the word "community." Is there a difference between community and fraternity? In Francis's world there is! The concept of people living in a particular place (Webster's first definition) is foreign to Francis's writings since he envisioned not only an itinerant way of life but also the reality that, wherever we might be, we are all related to one another as members of one family.

was it the center of his life, it was also the glue that held it together. His Earlier Rule, a vibrant description of his life as a brother written over a span of twelve years, is a collage of biblical phrases and images that speak eloquently of a gospel brotherhood. The Later Rule, a precise synthesis written for final papal approval, is called "the marrow of the gospel." Yet Francis would have his followers focus their energies on receiving the words of Scripture into their hearts each day and letting those words form and shape their lives and ministries. The Word of God was indeed a two-edged sword, he realized, that cut through the myths and fictions of their lives and enabled them to build upon the only foundation that was reliable, Christ.

It is difficult to determine to which characteristic Francis gave preference, poverty or fraternity. The one depends on the other: poverty demands dependence on others, while brotherhood and sisterhood become more tangible by the daily letting go of whatever makes us smug or comfortable not only materially but also in our relationships. In any case, poverty and fraternity are fundamentally at the service of the Word. This is the genius of Francis: a poor person conscious of his or her bond with others approaches the mystery of God differently.

At no time was this expressed so clearly as when Francis and his first two followers approached the Gospel Book to learn how God wanted them to live. These three men had already sold their possessions and given them to the poor. Poor themselves, they were united in a common enterprise, their journey to God. Yet as poor brothers they discovered God's Word anew; they heard the gospel as poor people who were related to and dependent on one another. There is a certain simplicity in that, a simplicity founded on discovering our humanity. Somehow poverty frees us to accept ourselves for what we truly are and empowers us to see one another as reflections of ourselves. Through the prism of simplicity, the gospel becomes ever more wonderful and the message of Christ ever more simple.

In the attic of a friary in northern Wales, the English poet Francis Thompson, struggling to overcome his addictions, wrote of what he had discovered was the unique trait of the followers of Francis, simplicity:

Franciscan simplicity itself needs definition. It is not an ignorant simplicity — the simplicity of the peasant. It consists, mainly, in the contentment of every man to be and appear just what he is. It matters not what his birth. He may be the son of a landowner or a ploughman; may have the refined speech of a cultivated man, or the rough speech of a peasant; equally he has the same unaffected dignified standing on his own basis — dignified, because it is unaffected. This unassertive taking for granted that he is just *himself* combined with matter-of-fact thoughtfulness of others, makes him a gentleman whatever his trick of speech or manner. It causes every stranger to feel himself domesticated with him. It is this lofty and unsought genuineness which makes the true poet take to the Franciscan and the true Franciscan to the poet. For the Franciscan embodies in himself the poet's ideal, which is sensitive and candid self-realization — the spontaneous candor of a child combined with adult consciousness while he has the native amity towards his fellow-mortals which, in the poet, is too often absorbed by egoism. Two things in this world *are* poetry — and luckily do not know it — the child and the Franciscan.

The simplicity of the gospel: the phrase captures Francis's approach to life. Nothing else mattered but living the gospel wholeheartedly. In doing so as a poor brother to all, Francis has continually captured the imagination of men and women throughout the world. The Kenyan, the Ilicano, the Colombian, the Hawaiian, the New Yorker: they are but a few who have struggled to incarnate the gospel simplicity of Francis of Assisi, for at heart everyone is indeed a Franciscan.

Who Is Francis of Assisi?

Francis di Bernardone was born in 1182 in Assisi, a small Umbrian city precariously perched on the borders of the Papal States and the Holy Roman Empire. While we know very little about Francis's childhood, an offhand comment of one of his later biographers, St. Bonaventure of Bagnoreggio, indicates that he received his primary education at the Church of San Giorgio, probably under the guidance of one of its priests, who would have attempted to train the boy in the liberal arts. The priest did not succeed in developing Francis's scholarly skills, but he certainly nurtured his sensitivity to languages, images, and the pros and cons of learning for learning's sake. For as the young man matured, so did his ability to observe, intuit, and express his experiences of the mysterious ways of an all-good God who continually surprised him.

As we read the history of Assisi during Francis's youth, we quickly sense how desirable and vulnerable it was. This must have been painfully obvious to the son of a cloth merchant whose business would have been so dependent on access to the Via Franca, the principal highway linking Assisi with cities — and, therefore, markets — north and south. Perched as it was on Monte Subasio, Assisi became increasingly strategic, and its citizens became adept at detecting any movement along this vital artery. We should not be surprised, then, that the citizens of Assisi, emboldened by their position, warded off any attempts to master them.

In 1198, when Francis was sixteen, the members of the Commune of Assisi attacked the Rocca Maggiore, the fortress of the feudal nobility, where only a year or so earlier Frederick II, the future emperor of the Holy Roman Empire, had been born. This was essentially an act of civil war that pitted members of Assisi's nobility against the newly powerful members of the rising merchant class. Ironically, the two sides represented not only Francis, son of the ambitious merchant, Pietro di Bernardone, but also Clare di Favarone, the young daughter of an aristocratic family whose ancestry could be traced to Charlemagne himself. Buoyed by this act of defiance, the Assisiani looked beyond their city walls, so that the ebb and flow of war touched almost every family. In 1202, however, things changed. The Battle of Collestrada was an engagement of two ancient rivals, the Assisiani and their archenemies, the hated men of Perugia. Arnaldo Fortini, who meticulously studied all the documentation of this period in Assisi's archives, maintains that this was the city's bloodiest skirmish. As the Perugians overwhelmed the Assisiani, they were literally beaten into the ground or dragged off to prison.

While we do not have any record of Francis's involvement in

the uprising of 1198, we can easily imagine the sixteen-year-old joining in the destruction of the Rocca, that symbol of feudal tyranny, and in the noisy proclamation of the new order. But we do have knowledge of the young man's role in the Battle of Collestrada; that is, we know that he was one of those imprisoned in Perugia. At his release, Francis returned to Assisi in broken health. But dreams of military glory continued to fill his imagination, so that the drudgery of working in his father's business made him increasingly restless.

In 1205 the twenty-three-year-old set off to join the military campaign of Walter of Brienne, a famous and dashing knight. He had traveled no further than Spoleto when he was laid low by illness. During his recovery, Francis had a dream that made him wonder if he were meant for a military career. He dreamt of a hall filled with military weapons and heard someone ask him: "Is it better to serve the lord or the servant?" "The lord," he replied. "Then why," he heard, "do you serve the servant?" The questions haunted the young man and initiated an intense, restless search that was characterized by periods of solitude, pilgrimage, and experimentation. At one moment we find him exchanging clothes with a beggar, at another wrestling with the unknown in a cave somewhere beyond Assisi.

Curiously, Francis tells us little about these events. We find nothing of his renunciation of a military or business career. Even the question of that significant dream is passed over. We can only discover reminiscences in his *Testament*, a curious document Francis seems to have written at various moments toward the end of his life. He describes the beginnings of his conversion in these simple words:

> The Lord gave me, Brother Francis, thus to begin doing penance in this way: for when I was in sin, it seemed too bitter for me to see lepers. The Lord Himself led me among them and I showed a heart full of mercy to them. When I left them, what had seemed bitter to me was turned into sweetness of soul and body. Afterwards I tarried a little and left the world.

While Francis tells us little about that departure from "the world," he does provide us with a remarkable insight into his understanding of penance. Unlike so many of his contemporaries who identified themselves as "penitents," Francis's first step toward God was the embrace of a human being who, at the time, was considered the most despicable: the leper. This was — and no doubt is — a primary characteristic of his approach to God: the search for the transcendent among the outcasts of society or even of one's family or friends.

Until this moment, Pietro and his wife, Pica, appear as supporting, even understanding, parents. It doesn't demand much imagination to conceive of the demands their restless son placed on their patience. A decisive moment occurred, however, while Francis was kneeling before a crucifix in the deteriorating chapel dedicated to St. Damian and heard yet another voice. "Francis," it said, "go and repair my house which, as you see, is falling into ruin." Responding to this call, Francis sold his horse and some cloth from his father's shop, trying Pietro's patience and alienating his support. Not only did Pietro have Francis denounced as a thief; he also appealed to the bishop of Assisi for justice. In a dramatic scene, Francis repudiated his father and returned even the clothes he was wearing. Standing naked before his friends and neighbors, he exclaimed: "No longer do I call Pietro di Bernardone my father, but the Father who is in heaven!" It was a decisive moment in which Francis began a new life and a far more penetrating search of what was God's will.

But once again we are bereft of any information beyond the sketchy facts of Francis's brief stay in Gubbio and his return to Assisi to fulfill the mandate he received from the crucifix, to rebuild the little Church of St. Damian. All Francis's early biographers suggest that rebuilding churches was a characteristic activity of Francis at this stage — he went from St. Damian's to St. Peter della Spina to Our Lady of the Angels, the "Portiuncula." In the last of these, Francis heard a proclamation of Matthew's Missionary Discourse that made a lasting impression upon him. "This is what I want!" his biographers tell us he proclaimed. "This is what I desire with my whole heart!" Perhaps more important than the actual words that the young Francis heard was the dynamic they initiated. For we find two concepts — life and gospel — coming together in a bold, creative way. Francis burst upon the world as a poor, itinerant evangelizer proclaiming a simple message of peace and salvation. He did so in such simplicity and with such energy that he was bound to attract followers. Within a short while three men joined him: Bernard of Quintavalle, a wealthy citizen of Assisi; Peter Catanii, a lawyer; and Giles, an illiterate Assisiano with a burning desire for prayer. Together these four men began a brotherhood dedicated to that poor, simple, itinerant life Francis had heard described at the Portiuncula.

We should turn to Francis's own description of what followed:

> After the Lord gave me some brothers, no one showed me what I had to do, but the Most High Himself revealed to me that I should live according to the pattern of the Holy Gospel. I had this written down simply and in a few words and the Lord Pope confirmed it for me. Those who came to receive life gave *whatever they had* (cf. Tob. 1:3) to the poor and were content with one tunic, patched inside and out, with a cord and short trousers. We desired nothing more. We clerical brothers said the Office as other clerics did; the lay brothers said the *Our Father*; and we quite willingly remained in churches. We were simple and subject to all.

The dynamic was important. Francis returned to the Scriptures to receive insight into God's will. But this time he was joined by those men he regarded as brothers, and together they discovered the pattern of gospel life that would be theirs. We will repeatedly notice this same approach: Francis points beyond himself to the Word of God, and his brothers form the context and highlight the profoundly relational spirituality that would become the Franciscan tradition.

By 1209 there were twelve brothers. They set off for Rome to receive papal approval for their "form of life." We do not know what the brothers showed Pope Innocent III. The biographers suggest what we would suspect: only a simple collection of quotations from the Gospels and some minor prescriptions necessary for their life together, for example, recitation of the Liturgy of the Hours, manual work to support themselves, and the like. In any case, the sincerity of Francis and his brothers inspired the pope to give them oral approval so that they could live under the protection of the church without fear of being accused of heresy, as were some of the other renewal groups of the day. Thus they returned to Assisi as a recognized, approved group of penitents and began to attract more and more followers, among them Clare of Assisi, a beautiful young woman who had already achieved a reputation for her commitment to the spiritual life.

A few years later, Innocent III announced his intention to convoke an ecumenical council. In November 1215, bishops, heads of religious orders, and members of royalty gathered in Rome to celebrate the Fourth Lateran Council and to respond to the pope's concerns. Christianity needed to be revitalized, he maintained, to stop the enervating heresies spreading throughout Europe and to organize a new Crusade that would prevent seizure of the Holy Land by the Muslims. We do not know anything of Francis's presence at what historians have called the "great council of the Middle Ages," but we can easily recognize its influence on him and his followers. Within a few years the brothers changed the direction of their lives to implement many of the council's mandates: regular chapters for the renewal of religious life, care and concern for the education of preachers, proper respect for the sacraments of the Eucharist and Penance, and so on. Francis himself embarked upon his own Crusade to the Near East, fearlessly dialogued with the sultan, and undoubtedly witnessed the fierce Battle of Damietta on August 29, 1219.

By the time of his return to Assisi in the fall of 1220, the number of Francis's followers had expanded. Not only were the brothers living in new and frequently challenging circumstances, but the Poor Ladies of St. Damian's (the Sisters of Clare) and the Brothers and Sisters of Penance (those lay followers unable to give themselves completely to a religious way) were encountering unfamiliar challenges as they attempted to live the gospel ideals underscored by their guide. Francis assisted them all. Clare tells us that he wrote many letters and words of encouragement to the Poor Ladies. The Brothers and Sisters of Penance received a commonitorium or reminder of the exhortation Francis had given them much earlier. In addition to recalling the principles of his approach to a penitential life, it highlighted the concerns of the council about the dangers of heretical influences in the evangelical movement of the day. But the brothers themselves joined Francis in developing their original form of life in light of the new circumstances and challenges that faced them. New structures had to be conceived so that the intimate sense of brotherhood could be maintained. Attention had to be paid to the physical needs of the growing fraternity and to the observance of the vision of poverty that inspired everyone. While the brothers had been addressing these and other issues from the very beginning, Francis's stay in the Near East undoubtedly caused them to value more highly his inspiration and insight. Thus the final additions to the Earlier Rule, a document incorporating and building upon the document presented to Pope Innocent III, reflect the collective wisdom of both Francis and his brothers: Francis recognizing their role in helping him understand the gospel, the brothers respecting his unique gifts in revealing the penetrating power of God's Spirit. As we read the writings from the period shortly after Francis's return from the Near East, we might wonder if they reveal a more refined, to-the-point expression of his ideals. The maturity and conviction that they exhibit unquestionably came from ten or more years of living intensely the gospel ideals that originally inspired him. The ideals were nurtured and refined so that the writings of this period reflect his commitment to the God he had discovered in the Gospels and whose presence he discerned in his fellow human beings, especially the poor and down-trodden. Within the following two years, 1222 and 1223, Francis was constrained to refine his vision of the brothers' gospel life. In the fall of 1223, Pope Honorius III placed the papal seal on the Later Rule, which has remained *the* rule of the Friars Minor to this day.

Now that the rule was firmly in place, Francis faced the deeper personal question of the direction of his own life. Drawn to a life of solitude and prayer but also to the gospel mandate of preaching, he turned to Clare and the Poor Ladies and to one of his earliest followers, Sylvester, asking their help in discerning God's will. Should he devote his life to prayer or to preaching? Their answer was clear: he should continue as he had begun, continuing his role of being a herald of Christ. Thus in the remaining years of his life we can discern an ongoing movement between contemplative listening to the Lord speaking to his heart and preaching the God whom he had encountered and experienced in his long hours of solitude. In both activities, Francis appears a man consumed by a humble and passionate love for Christ in his two principal mysteries: the Incarnation and the Redemption.

Two events of this period clearly bring this focus on Christ to our attention: the miracles of Greccio and LaVerna. The first occurred during the Midnight Mass of Christmas 1223, when visitors to the poor hermitage of Greccio saw, in Bonaventure's words, "a beautiful little boy asleep in the crib whom Francis embraced in both of his arms and seemed to awake from sleep." The second took place in September 1224, during a lengthy time of prayer on LaVerna, a mountain in Tuscany. Francis experienced a moment of ecstasy during which he was caught up in a mystical embrace of the Crucified Christ. When he returned to his senses, he discovered the stigmata, the marks of Christ's wounds, on his hands, feet, and side. Of all the countless portrayals of Francis that have appeared throughout the centuries, these two images — Greccio and LaVerna — have best captured the popular conception of his holiness and appeal. Throughout the centuries artists have depicted Francis kneeling tenderly over the manger with the Infant Jesus in his arms or kneeling in awe before the six-winged seraph in the form of the Crucified One.

Curiously, in Francis's writings we find very little about these events. His writings verify what Francis himself frequently emphasizes: a determination to hide the gifts the Lord has bestowed on him. The small piece of parchment that he left Brother Leo, the close companion who was with him on LaVerna, suggests the mystical experience he had enjoyed and through which he realized God's creative presence in every aspect of life. His "Praises of God" echoes with the simple phrase "You are..." and leaves the impression of a man who recognized that God's ever-present goodness was the sustaining power of his life. We can see the overflow of this consciousness most clearly in Francis's poetic masterpiece, the "Canticle of Creation," a hymn to God's grandeur and to that of all creation. "Most High, all powerful, good Lord,..." he sings, "Praised be You, my Lord, with all your creatures." Although exhausted by his physical austerities and blind from an eye-disease, the stigmatized mystic was able to burst into the praises of the creative God who was present in all things.

Slowly but surely the strength ebbed from his body. With his brothers gathered around him, Francis died at Our Lady of the Portiuncula, the very place where he had first heard the gospel call. It was the evening of October 3, 1226. His body was slowly carried to the city for burial in the Church of San Giorgio. (It was later moved to the magnificent basilica built in his honor.) Within two years, his friend Cardinal Hugolino, now Pope Gregory IX, canonized him and, in doing so, sang the praises of God whose marvelous deeds are renewed in every age.

How Do We Approach Francis's Writings?

Unfortunately we possess only thirty-eight of Francis's writings. While we know that he wrote many other pieces, we can only imagine what they might have contained. Even during Francis's life, they were neglected, set aside, and lost. But how do we approach those thirty-eight writings of Francis that we now possess? How we classify them says something about ourselves. Were we to approach them with a legalistic mind, we would undoubtedly begin with Francis's rules, placing all other writings — his letters and prayers, for example — in second place. As a historian, we might consider viewing the writings from the perspective of those who influenced them or through a prism of socioeconomic issues that were present in the thirteenth-century Umbrian Valley. If we were teaching spirituality, we might look at these texts thematically, choosing certain values or themes in order to ensure their presence in our consciousness. We might even approach them from a strictly literary viewpoint and divide them as works of poetry or prose.

For our purpose, it might be best to approach Francis's writings chronologically, beginning with his prayer of conversion, that is, the "Prayer before the Crucifix," and concluding with the last strophe of the "Canticle of the Creatures." In this way we can easily follow Francis's growth and the development of his insights and relate to him not as "the saint" but as one who, like ourselves, is eager to pursue a gospel way of life.

There is, however, one considerable disadvantage to this

method: many of Francis's writings cannot be accurately dated. Neither the biographical material nor the writings themselves provide any information concerning the circumstances or the time of their composition. In a sense, these writings stand in midair. The "Praises to Be Said at All the Hours" is an example. Not only does it not contain any clues as to the circumstances of its composition; we are also without any internal data that would help us place it in a definite period of Francis's life. It is somewhat timeless. But we can use this to our advantage because, with these writings, we have an opportunity to concentrate on their theological content. This is certainly not an ideal way to reflect upon Francis's thought, as if it simply dropped from heaven, but it does enable us to look more intently at the substance of this thought rather than at the forces or circumstances that shaped it. What we will probably discover is that our awareness of these more "abstract" theological themes will add to our understanding of the more historical texts.

But what is the most beneficial way to approach Francis's writings individually now that we have arranged them in a chronological order? Many people favor looking at them in a very literal way, analyzing the words Francis uses, the overall structure of each piece, and the precise meanings of words and phrases. Others prefer to place Francis's writings in their historical, socioeconomic contexts in order to perceive the effectiveness of his prophetic mission and the external forces that shaped his gospel vision. Still others attempt to study these writings from the perspective of mysticism, that is, as the reflections of one who was caught up in the presence of God and saw the world through its prism. Our threefold approach (described below) to Francis's simple writings embraces all of these tendencies and offers us an opportunity to reflect upon the writings from the three perspectives of spirituality highlighted by theologians such as Philip Scheldrake, Sandra Schneiders, and Bernard McGinn.

The approach used here is based upon the recognition that a person's spirituality must embrace three realities: personal experience, culture, and tradition. Obviously, our personal experiences influence our perceptions of God, of one another, and of the world in which we life, and they also influence our struggles to live virtuously. From this perspective we can see the formative influences of the Christian tradition as well as the socioeconomic culture of Assisi upon Francis's writings. But we should also consider how his own experiences of poverty, powerlessness, and fraternal life shaped his responses to that tradition and culture.

All of which suggests that any good spirituality reflects an ongoing dialogue between an individual, a tradition, and a culture. What is true of us is equally true of Francis of Assisi. Thus one of the most challenging aspects of reading his writings is that of discovering and identifying what forces are evident in them, whether those forces be passages from the Gospels, the affluence or power Francis experienced at some period of his life, or literary devices and expressions typical of his time.

If we keep this triad in mind, we will discover how the writings of Francis provide us not only a rich source of insights into his gospel spirituality but also an effective methodology in discerning what Christ asks of us in our journey in his footprints.

Part One

Writings from the Early Period to 1223

"A Prayer for Conversion"

Francis immediately places before us the prayer of his conversion. We most frequently associate it with that moment when, early in his life, he walked into the badly neglected Church of St. Damian and knelt before its crucifix. But praying this simple prayer with Francis, we might wonder if it would not be better to place it at an earlier period, for example, during those initial encounters with God when, as his biographers tell us, he struggled to know what God was asking of him. Thus it is an ideal piece with which to begin, for it prompts us to search for its meaning in a context to which we can relate rather than a time and place so distant from us.

> Most High,
> glorious God
> enlighten the darkness of my heart
> and give me
> correct faith,
> certain hope,
> and perfect love,
> sense and knowledge,
> Lord,
> that I may carry out
> Your holy and true command.

All of Francis's biographers characterize his early experiences as centered on knowing God's will. His earliest biographer, Thomas of Celano, describes those first agonizing periods as ones in which Francis frequented the caves on Monte Subasio. "He was so exhausted with the strain," Thomas writes, "that one person seemed to have entered, and another to have come out." Francis repeatedly urges us to discover the will of God. His writings convey the impression of someone whose life was an unending pursuit of knowing and fulfilling what God was asking of him. In fact, he summarizes his whole approach to life in his Earlier Rule when he tells us: "Now that we have left the world, we have nothing else to do but to follow the will of the Lord and to please Him." Even in the last years of his life, he wrote a prayer that expresses this: "Almighty, eternal, just and merciful God, give us miserable ones the grace to do for you alone what we know you want us to do and to desire always what pleases you." Thus he teaches us that our conversion is essentially linked with not only turning to God but also discovering God's will.

This is the only prayer, however, in which Francis uses the first-person singular; all his others are strikingly universal and all-embracing. If this prayer were uttered in some fashion at the time of his embrace of a leper, that decisive moment when, as he tells us, he "began to do penance," was that momentary brush with another's misery sufficient to make the young Francis realize his own sinful humanity? History is filled with individuals with similar experiences who have impressed us with their enormous capacity to enter into human pathos: Damien DeVeuster of Molokai, Dorothy Day, and Oscar Romero, to mention but a few of our more contemporary Christians. The "I" is replaced by "we." A smug, self-righteous judging of others is replaced by a consciousness of sharing the same sinful reality and an identification with the worst of sinners. Yet such an awareness demands a maturity that calls us continually beyond the narrow confines of our own world to that of another.

This makes Francis's request of his transcendent God so remarkably simple: "enlighten the darkness of my heart." How frequently he directs our attention to the struggles of our hearts! Forty-eight times he points to the heart, challenging us to discover its condition or its whereabouts. There is no formalism or tokenism in his notion of conversion. No, Francis offers us a journey of the heart as he continually leads us to give more generously and spontaneously out of love. By focusing on our heart, Francis encourages us to probe, to concentrate on, and to direct its mysterious ways. "Enlighten the darkness of my heart...." This is the prayer of someone who has learned that conversion is a lifelong process, one in which self-deception can so easily prevent us from coming to grips with the uncharted depths of our being.

Francis would have us pray for the theological virtues of faith, hope, and charity, the heart's fundamental strengths. What is striking, however, are the qualities that Francis would have adorn these virtues: "a *correct* faith, a *certain* hope, a *perfect* love." We might scoff at Francis's simple faith in the clergy of his day, many of whom were uneducated; or in theologians, some of whom he knew were caught in their own arrogance or personal agenda; or even in the hierarchy, some of whom he was well aware were overwhelmingly concerned about the use of their power. But this was the Francis who described himself as "stupid and simple"; he was confident that the Lord alone would provide him with a "correct faith." While we might be tempted to consider Francis's audacious poverty impractical and naive at least by today's standards, it is only understandable in light of the unshakable hope he placed in a totally good God who, he knew, would provide for his every need. "Only when things are hopeless," G. K. Chesterton maintains, "does hope have any meaning at all" (Chesterton 1925, 159). Francis embraced a poverty that forced him to turn away from his own resources to rely totally upon God. His was an attitude of unwavering hope, one that enabled him to let go of everything. Moreover, every page of his writings reveals a person eager to love God and his fellow human being ever more purely and selflessly. His was a restless, never-ending pursuit of a love that could be found only in and according to God, a flawless love without blemish, without any holding back. Thus he would direct our prayer for a *correct* faith, a *certain* hope, a *perfect* love.

What does Francis mean, however, when he would have us pray for "sense and knowledge to carry out [God's] command"? There is a temptation to interpret this as a request for the grace of discernment. But is it that refined? Probably not. It may well be simply a prayer for a sense of direction or an indication of where the Lord would lead us. How often we approach God in a quandary, not knowing what is expected of us and struggling with some decision. At such times, doesn't our prayer frequently become one for certitude or for a clear direction? Yet Francis would have us pray only for insight, an inkling or a sense of what God would have us do. Nothing could be simpler and more down-to-earth. Exactly what we would expect from the young Francis.

This prayer was overlooked for years; then, because of its somewhat polished style, friars embellished it and attempted to make it more relevant. Moreover, it has taken on the characteristics of a prayer associated more with a place, before the crucifix of St. Damian's, than with a period of one's life. Some authors have rejected this prayer, claiming that it is too cold and lacking in Francis's élan. Others prefer to see the influence of the liturgy upon this prayer, maintaining that Francis was only echoing the Roman Missal. In fact there is a similarity between this prayer and one offered on the twelfth Sunday after Pentecost: "Lord Jesus Christ, Who are the light of the world, Who enlighten the darkness of my mind, give me correct faith and perfect hope. Grant that I may always know, speak, and do your will. Amen." But why reject this prayer simply because it may have been influenced by the liturgy? Such an influence gives it more credence and even teaches us to listen more attentively to the liturgical formulas in order to ask God for the proper things.

In any case, Francis offers us a marvelous prayer of conversion, one that we might use continually as we attempt to deal with the shadows of our hearts and to turn more fully to the Lord. One of Francis's first followers, Clare, undoubtedly knew of this prayer; a passage of it appears in her *Testament* as she describes her own "conversion."

Clare, the "Little Plant"

Events moved quickly and decisively once Francis responded to the call of the Crucified One, "Rebuild my house which, as you see, is falling into ruin." The dramatic clash between father and son before Assisi's Bishop Guido, the impulsive flight to Gubbio after rejecting Pietro and all he represented, and the humble return to fulfill the Lord's command: these were three further steps that prepared the soil of Francis's heart for the seed of the gospel that was soon to be planted.

While laboring at St. Damian's, Francis began to invite those who passed by to join in his project. Although his companions describe the scene, Clare, Francis's *pianticella* (little plant), offers us a more powerful account in her *Testament.* "At that time," she writes, "climbing the wall of that church, [Francis] shouted in French to some poor people who were standing nearby: 'Come and help me in the work [of building] the monastery of St. Damian, because one day ladies will dwell here who will glorify our heavenly Father throughout His holy, universal Church by their celebrated and holy manner of life.'" It would be a while before Clare and her followers would move into St. Damian's and actualize Francis's prophetic vision of the neglected church, but we can't help imagining that, even as he was shouting to passers-by, he was looking for the women who would fulfill his dream.

Six or seven years after he heard the call of the Crucified Christ, Francis wrote a "form of life" for Clare and her few companions. We find it in Clare's rule with this simple introduction: "When the Blessed Father saw we had no fear of poverty, hard work, trial, shame, or contempt of the world, but, instead, regarded such things as great delights, moved by compassion he wrote a form of life for us as follows":

Because of divine inspiration you have made yourselves daughters and servants of the Most High King, the heavenly Father, and have taken the Holy Spirit as your spouse, choosing to live according to the perfection of the Holy Gospel, I resolve and promise for myself and for my brothers always to have the same loving care and solicitude for you as [I have] for them.

Is this simple statement the entire form of life that Francis gave to Clare? Hardly. Elsewhere she writes: "Afterwards he wrote a form of life for us, especially that we always persevere in holy poverty." What happened to his counsel on poverty? We will never know. Nevertheless, what little we have tells us a great deal of Francis's understanding of the spiritual life centered on the gospel.

Francis begins straightaway by calling us to look into our motivations. Are we moved, he asks, by *divine inspiration?* Medieval authors use the phrase "divine inspiration" in discussing the divine origin or inspiration of Sacred Scripture. They base its use upon 2 Tim. 3:16: "All Scripture is inspired by God and is useful for teaching the truth, rebuking error, correcting faults, and giving instruction for right living." In doing so, they underscore the close bond between the Word of God and the Holy Spirit. Francis, however, applies the phrase to Clare's life and those of her followers, as we will later see he also does to his followers. What does he mean by describing them as moved by "divine inspiration"? Undoubtedly Francis perceived the Spirit of God working in the same way: guiding them in the truth, correcting their errors and faults, and teaching them how to live. In a sense, he provides us a tool of discernment to guide us in knowing if we too are acting under the guidance of the Holy Spirit.

Only now does he invite us to share his profound vision of the spiritual life. It is really the first time that we see him offering the contours of the gospel life he envisions for all, a life that expresses quite simply the inner life of the triune God. To be a child of God, "the heavenly Father," is a dimension that Francis himself had openly declared as the foundation of his life when he proclaimed to all his fellow citizens that it was no longer Pietro di Bernardone who was his father but God. But that, he realized, is the call of all. This does not negate that "Old Testament call" to be a servant of the Most High King. On the contrary, it only focuses our attention more clearly on the life and example of Jesus, *the child* who pleased his heavenly Father by embracing the life of a slave. What could Francis mean, however, when he writes of taking the Holy Spirit as a spouse? The reference must be to the Virgin Mary, who, by her consent to the angel's call, was the espoused of the Spirit and then became the Mother of God. In fact, we will discover Francis speaking of Mary in the same way when we read the antiphon he addresses to her at the opening of the *Office of the Passion.* But now we encounter what will soon become obvious: the Marian foundations of Francis's spirituality. The choice, then, to pursue the perfection of the gospel has relational and dynamic reasons. What else could it mean to be a child of God than to model our lives on that of Jesus? With the power of divine love overwhelming us, how could we not strive continually to live the gospel life?

For years scholars and others were tempted to describe this Trinitarian vision from the perspective of the friars alone. In our day, however, a wonderfully new appreciation of Clare and her sisters allows us to see how Francis envisioned this life for all who came to him for insight into a life of penance. Even then his prophetic vision must have grasped how powerfully their enclosed, hidden life speaks eloquently of the indwelling of God in our souls and of the mystery of the pregnant Mother of God who carried within her womb God's presence. His promise of caring and showing solicitude for those who share that same trinitarian life flowed naturally because of his conviction that it made us all members of one family. This is so very clear when we look at the way in which he encouraged those men and women who came to him unable to be professional religious but who desired, nonetheless, to follow his gospel insights.

The Call to Penance

All of Francis's early biographers write of the power of his exhortations to penance. "Men were running, as were women," Thomas of Celano tells us, "clerics hastened and religious rushed to see and hear the holy man of God." Undoubtedly they heard this or some similar exhortation to a life of penance:

In the Name of the Lord!

Those Who Do Penance

All those who love the Lord *with their whole heart, with their whole soul and mind, with their whole strength* (cf. Mark 12:30) and love their neighbors as themselves (cf. Matt. 22:39), who hate their bodies with their vices and sins, who receive the Body and Blood of our Lord Jesus Christ, and who produce worthy fruits of penance (cf. Luke 3:8): O how happy and blessed are these men and women while they do such things and persevere in doing them, because *the Spirit of the Lord will rest upon them* (cf. Isa. 11:2) and *make* Its home and *dwelling-place* in them (John 14:23), and they are children of the heavenly Father (cf. Matt. 5:45) Whose works they do, and they are spouses, brothers, and mothers of our Lord Jesus Christ (cf. Matt. 12:50).

We are spouses when the faithful soul is joined by the Holy Spirit to our Lord Jesus Christ. We are brothers to Him when we do *the will of the Father Who is in heaven* (Matt. 12:50). We are mothers when we carry Him in our heart and body (cf. 1 Cor. 6:20) through a divine love and a pure and sincere conscience and give birth to Him through a holy activity that must shine as an example before others (cf. Matt. 5:16).

O how glorious it is to have in heaven a holy and great Father! O how holy, consoling to have such a beautiful and wonderful Spouse! O how holy and how loving, gratifying, humble, peace-giving, sweet, worthy of love, and, above all things, desirable: to have such a Brother and such a Son, our Lord Jesus Christ, Who laid down His life for His sheep (cf. John 10:15) and prayed to His Father, saying:

Holy Father, in your name, save those (John 17:11) *whom you have given me in the world; they were yours and you gave them to me* (John 17:6). The *words that you gave to me I have given to them, and they accepted them and* believed *in truth that I have come from you and* they have known *that you have sent me* (John 17:8).

I pray for them *and not for the world* (cf. John 17:9). Bless and sanctify them (John 17:17); *I sanctify myself for them* (John 17:19). *I pray not only for them, but for those who will believe in me through* their *word* (John 17:20) *that they might be* sanctified *in being one* (cf. John 17:23) *as we are* (John 17:11).

I wish, Father, that where I am, they also may be with me that they may see my glory (John 17:24) *in your kingdom* (Matt. 20:21). Amen.

Those Who Do Not Do Penance

All those men and women who are not living in penance, who do not receive the Body and Blood of our Lord Jesus Christ, who practice vice and sin and walk after the evil concupiscence and the evil desires of their flesh, who do not observe what they have promised to the Lord, and who in their body serve the world through the desires of the flesh, the concerns of the world and the cares of this life: They are held captive by the devil, whose children they are and whose works they do (cf. John 8:41). They are blind because they do not see the true light, our Lord Jesus Christ. They do not possess spiritual wisdom because they do not have the Son of God, the true wisdom of the Father. It is said of them: *Their wisdom has been swallowed up* (Ps. 107:27 [V 106:27]) and *Cursed are those who turn away from your commands* (Ps. 119:21 [V 118:21]). They see and acknowledge, know and do evil and knowingly lose their souls.

See, you blind ones, deceived by your enemies: the flesh, the world, and the devil, because it is sweet for the body to sin and it is bitter to serve God, for every vice and sin flow and *proceed from people's heart* as the Lord says in the Gospel (cf. Matt. 15:19ff.; Mark 7:21ff.). And you have nothing in this world or in that to come. And you think that you will possess this world's vanities for a long time, but you are deceived because a day and an hour will come of which you are not thinking, which you do not know, and of which you are unaware when the body becomes weak, death approaches, and it dies a bitter death. And no matter where, when or how a person dies in the guilt of sin without penance and satisfaction, if he can perform an act of satisfaction and does not do so, the devil snatches his soul from its body with such anguish and distress that no one can know [what it is like] except the one receiving it.

And every talent, ability, *knowledge and wisdom* (2 Chron. 1:12) they think they have will be taken away from them (cf. Luke 8:18; Mark 4:25). And they leave their wealth to their relatives and friends who take and divide it and afterwards say: "May his soul be cursed because he could have given us more and acquired more than what he distributed to us." Worms eat his body and so body and soul perish in this brief world and they will go to hell where they will be tortured without end.

In the love which is God (cf. 1 John 4:16) we beg all those whom these words reach to receive those fragrant words of our Lord Jesus Christ written above with divine love and kindness. And let whoever does not know how to read have them read to them frequently. Because *they are spirit and life* (John 6:63), they should preserve them together with a holy activity to the end.

And whoever has not done these things will be held accountable *before the tribunal of* our Lord Jesus *Christ* (cf. Rom. 14:10) *on the day of judgment* (cf. Matt. 12:36).

Francis offers us a disarming program of penance embracing five points: (1) a thorough love of God, (2) love of neighbor modeled on that of self, (3) consideration of the body infected with sin, (4) reception of the Eucharist, and (5) the blessing or results of such activities. This encouragement resonates deeply with similar ones of men and women who embraced a penitential way of life. Yet here we encounter the tremendously simple vision of Francis. Instead of presenting a life of penance filled with complicated austere practices and obligations, he goes no further than to provide a fundamentally Christian plan.

What is so appealing about Francis's understanding of penance, however, is the dividend it pays in enabling us to share in the inner life of God. "How happy are the men and women who do these things," he tells us, "for the Spirit of the Lord will rest upon them and make its home and dwelling place among them." Penance becomes a penetrating and ongoing emptying of one's self and a subsequent replenishment with the Lord. Francis teaches us that the embrace of penance brings about a profound change in our relationships with God, a change that we can understand only in light of the revelation of Jesus. Thus we again come face-to-face with the trinitarian patterns of Francis's thought: the Lord's Spirit dwelling within us brings us into consciousness of God as Father, a consciousness that flows from the revelation of Jesus as well as the realization of the Spirit's role in making us children of God. This trinitarian pattern is present at almost every turn. As we have suggested, it is as if his dramatic break with Pietro di Bernardone, his avaricious, ambitious father, heightened Francis's awareness of his heavenly, generous Father and drove him to emulate the pattern of sonship provided by Jesus.

Behind the establishment of these relationships, Francis sees the activity of the Spirit, the Spirit that makes us spouses, brothers or sisters, and mothers of Christ. Francis describes fundamental human relationships that marvelously embrace a well-rounded spiritual life: a spouse united to her lover; a brother or sister who, together with the firstborn, does the will of their Father; a mother who, while pregnant, carries her child within her, or who brings that child to birth, or in the Italian idiom, to the light of day. In light of this, Francis invites us to join him in expressing wonder and joy at these relationships or to echo the prayer of Jesus for his disciples and for those who will come to know him through them.

We might wonder about the influence of the image of the house or dwelling place that was brought to Francis's attention while at St. Damian's. Thomas of Celano and Bonaventure tell us that the voice of the Crucified Christ directed him to rebuild that *house* that was falling into ruin. From the first of the many references to houses or dwelling places that we find in Francis's writings, it becomes clear that the call haunted him throughout his life and that it gradually prompted him to think not only of the universal house of God, the church, but also of the house that is the dwelling place of God, each Christian. Could this be an indication that he envisioned the call to penance as containing the mystical call of St. Damian for all his followers? Possibly.

This bright, joy-filled, horizon-opening description of the penitential life contrasts sharply with the second part of Francis's exhortation. While in the first section he encourages us with totally other-centered expressions, now he speaks of a life that is quite self-centered and myopic. The Eucharist is ignored and promises are broken, but more is involved than that: self-gratification, concern for worldly success and profit, and a careless vision of the future become the very qualities of human life. Whereas he stressed being children of a living Father in the first section, he now describes what it means to be held captive by the devil. His reference to John 8:41 provides us with some insights into his thought as it focuses on the contrast highlighted by Jesus himself of being a child of God and one of the devil. Sin, he realizes, brings about a twisted, distorted way of looking at reality that causes us to be easily deceived and prone to act according to what seems to be immediately good or beneficial.

Throughout his challenging words, we can almost hear an echo of the "Prayer before the Crucifix": "enlighten the darkness of my heart." A biblical passage provides the key to opening this treasure trove of Francis's wisdom, in this case Matt. 15:19, which points to the human heart as the source of vice and sin. Throughout the Old and New Testaments our attention is drawn to the human heart. In the Old Testament the heart denotes the inner being, "the heart and the mind," which, as Jeremiah reminds us, the Lord judges (cf. Jer. 11:20). The New Testament builds on this notion and perfects it as the heart becomes the wellspring of good or evil. As Francis echoes this strong biblical image, he provides a key that unlocks the riches of the gospel life. Not only does he recognize that the penitential heart is the dwelling place of the Spirit; he also continually encourages us to have a clean heart and to become expressions or symbols of the Spirit's activities.

The first part of this simple exhortation is life-giving in its encouragement to embrace penance. The second part, however, dwells on the reality of death and its power in robbing us of those earthly possessions to which we have devoted much of our energy. The thought of death seems to haunt the latter part of this exhortation. In these early years, he is concerned about death's finality, and he fears that the cares and preoccupations of this world might distract us from paying attention to what is most important, the eternal life to which death leads us. We cannot help but wonder if some personal experiences of death may have influenced his thought.

Before we move on, we should take a closer look at the final lines of this exhortation. Francis begins the penultimate paragraph with a phrase from 1 John 4:16: "In the love which is God..." Not only does it appear to be one of his favorite biblical phrases; it also is his means of signaling us that what follows he considers most important. In this case, we find a plea for acceptance of his words, an acceptance characterized not simply by a request for "love and kindness" but by *"divine* love and kindness," that is, by sentiments brought about by God. Why? Because his words contain "the fragrant words of our Lord Jesus Christ." In fact, rereading this early exhortation, we discover it is simply a collage of scriptural quotations and allusions.

Awareness of this biblical tone, though, should make us sensitive to another Johannine allusion, this from John 6:63: "It is the spirit that gives life, the flesh is of no avail; the words that I have spoken to you are spirit and life." Even in this early work Francis seeks to contrast the spirit and the flesh and teaches us that, while the flesh is merely an outward manifestation of life, the spirit is life itself. He prompts us to cherish the Word of God as a channel or instrument of the Spirit itself and to see each word as a seed of divine life. As we continue to read his writings, their biblical character becomes more apparent and, with an ever-growing appreciation of the Scriptures, we marvel at how Francis challenges us to live them and to sustain ourselves with them. The Word and the words: in Francis they truly appear as Isaiah had said they would, as "the food of the poor" (Isa. 55:1–3). Thus it is not only a question of preserving them; it is also one of expressing their presence through "a holy activity."

A Conciliar and Postconciliar Man

Just as Francis's gospel intuitions were becoming more insightful and the number of his followers was growing, a decisive event in the history of the medieval world occurred. On April 19, 1213, Pope Innocent III announced his convocation of an ecumenical council to address the urgent need for reform within the church. This was a consolidating measure aimed at initiating a unified course of action against the encroaching powers of Islam and the spread of the Albigensian heresy. Four hundred and twelve bishops and more than eight hundred abbots, priors, and heads of religious orders gathered on November 11, 1215, to hear Innocent's address based on Luke 22:15, "I have eagerly desired to eat this Passover with you." The pope lamented the condition of the Holy Land as well as that of the church. "All of us who are members of the clergy," he announced, "must be ready to lay down our lives and give up all earthly goods for the sacred cause." Thus he challenged priests and religious to reform their lives and urged them to accept as their logo the tau, the sign of salvation used by Ezekiel and John.

It may be difficult for us to imagine that the Fourth Lateran Council, called by many historians the "Great Council," was completed by the end of that month. Nevertheless, the council fathers promulgated seventy decrees affecting church discipline and doctrine and initiated the Fifth Crusade. Almost every aspect of the church's life and ministry was touched: its sacramental worship, clerical discipline, religious life, and missionary activity. Many of the council's decrees influenced men and women such as Francis; Dominic Guzman, the founder of the Friars Preacher; and members of the numerous lay movements that Innocent III had continually encouraged during his pontificate. Some of its decrees, such as the demand to have chapters that would renew the religious spirit and, when necessary, restore discipline, affect religious communities to this day.

That such an ecclesial consolidation was necessary was most dramatically seen in the death of Innocent himself. Regarded by many as one of the strongest popes of the Middle Ages, his body was robbed and stripped on the night of July 16, 1216, as it lay in state in Perugia's Duomo. It must have not only scandalized the faithful but frightened the hierarchy responsible for the church's government. Immediately after Innocent's funeral, on July 18, 1216, the cardinals elected Cencio Savelli as his successor. Savelli, an elderly man with a history of long service to the Apostolic See, chose the name Honorius III and promised to continue the policies of his predecessor.

Faithful to his promise, Honorius III issued, in November 1219, his own exhortation to the bishops, clergy, and religious. The exhortation continued the teaching of his predecessor found in his *Ordo missae*, in his decree *De sacro altari mysterio*, and in the decrees of the council. Honorius's document, *Expectavimus hactenus* or *Sane cum olim*, helps us to understand the context of Francis's concerns:

> Since in times past the golden vessel full of manna prefigured the Body of Christ that contained the Godhead and since this vessel was placed below the Holy of Holies in the gold-covered Ark of the Covenant in order that it might be preserved decently in a holy place, we deplore and are grieved that in several provinces priests who are ignoring canonical sanctions and the judgment of God are reserving carelessly and irreverently touching with unclean hands the Sacred Eucharist. [And they do this] so that they neither fear the Creator nor love the Life-Giver nor tremble before the Judge of all, even though the Apostle sternly threatens that whoever disdains *the Son of God* or *considers the covenant-blood to be ordinary* or insults *the Spirit of grace* (cf. Heb. 10:29) will merit a worse punishment than one who transgresses the Law of Moses for which the penalty is the sentence of death.
>
> Therefore, lest the wrath of God blaze up in the future against the irreverent because of the carelessness of priests, We strictly enjoin by precept that the Eucharist be reserved always devotedly and faithfully in a place of honor that is clean and designated for It alone.

Every priest should teach his people frequently that
they should bow in reverence whenever the Life-Giving
Host is elevated at the celebration of Mass and that each
one should do the same when the priest is carrying It to the
sick. At the same time, the priest should carry It in becoming apparel covered with a clean veil and should bring It
back openly and honorably at his breast. The priest should
be preceded by a torch, since the Eucharist is the radiance
of Eternal Light, so that the faith and devotion of everyone
be increased.

If Prelates desire to escape the vengeance of God and
Ours, they should not delay in punishing seriously trans-
gressors of this precept. You should see that the foregoing
is so observed that you may be made partakers not of
punishment but of reward.

After his return from the Middle East, that is, sometime in
the spring of 1220, Francis wrote two exhortations that suggest
that the concerns of this papal exhortation struck deeply reso-
nant chords within him. The first of these he addressed to the
clergy:

Let all of us, clergymen, consider the great sin and the ignorance
some have toward the most holy Body and Blood of our Lord Jesus
Christ and His most holy names and written words that consecrate His Body. We know It cannot be His Body without first being
consecrated by word. For we have and see nothing corporally of
the Most High in this world except [His] Body and Blood, [His]
names and written words through which we have been made and
redeemed *from death to life* (1 John 3:14).

Let all those who administer such most holy ministries, however, especially those who administer them without discernment,
consider how very dirty the chalices, corporals and altar-linens are
upon which the Body and Blood of our Lord are sacrificed. It is
left in many dirty places, carried about unbecomingly, received unworthily, and administered to others without discernment. Even
His names and written words are at times left to be trampled
under foot; *for the carnal person does not perceive the things of
God* (1 Cor. 2:14).

Are we not moved by piety at these things when the good

Lord offers Himself into our hands and we handle Him and receive Him daily with our mouth? Do we refuse to recognize that we must come into His hands? Let us, therefore, amend our ways quickly and firmly in these and all other matters. Wherever the most holy Body and Blood of our Lord Jesus Christ has been unlawfully placed and left, let It be moved from there, placed in a precious place and locked up. Likewise, wherever the names and written words of the Lord may be found in unclean places, let them be gathered up and placed in a becoming place.

We know that we are bound to observe above all else all of these matters according to the precepts of the Lord and the constitutions of holy Mother Church. Whoever does not do this, let him know that, *on the day of judgment,* he will be bound *to render an account* of himself before our Lord Jesus Christ (cf. Matt. 12:36).

Let whoever makes copies of this writing so that it may be better observed know that they will be blessed by the Lord God.

More than anything else, Francis tells us of his own concern for the "little things" of worship, the chalices, corporals, and altar linens, even the Sacred Scriptures ("the names and written words") and the liturgical books ("the written words that consecrate His Body"). His encouragement undoubtedly comes in response to abuses that were prevalent during his day: carelessness, inappropriate use of churches and liturgical vessels, and indiscriminate distribution of the Eucharist. Yet many would be quick to note that Francis's day was no different than our own. More important than the historical context, though, are the reasons Francis offers for such visible care and concern for the Eucharist.

First, Francis does not use the word "Eucharist." Was it too abstract? Seemingly, for he consistently uses in its place the phrase "the Body and Blood of our Lord Jesus Christ" and reminds us that "we have nothing and see nothing corporally of the Most High in this world except [His] Body and Blood." Moreover, at least in this and the following writing, there is a close bond between the Lord's Body and Blood and his names and written words, hinting at what we will later see quite clearly in Francis's first admonition, his belief that the revelation of the Incarnation is somehow continued in the Eucharist.

Second, Francis envisions a significant activity of the Holy Spirit in our recognition of the Lord's presence. We'll see this too in his later writings. For the moment, we discover it expressed negatively: "the carnal person — that is, one without the Spirit — does not perceive the things of God." The passage, of course, comes from 1 Cor. 2:14, which refers to recognition of spiritual realities. Francis narrows the Spirit's activities, at least in this writing, to enabling the one who possesses it to break through appearance to perceive the Lord's Body and Blood, his names and written words. Although he expresses the Spirit's role negatively (that is, by its absence), as is appropriate in the context, Francis's encouragement is difficult to overlook: a way of discerning the Spirit's presence in our lives is by observing our spirit of reverence and respect for the Eucharist and what pertains to it.

We can see how intensely Francis feels about these matters from a letter that he sent to those who were called to serve. (In 1217 the number of Francis's followers had grown so large that they were divided into provinces and later into "custodies." Thus we begin to see distinctions in Francis's writings between a general minister, a provincial minister, and a custodian: all had the responsibility of ministering to the brothers of their geographical regions.)

To all the custodians of the Friars Minor whom this letter reaches, Brother Francis, your servant and little one in the Lord God, sends a greeting together with new signs of heaven and earth that are great and extraordinary in the sight of God yet regarded as of little importance by many religious and others.

I beg you with all that is in me and more that, when it is fitting and you judge it expedient, you humbly beg the clergy to revere the most holy Body and Blood of our Lord Jesus Christ and His holy name and written words that sanctify His Body above all else. They should hold the chalices, corporals, appointments of the altar, and everything that pertains to the sacrifice as precious. If the most holy Body of the Lord is very poorly reserved in any place, let It be placed and locked up in a precious place according to the command of the Church. Let It be carried about with great reverence and administered to others with discernment. Let the names and written words of the Lord, whenever they are found in dirty places, be also gathered up and kept in a becoming place.

In every sermon you give, remind people about penance and that no one can be saved unless he receives the most holy Body and Blood of the Lord (cf. John 6:54). When It is sacrificed on the altar by a priest and carried to any place, let all peoples praise, glorify and honor the Lord God living and true on bended knee (cf. 1 Thess. 1:9). May you announce and preach His praise to all nations in such a way that praise and thanks may always be given to the all-powerful God by all people throughout the world at every hour and whenever bells are rung.

Let my brother custodians who have received this writing, who have made copies of it and kept it for themselves and for the brothers who have the responsibility of preaching and the care of the brothers, and who have made known and preached about everything contained in it, know that they have God's blessing as well as my own. Let these be matters of true and holy obedience for them.

We might be tempted to pass quickly over this writing since it seems to repeat much of the liturgical thought expressed in the "Exhortation to the Clergy." It is an important statement, however, because of what Francis tells us of the intensity of his conciliar and postconciliar concerns. After a striking and unusual introduction, Francis continues: "I beg you with all that is in me and more...." He then proceeds to repeat the same exhortation he gave to the clergy. Does Francis suggest that his would-be followers have a special obligation or mission to fulfill those liturgical directives? Were there any doubt, we need only turn to the second paragraph, in which he stresses those very concerns of Pope Honorius III: the importance of receiving the Eucharist and of showing it respect. He even goes beyond the council's prescription by encouraging us not simply to bow before the Blessed Sacrament but to kneel.

There is one other thought-provoking passage in this writing: "May you announce and preach His praise to all nations in such a way that praise and thanks may always be given to the all-powerful God by all people throughout the world at every hour and whenever bells are rung." What prompted Francis to adopt this universal attitude? We see an indication of it in his

"Exhortation to the Clergy," which is surprisingly addressed to *all* the clergy. Yet now Francis speaks beyond his brothers to *all* nations and all peoples throughout the world. Undoubtedly his journey to the Middle East awakened a missionary consciousness in him; it also extended his understanding of the gospel calling to include evangelization of all peoples.

A Renewed Call to Penance

None of the writings of this period reflects this universal mission more eloquently than a brief, urgent message that, surprisingly, he addresses to "all mayors and consuls, magistrates and rulers throughout the world."

Brother Francis, your little and looked down upon servant in the Lord God, wishes health and peace to all mayors and consuls, magistrates and rulers throughout the world and to all others to whom these words may come.

Reflect and see that the day of death is approaching (cf. Gen. 47:29). I beg you with all possible respect, therefore, not to forget the Lord and turn away from His commandments because of this world's cares and preoccupation, for all those *who* leave Him in oblivion and *turn away from His commandments are cursed* (cf. Ps. 119:21 [V 118:21]) and *will be left in oblivion* by Him (Ezek. 33:13).

When the day of death does come, everything they think they have shall be taken from them (cf. Matt. 13:12; Mark 4:25; Luke 8:18). The wiser and more powerful they may have been in this world, the greater will be the punishment they will endure in hell (cf. Wis. 6:7).

Therefore I strongly advise You, my Lords, to put aside all care and preoccupation and receive the most holy Body and Blood of our Lord Jesus Christ fervently in holy remembrance of Him. May you stir up such honor to the Lord among the people entrusted to you that every evening an announcement may be made by a messenger or some other sign that praise and thanksgiving may be given by all people to the all-powerful Lord God. If You do not do this, know that, *on the day of judgment,* You must render *an account* before the Lord Your God, Jesus Christ (cf. Matt. 12:36).

Let those who keep this writing with them and observe it know that they will be blessed by the Lord God.

What prompted this somewhat audacious message to the civil authorities? There is a prophetic tone to this letter that we can discern immediately: its address of a universal audience that is not limited to the rulers but to all those who have responsibilities in the governance of peoples; its approach of accentuating the reality of death; and its emphatic caution not to forget the Lord or his commandments. Did Francis's presence at the Siege of Damietta inspire this message? The siege, slaughter, and pillage provide a dramatic background for Francis's thought and also help us to understand the new, fearless drive that appears in this letter, as well as the simplicity of its "back-to-basics" message: put aside all care and anxiety, receive the Eucharist, and lead your people to honor and praise God. "Know that in the sight of God," he writes reflecting possibly on the Damietta experience, "there are certain very lofty and sublime things that people think of as worthless and contemptible; there are others that are precious and remarkable to people that God considers extremely worthless and contemptible."

What influenced Francis to join his exhortation to receive and reverence the Eucharist with announcing the divine praise? Could this be the influence of the Islamic *salât*, the prayer offered five times daily and announced by a muezzin or herald? Anyone who has spent time in an Islamic country will immediately recall hearing that plaintive announcement: "Allah is god and Mohammed is his prophet!" Thus such speculation makes a great deal of sense when we consider that this letter was written shortly after Francis's return from the Middle East. If this speculation has any grounds, we can only wonder what Francis's response would be in these days to the Second Vatican Council's concerns for dialogue with other religions and for finding what unites rather than divides us. Indeed, the conciliar and postconciliar Francis unwittingly urges us to examine our own response or our hesitancy or sluggishness in responding to an ecumenical council that finds many parallels in that of his time.

In the light of the Letter to the Rulers of the People, we are in a better position to read the second version of the Letter to the Faithful. While we refer to this as a letter, the medieval manuscripts repeatedly call it a *commonitorium,* that is, a writing that reminds its reader to carry out a directive. In other words, its principal purpose is that of recalling an earlier message, in this case: the call to penance that Francis made at the outset. When we notice the frequent use of Scripture and notice many of the conciliar themes, especially those of being Catholic and receiving the Eucharist, we might wonder if Francis were also attempting to remind us of the sources of penitential life.

In the name of the Father and of the Son and of the Holy Spirit. Amen.

Brother Francis, their servant and subject, sends esteem and reverence, true peace from heaven and sincere love in the Lord to all Christian religious people: clergy and laity, men and women, and to all who live in the whole world.

Because I am the servant of all, I am obliged to serve all and to administer the fragrant words of my Lord to them. Therefore, on reflecting that I cannot visit each one of you personally because of sickness and the weakness of my body, I proposed to offer you in this letter and message the words of our Lord Jesus Christ, Who is the Word of the Father, and the words of the Holy Spirit, which *are spirit and life* (cf. John 6:63).

What prompted this writing? In the first place, we have to look at the information Francis provides. At the beginning of the exhortation he writes: "on reflecting that I cannot visit each of you personally because of sickness and the weakness of my body...." His companions tell us that he "suffered for a long time from his liver, spleen, and stomach, right up to the time of his death. In addition to that, in the course of his voyage to preach to the Sultan of Babylonia and of Egypt, he had contracted a very serious disease of the eyes caused by fatigue and especially by the excessive heat he had to endure both in going and in returning." A few paragraphs later, they also provide another detail about his illness. He suffered, they tell us, *febris quartana,* a type of malaria in which paroxysms occur every fourth day. From these indications, then, we can safely assume that Francis wrote this exhortation after his return from the Middle East and imagine that he was suffering from those sicknesses that were to remain with him until his death.

Moreover, Francis's followers were growing in number. No doubt they were also attracting more attention. During these years, Cardinal Hugolino dei Conti di Segni took more and more interest in the brothers, then in Clare and her Poor Ladies, and, finally, in the Brothers and Sisters of Penance. In 1219, Hugolino presented a simplified version of the Benedictine rule to the Poor Ladies and two years later a set of guidelines to the Brothers and Sisters of Penance. *Memoriale propositi,* this latter document, bore little resemblance to Francis's earlier call to penance. It was more reflective of the canonical mind of its author. Did Hugolino consult with Francis and perhaps ask him to write his own set of guidelines? Could this have been the reason for Francis's issuance of a renewed call to penance? Or could it have been prompted by the experience of Damietta and the prophetic drive to call people to penance that we saw in the Letter to the Rulers of the People?

Whatever is the case, there is a sense of urgency in this writing, just as there is a deeper, more mature awareness of the mystery of Christ and of the importance of welcoming the Word of God. From the outset Francis encourages us to be ever more sensitive to the passages and allusions of Sacred Scripture that permeate his writings. He provides a key to his thoroughly biblical spirituality when he writes that he is simply offering us "the words of our Lord Jesus Christ, Who is the Word of the Father, and the words of the Holy Spirit, which *are spirit and life* (cf. John 6:63)." From his perspective, then, this writing contains not his words but those of the Father, Son, and Holy Spirit. This occurs at least six different times as Christ is seen as the Word of the Father and his words as the principle of salvation, of the Holy Spirit, and of life. We certainly have an echo of the Gospel of John here, the Word who speaks words bringing the Spirit. But we also have an example of how thoroughly Francis absorbed and reflected the Sacred Scriptures. Twenty times in this "Later Exhortation" Francis writes of speaking, and in all but four instances he refers to Jesus. Correspondingly, there are sixteen references to receiving or accepting the words or the Body and Blood of the Lord. In a sense, he calls us to transparency, to expressing through every fiber of our being the Word of God. Thus he emphasizes one of his prominent themes: welcoming that Word. Is it any wonder that there is such a strong emphasis in the Franciscan tradition on interior prayer? In fact, some authors consider that the greatest contribution made by the followers of Francis to the history of contemplative prayer is their efforts to make its daily practice accessible to the people.

Francis is not proposing any particular words of Christ but the very person of the Word of God:

The Most High Father made known from heaven through his holy angel Gabriel this Word of the Father — so worthy, so holy and glorious — in the womb of the holy and glorious Virgin Mary, from whose womb He received the flesh of our humanity and frailty. Though He was rich beyond all things (cf. 2 Cor. 8:9), He, together with the most Blessed Virgin, His mother, wished to choose poverty in the world.

And as His Passion was near, He celebrated the Passover with His disciples and, taking bread, gave thanks, blessed and broke it, saying: *Take and eat: this is My Body* (Matt. 26:26). And taking the cup He said: *This is My Blood of the New Covenant which will be poured out for you and for many for the forgiveness of sins* (Matt. 26:28). Then He prayed to His Father, saying: *Father, if it can be done, let this cup pass from me* (Luke 22:42). *And His sweat became as drops of blood falling on the ground* (Luke 22:44). Nevertheless He placed His will in the will of His Father, saying: *Father, let your will be done* (Matt. 26:42); *not as I will, but as You will* (Matt. 26:39). His Father's will was such that His blessed and glorious Son, Whom He gave to us and Who was born for us, should offer Himself through His own blood as a sacrifice and oblation on the altar of the cross: not for Himself through Whom all things were made (cf. John 1:3), but for our sins, leaving us an example that we might follow His footprints (cf. 1 Pet. 2:21).

And He wishes that all of us be saved through Him and receive Him with our heart pure and our body chaste. But there are few who wish to receive Him and be saved through Him, even though His *yoke is easy* and His *burden light* (Cf. Matt. 11:30). Those who do not wish to taste how sweet the Lord is (cf. Ps. 34:9 [V 33:9]) and who love *the darkness more than the light* (John 3:19), not wishing to fulfill God's commands, are cursed; it is said of them by the prophet: *Cursed are those who stray from your commands* (Ps. 119:21 [V 118:21]).

There is a striking contrast within his vision. On the one hand, Francis would have us focus on the Lord who is "so worthy, so holy and glorious"; on the other hand, he directs our attention to one who assumed "the flesh of our humanity and frailty." He encourages us never to lose sight of the dignity, holiness, and glory of the divine Word, but at the same time, he does not want us to overlook the frailty of the Word's human flesh. This initial contrast, however, simply introduces that of the Word of the Father who abandoned divine riches to be clothed in our human poverty, and of the blessed and glorious Son of God who shed his blood on the cross, and of the Creator of all things who offered himself for us sinful human beings. Francis would not have us forget that the Incarnation is a powerful expression of descent embraced by the Word of the Father who emptied himself of divine glory to become a poor human being in our midst. In all of the self-emptying to which he calls us, Francis keeps those contrasts before our eyes. The Son of God left us an example, he reminds us, and "wishes that all of us be saved through Him." It is as simple as that.

In light of the mystery of Christ, Francis gives us a far greater sense of direction in this exhortation than in his earlier one. In fact, he seems to give us a series of ten specific directives together with explanations of what is implied in each. For example, he again places before us the love of God as a primary obligation, but now he adds a significant passage describing how we should fulfill it by adoring the Father:

But how happy and blessed are those who love God and do as the Lord Himself says in the Gospel: *You shall love the Lord your God with all your heart* and all *your mind,* and *your neighbor as yourself* (Matt. 22:37, 39). Let us love God, therefore, and adore Him with a pure heart and a pure mind, because He Who seeks this above all things has said: *True adorers adore the Father in Spirit and Truth* (John 4:23). For all *who adore Him should adore Him in the Spirit* of truth (cf. John 4:24). And *Day and night* let us direct praises and prayers to Him (cf. Ps. 32:4 [V 31:4]), saying: *Our Father, Who art in heaven...*(Matt. 6:9) for we *should pray always and not become weary* (Luke 18:1).

In the remaining nine directives, Francis urges us on with the word *debere*, to be bound or to be under obligation. Of all the times this Latin word occurs in Francis's writings, it appears most frequently in this text (fourteen times). Yet that is not as significant as the fundamental gospel teachings of Francis that we find in six of these prescriptions and the teaching of the Fourth Lateran Council in the remaining three:

We must indeed confess all our sins to a priest and receive the Body and Blood of our Lord Jesus Christ from him. Whoever does not eat His flesh and drink His blood (cf. John 6:54, 57) *cannot enter the kingdom of God* (John 3:5). But let him eat and drink worthily because anyone who receives *unworthily, not distinguishing*, that is, not discerning, *the Body of the Lord, eats and drinks judgment on himself* (1 Cor. 11:29).

Let us, moreover, produce worthy fruits of penance (cf. Luke 3:8).

And let us love our neighbors as ourselves (cf. Matt. 22:39). And if anyone does not want to love them as himself, let him at least not do them any harm, but let him do good.

Let whoever has received the power of judging others pass judgment with mercy, as they would want to receive mercy from the Lord. For *judgment will be without mercy* for those *who have not shown mercy* (James 2:13).

Let us, therefore, have charity and humility and give alms because it washes the stains of our sins from our souls (cf. Tob. 4:11; 12:9). For though people lose everything they leave behind in this world; they carry with them, however, the rewards of charity and the alms they have given for which they will receive a reward and a fitting payment from the Lord.

We must also fast and abstain from vices and sins (cf. Sir. 3:32) and from an excess of food and drink and be Catholics.

We must also frequently visit churches and venerate and revere the clergy not so much for themselves, if they are sinners, but because of their office and administration of the most holy Body and Blood of Christ which they sacrifice upon the altar, receive and administer to others. And let all of us know for certain that no one can be saved except through the holy words and Blood of our Lord Jesus Christ which the clergy pronounce, proclaim and minister. And they alone must minister and not others. Religious, however, who have left the world, are bound to do more and greater things but not to overlook these.

We must hate our bodies with their vices and sins because the Lord says in the Gospel: All evils, vices and sins *come from the heart* (cf. Matt. 15:18–19; Mark 7:23).

We must love our *enemies* and do good *to those who* hate us (cf. Matt. 5:44; Luke 6:27).

We must observe the commands and counsels of our Lord Jesus Christ.

We must also deny ourselves (cf. Matt. 16:24; Mark 8:34; Luke 9:23) and place our bodies under the yoke of servitude and holy obedience as each one has promised to the Lord. And let no one be bound to obey another in anything in which a crime or sin would be committed. Instead, let the one to whom obedience has been entrusted and *who is* considered *the greater* be the *lesser* and the servant of the other brothers (cf. Matt. 20:26–27; Mark 10:43–44; Luke 22:26). And let him have and show mercy to each of his brothers as he would want them to do to him were he in a similar position (Matt. 7:12; Luke 6:31). Let him not become angry at the fault of a brother but, with all patience and humility, let him admonish and support him.

We must not be wise and prudent according to the flesh (cf. 1 Cor. 1:26), but, instead, we must be simple, humble and pure. And let us hold our bodies in scorn and contempt because, through our own fault, we are all wretched and corrupt, disgusting and worms, as the Lord says through the prophet: *I am a worm and not a man, the scorn of men and the outcast of the people* (Ps. 22:6 [V 21:7]).

We must never desire to be above others, but, instead, we must be servants and subject *to every human creature for God's sake* (1 Pet. 2:13).

Could these be Francis's Ten Commandments, that is, his attempt at expressing a more structured gospel and ecclesial way of life for us? He certainly spells out the implications of the earlier exhortation to a penitential life and makes it clear that they flow from Christ himself. The results are similar:

And *the Spirit of the Lord will rest* upon all those men and women who have done and persevered in these things (Isa. 11:2; cf. Luke

4:18) and It shall make a home and *dwelling-place in them* (cf. John 14:23). And they will be the children of the heavenly Father (cf. Matt. 5:45), Whose works they do. And they are spouses, brothers and mothers of our Lord Jesus Christ (cf. Matt. 12:50; Mark 3:35; Luke 8:21).

We are spouses when the faithful soul is united by the Holy Spirit to our Lord Jesus Christ. We are brothers, moreover, when we do *the will of* His *Father Who* is in heaven (cf. Matt. 12:50; Mark 3:35); mothers when we carry Him in our heart and body (cf. 1 Cor. 6:20) through love and a pure and sincere conscience; and give Him birth through a holy activity, which must shine before others by example (cf. Matt. 5:16).

O how glorious and holy and great to have a Father in heaven! O how holy, consoling, beautiful and wonderful to have such a Spouse! O how holy and how loving, gratifying, humbling, peace-giving, sweet, worthy of love, and above all things desirable it is to have such a Brother and such a Son: our Lord Jesus Christ, Who laid down His life for His sheep (cf. John 10:15) and prayed to His father, saying:

Holy Father save in your name, those whom you have given me (John 17:11). Father, all those *whom you have given me in the world were yours and you have given them to me* (John 17:6). *The words that you gave me, I have given to them; they have accepted them and known in truth that I have come from you and they have believed that you have sent me* (John 17:8).

I pray for them and *not for the world* (cf. John 17:9); bless and sanctify them (John 17:17). *I sanctify myself for them that they may be sanctified in* (John 17:19) *being one as* we are *one* (John 17:11).

And I wish, Father, *that where I am, they may be with me that they may see my glory* (John 17:24) *in your kingdom* (Matt. 20:21).

Francis reminds us that the same blessing redounds upon us as we struggle to live that life of penance or *metanoia* (conversion) that he describes: the Spirit enters deeply into our lives providing us with a spiritual life that is caught up in relationships that incredibly transcend our dreams. As he presents his own version of Jesus' prayer at the Last Supper, Francis bursts once again into praising the wonders of the triune God in a way that is contagious: "O how glorious and holy and great to have a Father in heaven! O how holy, consoling, beautiful and wonderful to have such a Spouse! O how holy and how loving, gratifying, humbling, peace-giving, sweet, worthy of love, and above all things desirable it is to have such a Brother and such a Son: our Lord Jesus Christ, Who laid down His life for His sheep (cf. John 10:15) and prayed to His Father." Now, however, Francis breaks into one of those invitational prayers that, as we will see, characterize his entire approach to God:

Let *every creature*
    in heaven, on earth, in the sea and in the depths,
        give praise, *glory, honor and blessing*
To Him Who suffered so much,
        Who has given and will give in the future every good,
            for He is our power and strength,
        Who *alone is good,*
        Who alone is almighty,
        Who alone is omnipotent, wonderful, glorious
            and Who alone is holy,
                worthy of praise and blessing
                    through endless ages. Amen.

While Francis extends his call to penance beyond us to all creatures, he does not lose sight of his Christ-centered focus. In fact, in this brief invitational prayer not only does Francis see a particular role for Christ in the Incarnation and in his sufferings on the cross; he also portrays Christ as continuing the work of the Creator's gift of goodness. Thus he introduces a theme that appears frequently in his other writings: Christ, under the title of God's Son, is beside the Father and the Spirit in the common work of creation.

Such a positive, other-centered vision only intensifies the contrast that Francis repeats in the last section of his exhortation:

All those, however, who are not living in penance, who do not receive the Body and Blood of our Lord Jesus Christ, who practice vice and sin and walk after evil concupiscence and wicked desires, who do not observe what they have promised, and who bodily serve the world, the desires of the flesh, the cares and anxieties of this world, and the preoccupation of this life are deceived by the devil whose children they are and whose works they do (cf. John 8:41). They are blind because they do not see the true light, our Lord Jesus Christ. They do not have spiritual wisdom because they do not possess the Son of God, the true wisdom of the Father within them. It is said of them: *Their wisdom has been swallowed up* (Ps. 107:27 [V 106:27]). They see, recognize, know and do evil; and, knowingly, they lose their souls.

See, you blind ones, deceived by your enemies, that is, the flesh, the world and the devil because it is sweet for the body to commit sin and bitter to serve God, for every evil, vice and sin flow and *proceed from people's heart,* as the Lord says in the Gospel (cf. Mark 7:21ff.; Matt. 15:19ff.). And you have nothing in this world or in that to come. You think you possess the vanities of the world for a long time, but you are deceived because a day and an hour are coming of which you do not think, do not know, and are not aware.

The body becomes weak, death approaches, relatives and friends come saying: "Put your affairs in order." Look, his wife and children, relatives and friends pretend to cry. Looking around, he sees them weeping and is moved by an evil impulse. He says, thinking to himself, "See, I place my soul and body, all that I have in your hands." In fact, that man is cursed who entrusts and places his soul and body and all he has in such hands; for, as the Lord says through the prophet, *Cursed is the one who trusts in another* (Jer. 17:5). And immediately they make a priest come. The priest says to him: "Do you want to receive penance for all your sins?" "I do," he responds. "Do you wish to make satisfaction, as far as you can, out of your wealth, for what you have done and the ways in which you have cheated and deceived people?" "No," he responds. "Why not?" the priest asks. "Because I have placed everything in the hands of my relatives and friends." And he begins to lose his speech and so the wretched man dies.

But let everyone know that whenever and however someone dies in mortal sin without making amends when he could have and did not, the devil snatches his soul from his body with such anguish and distress that no one can know [what it is like] except the one experiencing it.

And every talent and power and knowledge that he thought he had *will be taken away from him* (Mark 4:25; Luke 8:18; Matt.

13:12). And he leaves his relatives and friends and they take and divide his wealth and, afterwards, they say: "May his soul be cursed because he could have given us more and acquired more than he distributed to us!" Worms eat his body and so he loses his body and soul in this brief world and goes to hell where he will be tortured without end.

Christ, Francis teaches us, is not merely the teacher who, like a schoolmaster, teaches us some lesson. He is not external to his followers. No, he is the wisdom and light that dwell within their hearts. Those who do not turn to him, Francis maintains, are blind slaves. They are slaves because they are completely bound by the power of their carnal desires and thus by the devil himself; and blind because they are easily deceived and led astray. Francis dramatically exemplifies this by telling us the story of the sick man who finds himself at the point of death. But Francis now tells the story with far more details and drama so that we cannot miss his point.

There are so many questions surrounding this writing, not the least of which is the detailed version of the hard-heartedness of the dying man. Who was the dying man? Is John of Capistrano correct in suggesting that Francis's father, Pietro, died during these years and became his model of the rich but unrepentant dying man? Or with this more dramatic account did Francis wish to remind us of the stark reality of death and the ultimate tragedy of dying unrepentant in the state of mortal sin? If so, what prompted this dramatic rendition of what was a more simple example in the "Earlier Exhortation"? So often experiences of tragedy or sudden death bring us face-to-face with the ultimate realities of life and prompt us not only to return to a faith that we might have neglected but even to practice that faith as never before. In light of his experiences of the war, Francis calls us all to a vibrancy of faith, to an intensity of love. As we have seen, he may have witnessed the Siege of Damietta, August 29, 1219, and been reminded of the slaughter of his own compatriots at the Battle of Collestrada seventeen years earlier. Whatever the cause, the theme of death confronts us, as it did Francis, with a reality that should deter us from the grasping, narcissistic behavior that so often plagues the rich and comfortable.

He comes to the end of his exhortation by fittingly invoking the Trinity in whose very inner life we have been involved. In these final words, though, he expresses that urgency or passion that we can find in so many other passages.

In the name of the Father and of the Son and of the Holy Spirit. Amen.

I, brother Francis, your lesser servant, beg and implore you in the love that is God (cf. 1 John 4:16), and with a wish to kiss your feet, to receive, to put into practice, and to observe, as you should, these words and the others of our Lord Jesus Christ with humility and charity. And may the Father and the Son and the Holy Spirit bless all those men and women who receive them with kindness, understand them and send copies of them to others, if *they have persevered to the end* in them (cf. Matt. 24:13).

Amen.

Were we to possess no other writing of Francis, in this one alone he permits us to enter into his heart and to discover the core of his belief.

The Life of the Gospel of Our Lord Jesus Christ

For the most part, we have been reading texts that Francis addressed to a wide audience: the faithful whom he called to embrace a life of penance, the clergy with whom he shared a special responsibility in caring for the worship of God, and the rulers of the people to whom he addressed a prophetic message to shake them from their spiritual lethargy. We should now turn our attention to his words to the brothers whom, in his own words, "the Lord gave to [him]." In a sense, this is the most difficult part of reading the writings of Francis, for it demands a sense of the three perspectives that we mentioned at the outset: tradition, personal experience, and culture. To unlock the richness of his vision, we should be sensitive to the religious traditions to which Francis was heir, especially that of the monastic *lectio divina*, which undoubtedly inspired him to follow the will of God through an ever-deepening knowledge of Sacred Scripture. We must understand that and also be aware of Francis's own struggles or experiences of the church and of the society in which he lived. Both of these perspectives, however, must be studied in light of the culture of twelfth- and early thirteenth-century Assisi.

In the Earlier and Later Rules, we have two documents that Francis wrote with the help of others: his brothers, who undoubtedly helped him articulate, clarify, or affirm certain gospel values in light of lived situations; other religious, such as those Cistercians present at the gatherings of the brothers, Cardinal Hugolino, Popes Innocent III and Honorius III themselves, and possibly Clare and the Poor Ladies; and, as we have already seen, the Fourth Lateran Council. As we struggle — and struggle we must — to discern the different layers of Francis's thought, we will grow in appreciation of how he teaches us to follow the Lord's will by deepening our insights into the gospel life as it unfolds each day. In his *Method in Theology*, Bernard Lonergan offers an insight that is very apropos of our attempts to understand the rules of Francis: "As intelligent, the subject seeks insight and as insights accumulate, he reveals them in his behavior, his speech, his grasp of situations, his mastery of theoretic domains" (Lonergan 1972, 10). Lonergan's statement expresses perfectly what Francis would have us do: struggle with insight until we understand what it means to be and to live as a child of God. Only as those insights develop will we express them in our behavior, speech, and patterns of thought. In fact, we will begin to think biblically.

Before we read the lengthy description of the brothers' life, however, we should turn our attention to an intermediate document, a blueprint or design of living for those who desire to live a more solitary form of gospel life. (At the time of its composition, between 1217 and 1221, some of Francis's followers were undoubtedly living in out of the way hermitages such as Poggio Bustone, Monte Casale, or Monte LaVerna.) With our contemporary emphasis on fraternity, this document is difficult to understand. The pursuit of solitude has become obsolete in favor of deepening the bonds of brotherhood. Nevertheless, Francis offers us a formula in which the two blend together.

Let those who wish to dwell in hermitages in a religious way be three brothers or, at the most, four; let two of these be "the mother" and have two "sons" or at least one. Let the two who are "mothers" keep the life of Martha and the two "sons" keep the life of Mary (cf. Luke 10:38–42) and have one enclosure in which each one may have his cell in which he may pray and sleep.

And let them always recite Compline of the day immediately after sundown and strive to maintain silence, recite their Hours, rise for Matins, and *seek first the kingdom of God and His justice* (Matt. 6:33). And let them recite Prime at the proper hour and, after Terce, they may end their silence, speak with and go to their mothers. And when it pleases them, they can beg alms from them as poor little ones out of love of the Lord God. And afterwards let them recite Sext, None and, at the proper hour, Vespers.

And they may not permit anyone to enter or eat in the enclosure where they dwell. Let those brothers who are the "mothers" strive to stay far from everyone and, because of obedience to their minister, protect their "sons" from everyone so that no one can speak with them. And those "sons" may not talk with anyone except with their mothers and with the minister and his custodian when it pleases them to visit with the Lord's blessing.

The "sons," however, may periodically assume the role of the "mothers," taking turns for a time as they have mutually decided. Let them strive to observe conscientiously and eagerly everything mentioned above.

What is remarkable about this simple blueprint is that it contains the basic elements of Francis's view of life. It is a life based on following the Lord's will as did Martha and Mary; lived in celebrating God's Word in fraternal love and dependence on one another; and dedicated to service and prayer or to the pursuit of God for the sake of others. Some of the text's words and phrases appear frequently in Francis's writings: "mother," "son," "as little poor ones," "when it pleases them." Thus Francis tells us quite simply how he envisions a gospel life centered on the pursuit of God in solitude: a fraternal caring for one another that can be characterized only by a mother's love and a child's simple acceptance, an identification with the poor and little ones of the earth, and a sense of freedom and mutual respect. All of these fraternal expressions centered on the celebration of the Word, the Liturgy of the Hours. Francis teaches us that we can be living alone yet fraternally by caring for one another and by learning to receive from one another. Perhaps this is the genius of Francis: his vision of brotherhood in which he teaches us to be more concerned about each other than about the places or structures in which we live. If we had no other statement of how he envisions the gospel life lived by his brothers, this would suffice in presenting the ideals of its inner life.

Now we must return to 1209, when Francis was beginning to attract followers and, with them, went to the Gospel Book of San Nicolao in order to discern God's will for them. The *Anonymous of Perugia*, the oldest account of this event, tells us that these first brothers opened the Gospel Book to Matt. 19:21 ("If you would be perfect, go, sell all that you possess and give to the poor; and you will have treasure in heaven"), then to Matt. 16:24 ("If any man would come after me, let him deny himself and take up his cross and follow me"), and finally to Luke 9:3 ("Take nothing for your journey, no staff, nor bag, nor bread, nor money; and do not have two tunics."). The anonymous author tells us that after Francis read these passages, he cried out, "This will be our rule!" The author of the *Legend of the Three Companions*, a redaction of the earlier text, broadens Francis's statement to: "This will be our life and our rule and of those who want to join us!" Shortly afterward, Francis and his first twelve followers made their way to Rome and presented to Pope Innocent III their proposal of life, a simple work composed of texts from the Gospels and some points necessary for common life. We will probably never discover the exact wording of this original rule, which Innocent III approved in 1209. The prologue and first chapter of the Earlier Rule suggest that somehow the original document was gradually absorbed into the Earlier Rule. The latter began with a simple gospel foundation and grew with the number of Francis's followers: "This is the life of the Gospel of our Lord Jesus Christ that Brother Francis petitioned the Lord Pope to grant and confirm for him; and he did grant and confirm it for him and his brothers present and to come."

Many call this document the Rule of 1221 and in doing so give the impression that it was composed in that year. Others write of it as the First Rule, which can easily prompt us to consider it as the text that Francis and his first brothers brought to Innocent III in 1209. In both instances, the titles are misleading. The primitive proposal of 1209 became part of a much larger document, or, to put it another way, the original description of the gospel life was expanded as the number of brothers increased and their experiences became more varied. But the last period of the text's development came to an end in 1221 when all the brothers gathered to discuss their way of life. We have, then, a description of gospel life that includes many stages of development, one that reflects the developments of the primitive fraternity itself. We call it the Earlier Rule to distinguish it from the Later Rule, which Francis and his brothers wrote and submitted to Pope Honorius III in November 1223 for his approval.

The description of life that Francis brought to Pope Innocent in 1209, however, was a very straightforward collection of texts from the Gospels. Thomas of Celano tells us that certain things were added for the sake of uniformity, probably the manner of reciting the Liturgy of the Hours and of performing manual work. We can see the traces of this simple proposal at the beginning of the Earlier Rule:

The rule and life of these brothers is this: to live in obedience, in chastity, and without anything of their own, and to follow the teaching and footprints of our Lord Jesus Christ (cf. 1 Pet. 2:21), Who says: *If you wish to be perfect, go* (Matt. 19:21), *sell everything* (Luke 18:22) *you have and give it to the poor, and you will have treasure in heaven; and come, follow me* (Matt. 19:21). And, *If anyone wishes to come after me, let him deny himself and take up his cross and follow me* (Matt. 16:24 E). Again: *If anyone wishes to come to me and does not hate father and mother and wife and children and brothers and sisters, and even his own life, he cannot be my disciple* (Luke 14:26 E). And: *Everyone who has left father or mother, brother or sisters, wife or children, houses or lands* (Matt. 19:29 E) *because of me* (Mark 10:29), *will receive a hundred fold and will possess eternal life* (cf. Matt. 19:29 E; Mark 10:29; Luke 18:30).

In this simple collection of passages from the Gospels, we come across a formula articulating the three evangelical counsels of poverty, chastity, and obedience, which might prompt us to wonder if this was part of the original document. In fact, the passage reflects one inserted into the rule of the Trinitarians, which was approved by Pope Innocent III nine years earlier. It also reflects Innocent's letter to the Benedictine abbot of Subiaco, a letter that teaches that the essence of religious life consisted in these three evangelical councils. That might make us wonder if Francis, arriving at the papal court with his collection of passages from the Gospels, learned that he would be smart to insert that formula into his proposal. Whether this is the case or not, we can imagine that he saw no contradiction between what he was proposing and the more limited concepts of the three counsels.

How does Francis envision entrance into his fraternity? The answer given us in the second chapter of the Earlier Rule is more complicated than it appears because, as we have said, it was originally composed of texts from the Gospels that were elaborated upon as circumstances warranted. We can suppose that the original text looked like this:

If anyone, wishing by divine inspiration to accept this life, comes to our brothers, let him be received by them with kindness. After this has been done, let the above-mentioned person — if he wishes and is capable of doing so spiritually without any difficulty — sell all his belongings and be diligent in giving everything to the poor (cf. Matt. 19:21; Luke 18:22). Let all the brothers wear poor clothes and, with the blessing of God, they can patch them with sackcloth and other pieces, for the Lord says in the Gospel: *Those who wear expensive clothing and live in luxury* (Luke 7:25) and *who dress in fine garments are in the houses of kings* (Matt. 11:8). Although they may be called hypocrites, let them nevertheless not cease from doing good and let them not seek expensive clothing in this world that they might have a garment in the kingdom of heaven (cf. Matt. 22:11).

Notice the simplicity of the statement and its gospel focus. Francis describes our sole motivation with a term — "divine inspiration" — that was used primarily by medieval scholars to refer to the origin of Revelation. It is an echo of 2 Tim. 3:16: "All Scripture is inspired by God and is useful for teaching the truth, rebuking error, correcting faults, and giving instruction for right living." Thus Francis presumes that our wish is an expression of the same Spirit that guided the prophets, the evangelists, and all the human authors of Sacred Scripture. The way to ascertain if that is the case is to look carefully at the gospel orientation and expression of our lives. This being the case, the brothers are directed to receive newcomers with kindness. At first this may not seem to be an exceptional directive, yet it is in direct contrast with the Benedictine approach, which permitted a newcomer to enter only after a period of trial. "Do not grant newcomers to the monastic life an easy entry, but, as the apostle says, 'Test the spirits to see if they are from God' (1 John 4:1)." Francis, in contrast, would have newcomers received with kindness. Even at this early stage, it seems, he realized that we are all God's gifts to one another and instruments opening God's mysterious presence.

There is only one condition: selling all our belongings and giving the proceeds to the poor. Those are clearly the words Francis himself heard. What more could he ask of those who wish to follow him? This means quite simply that we enter his company materially poor, without any claims to what would give us security or make us comfortable. It is our passport to the kingdom of heaven, which is promised only to the poor. So Francis would have us dress as the poor. We find no description of a religious garb or an official insignia. No, only our poor clothes, patched and mended as they show their wear by sackcloth and other pieces. His reasons for this? The words of the Gospels themselves, which are quite explicit about those who wear expensive clothing and live in luxury.

But as the number of those asking to join the primitive fraternity steadily increased, Francis and his brothers added to the gospel ideals to refine the process of admitting one to their number. Thus these verses seem to have been added to that core that we just read:

If he is determined to accept our life, let the brothers be very careful not to become involved in his temporal affairs, but let them present him to their minister as quickly as possible. Let the brothers and the minister of the brothers be careful not to interfere in any way in his temporal affairs; let them not accept money either by themselves or through an intermediary. Nevertheless, if they are in need, the brothers, like other poor people, can accept, instead of money, whatever is needed for the body.

How this addition reflects the weakness of human nature! It is a caution for those responsible not to become involved in the negotiations of aspirants in selling and giving away their goods. We easily can imagine some of the experiences that prompted the brothers to be more precise in following the simple prerequisites of the gospel. Human nature being what it is, there are inevitably temptations to suggest that certain needs could easily be remedied by the generosity of those who wished to join us. A word here, a gesture there, all could lead to persuading those wishing to join our company to donate their goods to the fraternity. Francis would have none of it.

By 1220, however, Cardinal Hugolino had undoubtedly become involved in guiding the brothers and quite possibly went to Honorius III for a papal document that would protect the expanding brotherhood. On September 22, 1220, the pope issued a papal decree, *Cum secundum consilium,* in which he states: "[S]o that those who are about to undertake regular observance may first try it and be themselves tried in it,... [the brothers] are strictly forbidden to admit anyone to profession unless he has been under a year of probation." We can see that this piece of legislation influenced yet another stage of development:

When he has returned, the minister may give him the clothes of probation for a year, that is, two tunics without a hood, a cord, trousers, and a small cape reaching to the cord. When the year and term of probation has ended, let him be received into obedience. After this it will be unlawful for him to join another Order or to "wander outside obedience" according to the decree of the Lord Pope and the Gospel, for *no one putting his hand to the plow and looking to what was left behind is fit for the kingdom of God* (Luke 9:62). If anyone comes, however, who cannot give away his belongings without difficulty and has the spiritual will to do so, let him leave them behind, and it will suffice for him. Let no one be received contrary to the rite and practice of the Holy Church. Let all the other brothers who have already promised obedience have one tunic with a hood and, if it is necessary, another without a hood and a cord and trousers.

Suddenly we find the introduction of "the clothes of probation," which are given to aspirants for a year. At the end of the year, they are accepted into obedience and forbidden thereafter to wander outside of its limits. They also receive a new set of clothes. We also find an indictment of those who turn back to their former way of life. The simple gospel vision of Francis became more sophisticated and complex as did the size of his primitive fraternity. Is that so unusual? Benedict begins his rule with the simple invitation: "Listen carefully, my child, to my instructions, and attend to them with the ears of your heart." What follows, however, is a lengthy description of Christian life that encompasses seventy-three chapters. The problem is not with the gospel; it is with us. Because of our sinfulness, we tie ourselves up in unending questions and complicated procedures.

Now Francis directs our attention beyond the externals and the fear of being called hypocrites to the sincerity of looking intensely for the kingdom of God.

The Lord says: *This kind* of devil *cannot come out except* through fasting and prayer (cf. Mark 9:29 [V 9:28]); and again: *When you fast do not become gloomy like the hypocrites* (Matt. 6:16). For this reason let all the brothers, whether clerical or lay, recite the Divine Office, the praises and prayers, as is required of them.

Let the clerical brothers recite the Office and say it for the living and the dead according to the custom of clerics. For the failings and negligence of the brothers, let them say each day the *Have mercy on me, O God* (Psalm 51 [V 50]) with the *Our Father* (Matt. 6:9–13); and for the deceased brothers let them say the *Out of the depths* (Psalm 130 [V 129]) with the *Our Father*. They may have only the books necessary to fulfill their office.

The lay brothers who know how to read the Psalter may have one. Those who do not know how to read, however, may not be permitted to have any book. Let the lay brothers say the *Creed* and twenty-four *Our Father's* with the *Glory to the Father* for Matins; for Lauds, let them say five; for Prime, the *Creed* and seven *Our Father's* with the *Glory to the Father*; for each of the hours, Terce, Sext and None, seven; for Vespers, twelve; for Compline, the *Creed* and seven *Our Father's* with the *Glory to the Father*; for the deceased, seven *Our Father's* with the *Eternal Rest*; and for the failings and negligence of the brothers three *Our Father's* each day.

Similarly, let all the brothers fast from the feast of All Saints until the Nativity, and from the Epiphany, when our Lord Jesus Christ began to fast, until Easter. However, at other times, according to this life, let them not be bound to fast except on Fridays. Let it be lawful for them, according to the Gospel, to eat of all the food that is placed before them (cf. Luke 10:8).

Our contemporary approach to the Liturgy of the Hours echoes that of the centuries. It is quite simply the sanctification of each day binding us together in praising God and in centering our lives on the Word of God. Francis would have all of us do the same. As we saw in the Rule for the Hermitages, he invites us to leave our individual concerns, holy as they might be, to come together to pray the Our Father. It is inspirational to imagine his first companions traveling throughout the Italian countryside and stopping to pray Midday Prayer. That is precisely what he would have us do: drop what we are doing to unite with one another in God's Word.

This centering of our lives in the Word leads us to grapple with the demands of our appetites and desires. Asceticism used to receive a great deal of attention in the pursuit of spiritual growth. Now we tend to overlook many of its century-old practices in order to accentuate more positive values. Nevertheless, Francis quite rightly suggests that the Word teaches us throughout the day how self-centered and needing of discipline we truly are. His encouragement to fast and abstain flows not from the pursuit of achieving perfection for its own sake but from an awareness of what God's Word teaches us about our shortcomings. Together, the Word and our expressions of self-discipline overcome any tendencies to be caught up in externals or to be concerned about what others see as hypocrisy. No, they provide us with tools necessary for authenticity, for re-creating ourselves in God's image and likeness.

Nowhere should the consequences of this Word-centered life be more obvious than in our life together. "There are as many centers to the universe," Alesandr Solzhenitsyn once wrote, "as there are human beings in it." What a different picture Francis presents in the next section of the Earlier Rule, chapters 4, 5, and 6, as he molds our lives according to the gospel. Unfortunately we encounter the same difficulty with these chapters as we did with chapter 2 — that is, there are a number of historical layers. For example, the brothers did not divide the fraternity into provinces until 1217, when they also appointed provincial ministers who became responsible for the well-being of their brothers. Moreover, the document that established the novitiate in 1220 also suggested that some brothers not only were wandering about as they wished but were also falling into sin. We can find traces then of Francis's struggle to maintain his simple gospel vision as his followers were increasing and as his idealism confronted the reality of our sinful human nature.

In the name of the Lord!

Let all the brothers who have been designated the ministers and servants of the other brothers assign their brothers in the provinces and places where they may be, and let them frequently visit, admonish and encourage them spiritually. Let all my other brothers diligently obey them in those matters concerning the well-being of their soul and which are not contrary to our life.

Let them behave among themselves according to what the Lord says: *Do to others what you would have them do to you* (Matt. 7:12); and "Do not do to another what you would not have done to you."

Let the ministers and servants remember what the Lord says: I have *not* come *to be served, but to serve* (Matt. 20:28); and because the care of the brothers' souls has been entrusted to them, if anything is lost on account of their fault or bad example, they will have *to render an account* before the Lord Jesus Christ *on the day of judgment* (cf. Matt. 12:36).

Protect your soul, therefore, and those of your brothers, because *it is a fearful thing to fall into the hands of the living God* (Heb. 10:31). If anyone of the ministers commands one of the brothers something contrary to our life or to his soul, he is not bound to obey him because obedience is not something in which a fault or sin is committed.

However, let all the brothers subject to the ministers and servants reasonably and attentively consider the deeds of the ministers and servants. If they see any of them walking according to the flesh and not according to the Spirit in keeping with the integrity of our life (cf. Rom. 8:4), if he does not improve after a third admonition, let them inform the minister and servant of the whole fraternity at the Chapter of Pentecost regardless of what objection deters them.

Moreover, if, anywhere among the brothers, there is a brother who wishes to live according to the flesh and not according to the Spirit (cf. Rom. 8:4), let the brothers with whom he is living admonish, instruct and correct him humbly and attentively. If, however, after the third admonition he refuses to improve (cf. Matt. 18:15–17), let them send or report him, as soon as they can, to their minister and servant; and let the minister and servant deal with him as he considers best before God.

Let all the brothers, both the ministers and servants as well as the others, be careful not to be disturbed or angered at the sin or the evil of another because the devil wishes to destroy many because of the fault of another. But let them spiritually help the one who has sinned as best they can, because *those who are well do not need a physician, but the sick do* (cf. Matt. 9:12; Mark 2:17).

Likewise, let all the brothers not have power or control in this instance, especially among themselves; for, as the Lord says in the Gospel: *The rulers of the Gentiles lord it over them and the great ones make their authority over them felt* (Matt. 20:25); *it shall not be so among the brothers* (Matt. 20:26a). Let whoever *wishes to be the greater* among them *be* their *minister* (cf. Matt. 20:26b) and *servant* (Matt. 20:27). *Let whoever is the greater among them become the least* (Luke 22:26).

Let no brother do or say anything evil to another; on the contrary, *through the charity of the Spirit, let them serve* and obey *one another* voluntarily (Gal. 5:13; cf. 1 Pet. 1:22; 2:13–15). This is the true and holy obedience of our Lord Jesus Christ.

Let all the brothers, as often as *they have turned away from the commands of the Lord* and "wandered outside obedience," as the Prophet says, know they are cursed outside obedience as long as they knowingly remain in such a sin (Ps. 119:21 [V 118:21]). When they have persevered in the Lord's commands as they have promised by the Holy Gospel and their life, let them know they have remained in true obedience and are blessed by the Lord.

If they cannot observe this life, let the brothers, wherever they may be, have recourse to their minister, as soon as they can, making this known to him. Let the minister, on his part, strive to provide for them as he would wish to have done for him were he in a similar position (cf. Matt. 7:12).

Let no one be called *prior* (cf. Matt. 20:27), but let everyone in general be called a lesser brother (cf. Matt. 23:8; Luke 22:26). Let one wash the feet of the other (cf. John 13:14).

It was Pope Paul VI who first wrote of a "civilization of love," a phrase used repeatedly by his successor, John Paul II. These words of Francis may well provide the blueprint as they describe a society in which there is no power or control over one another, in which authority is converted into loving service. Is this Francis the dreamer? On the contrary, this is the gospel life that he envisions for all who, like him, would revel in the revelation of Jesus. "Do to others what you would have them do to you," he tells them in the words of Jesus. And lest the message be lost, he repeats it in a negative way: "Do not do to another what you would not have done to you." "Let no one be called the first," he reminds us again in the words of Matthew's Gospel, "but let everyone in general be called a lesser brother." This is Francis's first call to minority, a call to be less than those with whom one is living, to be their servant. Were these words not enough, he places before us the image of Jesus himself: "Let one wash the feet of the other." What could be simpler?

Yet Francis would not have us be dreamy idealists. The reality of sin twists and distorts our gospel dreams and prompts our weakened human nature to turn in on itself. We can easily imagine Francis continually reminding his brothers and encouraging them in their struggles. Now he would have those who take his place do the same, that is, visit, admonish, and encourage their companions spiritually. Yet there is no hint that Francis sees those responsible for others in a superior position. The suggestion never appears in his writings. No, they are not only ministers but servants as well, entrusted with the responsibility of caring for others' spiritual growth, of ensuring that they walk not "according to the flesh" but "according to the Spirit." We will see how demanding a responsibility this is when we read Francis's powerful Letter to a Minister, a letter to an unknown brother who suffered because of that responsibility. Now we must continue reading this description of gospel life.

Chapter 7 is one of the oldest sections of the Earlier Rule

and may well have been part of the document that Francis and the first brothers presented to Pope Innocent III in 1209. In these verses we perceive a style of life totally different from the more structured life of traditional religious. The brothers did not yet have their own community dwelling places and probably lived among others. Nor were they involved in any typically religious or clerical ministries; on the contrary, they seemed to have sustained themselves by working for others as laborers or servants. This chapter, in other words, presents a picture of men who were living a life that was guided more simply by the gospel than by any principles of established religious life:

None of the brothers may be treasurers or overseers in any of those places where they may be staying to serve or work among others. They may not be in charge in the houses in which they serve; nor may they accept any office which would generate scandal or *be harmful to their souls* (cf. Mark 8:36); Let them, instead, be the lesser ones (cf. Luke 22:26) and be subject to all in the same house (cf. 1 Pet. 2:13).

Let the brothers who know how to work do so and exercise that trade they have learned, provided it is not contrary to the good of their souls and can be performed honestly. For the prophet says: *You shall eat the fruit of your labors; you are blessed and it shall be well for you* (Ps. 128:2 [V 127:2]). The Apostle says: *Whoever does not wish to work shall not eat* (cf. 2 Thess. 3:10); and *Everyone should remain* in that trade and office *in which he has been called* (cf. 1 Cor. 7:24).

For their work they can receive whatever is necessary excepting money. When it is necessary, they may seek alms like other poor people. It is lawful for them to have the tools and instruments suitable for their trades.

Let all the brothers always strive to exert themselves in doing good works, for it is written: "Always do something good that the devil may find you occupied." And again: "Idleness is an enemy of the soul." Servants of God, therefore, must always apply themselves to prayer or some good work.

Let the brothers, wherever they may be, either in hermitages or other places, be careful not to make any place their own or contend with anyone for it. Whoever comes to them, friend or foe, thief or robber, let him be received with kindness.

Wherever the brothers may be and in whatever place they may meet, they should revere one another, spiritually and attentively, and *honor one another without complaining* (1 Pet. 4:9). Let them be careful not to appear outwardly as sad and gloomy hypocrites; but let them show themselves *joyful*, cheerful and consistently gracious *in the Lord* (cf. Phil. 4:4).

Now we see that the principles that govern the relations among the brothers themselves are extended to their relations with those who are in different realities and circumstances. "Let them, instead, be the lesser ones (cf. Luke 22:26)," Francis repeats, "and be subject to all in the same house (cf. 1 Pet. 2:13)." He calls us all to that same minority that he envisions for the brothers. Now he encourages us to be less than those among whom we find ourselves — in this first instance, in the context of day-to-day work. This is not only living among others and working as their peers. It is not simply the assumption of equality or of sharing the condition of work. It is serving and being dependent upon them. Here again, there is no question of having dominion or power over others; on the contrary, Francis would have us be subject to others. This is what it means to be a minor.

Of course, the first two paragraphs of this chapter take for granted that the brothers are working. But this is not something remarkable for Francis; it is simply the teaching of the Old and New Testaments. Moreover, it reflects the wisdom of monasticism as quotations from Benedict, Jerome, and Gregory the Great aptly suggest. Work is simply part of living.

In between these biblical and monastic quotations, however, we encounter what may be as much of a stumbling block as social advancement was for any gospel idealist: payment for work. The document is quite clear: "For their work they can receive whatever is necessary." But immediately a restriction is added: money. Why? We are not told. Nevertheless, the following chapter continues the prohibition even more forcefully:

The Lord teaches in the Gospel: *Watch, beware of all* malice and *greed* (cf. Luke 12:15). *Guard yourselves* against the anxieties of this world and *the cares of this life* (cf. Luke 21:34; Matt. 13:22).

Let none of the brothers, therefore, wherever he may be or go, carry, receive, or have received in any way coin or money, whether for clothing, books, or payment for some work — indeed, not for any reason, unless for an evident need of the sick brothers; because we should not think of coin or money having any greater usefulness than stones. The devil wants to blind those who desire or consider it better than stones. Let us who have left all things (cf. Matt. 19:27), then, be careful of not losing the kingdom of heaven for so little.

If we find coins in some place, let us pay no more attention to them than to the dust we trample underfoot, for *vanity of vanities and all is vanity* (Eccles. 1:2). If by chance, which God forbid, it happens that some brother is collecting or holding coin or money, unless it is only for the aforesaid needs of the sick, let all the brothers consider him a deceptive brother, an apostate, a thief, a robber, and as the one who held the money bag (cf. John 12:6), unless he has sincerely repented.

Let the brothers in no way receive, arrange to receive, seek, or arrange to seek money for leprosaria or coins for any houses or places; and let them not accompany anyone begging money or coins for such places. The brothers can perform for those places, however, other services not contrary to our life with the blessing of God. Nevertheless, the brothers can beg alms for a manifest need of the lepers. But let them beware of money. Similarly, let all the brothers be careful of going throughout the world for filthy gain.

Why is Francis so vehement about the use of money? He even prefaces his prohibition with Jesus' words concerning greed and anxiety. The reason may be found in the fact that money had not yet become the medium of exchange that it is for us; it was more a means of what we would consider capital investment. Nevertheless, the economic world in which Francis and the brothers lived was similar to our own. As our use of computers becomes more sophisticated, money is changing by losing its significance in favor of a system of credit cards. Each day credit cards are becoming more important for us. Not only do they enable us to purchase items; they also provide instant information concerning our assets or savings. In other words, they are signs of our worth. In Francis's day, money was still considered a sign of financial security and strength, a luxury that the poor lacked.

Thus we find that now familiar phrase, "like other poor people." Echoing biblical themes, Francis tells the brothers that to have what is necessary, the first thing they (the "lesser ones") must do is to work: this is as much as "other poor people" seek to do. If we cannot work because we are not in a position to do so or because we cannot find work or because our work is not adequately rewarded, then we should go seeking alms as the poor do. Francis proposes for us lesser ones a social, concrete point of reference, one that is established by the poor.

From this perspective, Francis offers us two wonderful characteristics, hospitality and joy. At first, they seem to be in opposition to the poor life we are to embrace. Yet there is no greater contribution that Francis makes to the spirituality of gospel poverty than the strong bond that he establishes between poverty and fraternity, especially a fraternity that is open to all. We can trace this as a thread throughout his writings, as we have already seen in his Rule for the Hermitages. Poverty, he realized, was the great leveler in that it made everyone dependent on and open to the other. Notice the almost carefree abandon that is expressed in this passage: "Let the brothers, wherever they may be, either in hermitages or other places, be careful not to make any place their own or contend with anyone for it. Whoever comes to them, friend or foe, thief or robber, let him be received with kindness." Not only would Francis have us avoid the tendencies to claim some place as our own and to dispute about it; he goes further in suggesting that we open it to everyone, even those who would do us harm or steal from us. If this is our attitude toward "outsiders," then this attitude should be amplified in our relations with one another. Hospitality, respect, and mutual deference — these are the characteristics that should be obvious in all our dealings: "Wherever the brothers may be and in whatever place they may meet, they should revere one another, spiritually and attentively, and *honor one another without complaining* (1 Pet. 4:9)."

No religious rule before that of Francis had ever contained a sentence such as this: "Let them be careful not to appear outwardly as sad and gloomy hypocrites; but let them show themselves *joyful*, cheerful and consistently gracious *in the Lord* (cf. Phil. 4:4)." How could anyone attempt to legislate joyfulness? Yet Francis definitely saw it as a characteristic that should be evident to everyone. This is an essential ingredient of the minority embraced by Francis and his followers. We might interpret it as an antidote to the severe, somber expressions of penance found in some of the penitential movements contemporary with Francis. Yet it flows from a much more profound reason, our identification with the humility and poverty embraced by Jesus.

Let all the brothers strive to follow the humility and poverty of our Lord Jesus Christ and remember that we should have nothing else in the whole world except, as the Apostle says: *having food and clothing, we are content with these* (cf. 1 Tim. 6:8).

They must rejoice when they live among people considered of little value and looked down upon, among the poor and the powerless, the sick and the lepers, and the beggars by the wayside.

When it is necessary, let them go for alms. Let them not be ashamed and remember, moreover, that our Lord Jesus Christ, *the Son of the* all powerful *living God, set His face like flint* and was not ashamed (cf. John 11:27; Isa. 50:7). He was poor and a stranger and lived on alms, He, the Blessed Virgin, and His disciples. When people reproach them and refuse to give them alms, let them thank God for this because they will receive great honor before the tribunal of our Lord Jesus Christ for such insults. Let them know that reproach is charged not to those who suffer it but to those who caused it. Alms are a legacy and a justice due to the poor that our Lord Jesus Christ acquired for us. The brothers who work to acquire them will receive a great reward and enable those who grant them to gain and acquire one; for all that people leave behind in the world will perish, but they will have a reward from the Lord for the charity and almsgiving they have done.

Let each one confidently make known his need to another that the other might discover what is needed and minister to him. Let each one love and care for his brother as a mother loves and cares for her son in those matters in which God has given him the grace (cf. 1 Thess. 2:7). *Let the one who does not eat not judge the one who does* (Rom. 14:3b).

Whenever a need arises, all the brothers, wherever they may be, are permitted to consume every food that people can eat, as the Lord says of David who ate *the loaves of offering* (cf. Matt. 12:4) *that only the priests could lawfully eat* (Mark 2:26).

Let them remember what the Lord says: *Be careful that your hearts do not become drowsy from carousing, drunkenness and the anxieties of daily life, and that the day catches you by surprise; for that day will assault everyone who lives on the face of the earth like a trap* (Luke 21:34–35). Similarly, in time of a manifest necessity, let all the brothers do as the Lord has given them the grace to satisfy their needs, because necessity has no law.

Thus far, Francis has provided us with a practical, day-to-day form of life. As a community of faith centered on God's Word, we live as brothers and sisters. In order to sustain ourselves, we work and receive whatever is necessary; if that is not given to us, we beg and depend on the goodness and generosity of God. Now, however, Francis presents another gospel foundation that transcends these practical norms. In all things we must identify with the poor and humble Jesus. There is no question of circumstances or social climate, no discussion of acceptance or rejection by others. No, we are confronted with a simple, straightforward principle of daily life: Jesus Christ. In light of this, Francis would have us rejoice when we live among the *anawim:* those "considered of little value and looked down upon,...the poor and the powerless, the sick and the lepers, and the beggars along the wayside." It is not a question of rejecting others. It is a question of rejoicing when we can live poorly among the poor. Why embrace such a way of life? For no other reason than out of love of Christ who chose it out of love of us.

Once again Francis returns to having confidence in the generosity of others. In this instance, however, he deepens our motivation by placing before us the Son of God and by offering us a direct reference to the Suffering Servant of God. Because of Christ, Francis tells us, the poor have a right to the care of those who are well-off, and, by taxing their generosity, they provide an occasion of grace for them. It is an extraordinary social doctrine, which is rooted in Francis's profound belief in God's choice of poverty as a means of making us rich. We certainly have another aspect of the blueprint for his "civilization of love" provided by the Earlier Rule, one that goes far beyond our contemporary quest for solidarity with the poor. Our identification with the poor Christ, moreover, gives us the freedom to turn to one another, to express our needs, and to expect satisfaction. It provides, in other words, a foundation for our life of fraternity in which we become instruments of grace for one another. Poverty, in Francis's view, becomes a language of love, of concern for one another. It breaks down the barriers that our pride and independence build to protect us from being too vulnerable. It provides an environment of freedom in which true happiness consists in the love expressed by another and, ultimately, by God. "This vocation to poverty," suggests Paul VI, "witnesses to the authenticity of the Gospel."

If any of the brothers falls ill, wherever he may be, let the other brothers not leave him behind unless one of the brothers — or several of them, if that is necessary — is designated to serve him as "they would want to be served themselves." In case of the greatest need, however, they can entrust him to some person who should do what needs to be done for his sickness.

I beg the sick brother to thank God for everything and to desire to be whatever the Lord wills, whether sick or well, because God teaches all those He *has destined for eternal life* (Acts 13:48) "by the torments of punishments," sicknesses, "and the spirit of sorrow," as the Lord says: *Those whom I love, I correct and chastise* (Rev. 3:19).

If anyone is disturbed or angry at either God or his brothers, or perhaps anxiously and forcefully seeks medicine with too much of a desire to free the flesh that is soon to die and is an enemy of the soul: this comes to him from the Evil One and is carnal. He does not seem to be one of the brothers for he loves his body more than his soul.

Perhaps no one experiences poverty and the need to rely on another as much as the sick. It is only natural then that Francis, who himself experienced the ravages of sickness at this time, encourages us not only to be sensitive to those who are sick but even to thank God for sickness when it comes to us. A chronicle of an ancient Franciscan friary contains a passage stating: "We have had few blessings this year since there have been no sick among us." What a consoling thought! Not only does sickness bring its own kind of blessing; it also brings untold blessings for those who care for the sick. Yet we can see Francis's lofty idealism in this paragraph, especially as he encourages the sick not to be disturbed or angry at God or at another because of their sickness. He even cautions them against anxiety and force in seeking the medicines that will cure them. These are attitudes that are signs of the spirit of the flesh or of the presence of the Evil One. No, the truly spiritual person, Francis suggests, accepts sickness as God's blessing and love.

This prompts Francis to call us to reflect upon the dynamics of fraternal life. His words remind us that fraternity is not a matter of buildings or structures. No, it is simply about ourselves — sinful human beings with weaknesses and failings as well as gifts and blessings.

Let all the brothers be careful not to slander or engage in disputes (cf. 2 Tim. 2:14); let them strive, instead, to keep silence whenever God gives them the grace. Let them not quarrel among themselves or with others, but let them strive to respond humbly, saying: *I am a useless servant* (cf. Luke 17:10). Let them not become angry because *whoever is angry with his brother is liable to judgment; whoever says to his brother "fool" shall be answerable to the Council; whoever says "fool" will be liable to fiery Gehenna* (Matt. 5:22).

Let them love one another, as the Lord says: *This is my commandment: love one another as I have loved you* (John 15:12). Let them express the love they have for one another by their deeds (cf. James 2:18), as the Apostle says: *Let us not love in word or speech, but in deed and truth* (1 John 3:18).

Let them revile no one (cf. Titus 3:2). Let them not grumble or detract from others, for it is written: *Gossips* and *detractors* are *detestable* to God (cf. Rom. 1:29–30). Let them be *modest by showing graciousness toward everyone* (cf. Titus 3:2). Let them not judge (cf. Matt. 7:1) or condemn. As the Lord says, let them not consider the least sins of others (cf. Matt. 7:3; Luke 6:41); let them, instead, reflect more upon their own sins *in the bitterness of their soul* (Isa. 38:15). Let them struggle *to enter through the narrow gate* (Luke 13:24), for the Lord says: *The gate is narrow and the road that leads to life constricted; those who find it are few* (Matt. 7:14).

This is a chapter concerning relationships, those that Francis sees characterizing our attempts to build a gospel unity. Yet it is also a chapter of contrasts as he envisions our positive efforts of caring and respecting one another overcoming the negative attitudes brought about by our weakened, sinful nature. As we can see, the entire chapter is a collage of New Testament quotations. At its very heart, though, is Jesus' command at the Last Supper, "This is my commandment: love one another as I have loved you." The words resonate deeply with those in which Francis reminds us of our obligation to serve one another as Christ did by washing the feet of his disciples or of the Golden Rule of the Beatitudes, "Do to others as you would have them do to you." Two years after Francis's death, Thomas of Celano described his first followers. "Truly, upon a foundation of constancy," he writes, "a noble structure of charity arose, in which the living stones, gathered from all parts of the world, were gathered into a dwelling place of the Holy Spirit." His words must have flowed from his reflections on the attempts of those first followers to live up to the lofty vision Francis offered them.

What follows, however, undoubtedly flows from the difficulties Francis and his first brothers must have encountered while traveling about the Italian countryside.

Let all the brothers, wherever they may be or may go, avoid evil glances and association with women. No one may counsel them, travel alone with them or eat out of the same dish with them. When giving penance or some spiritual advice, let priests speak with them in a becoming way. No woman whatsoever may be received to obedience by any brother, but after spiritual advice has been given to her, let her do penance wherever she wants.

Let us all keep close watch over ourselves and keep all our members clean, for the Lord says: *Whoever looks at a woman with lust has already committed adultery with her in his heart* (Matt. 5:28); and the Apostle: *Do you not know that your members are a temple of the Holy Spirit?* (cf. 1 Cor. 6:19); therefore, whoever *violates God's temple, God will destroy* (1 Cor. 3:17).

While these words seem so foreign to our contemporary approach, they reflect abuses described and forbidden in many twelfth- and thirteenth-century manuals of canon law. When we look at Francis's biographies, we quickly see his respect and courtesy for women. Clare, Lady Jacoba, the mothers of some of his brothers, the five women he directed to join the Poor Ladies in St. Damian's: these are but a few of those who received Francis's attention. He truly emerges as a man of chivalry. Yet he strongly directs the brothers to avoid looking at women as mere objects of passion and encourages them to avoid any circumstance that might be suspect or that might lead to compromise. Where that could lead we can quickly see in the following chapter:

If any brother commits fornication at the instigation of the devil, let him be deprived of the habit he has lost by his wickedness, put it aside completely, and be altogether expelled from our Order. Afterwards he may do penance (cf. 1 Cor. 5:4–5).

It is difficult to fathom the strength of the words. They are so unlike the compassionate, caring Francis whom we have encountered. Yet here he proposes that someone who has fallen be deprived of the habit and be thrown out of the fraternity. Only then may the sinner do penance. As we will see, the prescription must have caused consternation among the brothers, for within a short time they were clamoring for a clearer direction concerning those who sinned mortally. These words say more about Francis's vision of what unites us than about his attitude toward the one who sins. In the previous chapter we can clearly see his quotation of 1 Corinthians, "Do you not know that your members are a temple of the Holy Spirit?" This simply reinforces what we have seen earlier — that divine inspiration moves someone to ask for a deeper share in gospel life, that is, the Spirit. To commit a sin of the flesh, Francis proposes, is to act contrary to the Spirit. It results in severing the bond of unity. These words, therefore, reveal once again that lofty gospel idealism we have encountered so often. Now we can understand it as an example of the difficulties Francis and his first followers encountered while living a new expression of religious life, one that was not protected by monastic walls but that was lived in the world. In a sense it is appropriate that such realism appears before we return to those lofty ideals, for now Francis calls us to reflect upon our gospel mission in the world:

When the brothers go through the world, let them take *nothing* for the journey, *neither knapsack, nor purse, nor bread, nor money, nor walking stick* (cf. Luke 9:3; 10:4; Matt. 10:10). *Whatever house they enter,* let them *first* say: *Peace to this house* (cf. Luke 10:5). Let them eat and drink *what is placed before them* for as long as they stay *in that house* (cf. Luke 10:7). Let them not resist anyone evil, but whoever strikes them on one cheek, let them offer him the other as well (cf. Matt. 5:39; Luke 6:29). *Whoever takes their cloak, let them not withhold their tunic* (cf. Luke 6:29). *Let them give to all who ask of them and whoever takes what is theirs, let them not seek to take it back* (cf. Luke 6:30).

These words draw our attention away from the more inner dynamics of the fraternity to the missionary dimension of life. It is a clear statement of the gospel ideals that we can discover in chapters 1, 4, 6, and 12: Our starting point should definitely be the description of Thomas of Celano that portrays Francis's discovery of God's will through listening to the Missionary Discourse of Matthew's Gospel. This paragraph is a patchwork of quotations from the Missionary Discourse and the Sermon on the Mount in both Matthew and Luke. Why, we might ask, did Francis and his brothers choose these texts and not others? Why, for example, does Francis overlook the passage "the laborer deserves his keep" (Matt. 10:10) or that of "shaking the dust from your feet" (Matt. 10:14)? More surprisingly, why does Francis omit those consoling verses of Matt. 10:29–30 that tell of the Father's care for those who have been sent in the name of Jesus?

The biblical instructions are directed without any qualification to "the brothers when they go through the world." There is no question of models of social interaction or of productivity; nor is there a discussion of the socioeconomic significance of peace, as some might suggest. This directive is biblical through and through and is placed before every one of Francis's followers suggesting not simply a geographical-spatial context as much as one that is socio-theological. Francis takes lines word-for-word from the Missionary Discourse. The text alone speaks to us, and from it we can draw the image of the missionary according to the "gospel of Francis."

What follows, however, offers us some concrete examples of this gospel idealism:

I direct all my brothers, both cleric and lay, that when they go through the world or dwell in places they in no way keep any animal either with them, in the care of another, or in any other way. Let it not be lawful for them to ride horseback unless they are compelled by sickness or a great need.

Our temptation in reading this text might be simply to dismiss it as a piece of medieval legislation that has no meaning for our world. In fact, it does echo the laws governing some other religious communities contemporary with that of Francis. Yet Francis directs this to *all* who travel throughout the world or take up residence. That all-embracing formula, "all my brothers, both cleric and lay," suggests the importance of this directive, for Francis uses it only in passages that he considers significant. In this instance, therefore, to live the gospel mandate seriously is to "take nothing for your journey." Our understanding of mission, in other words, must be considered in light of the poverty that each of us as proclaimers of the gospel must exemplify.

This introduces Francis's vision of the evangelization of nonbelievers, one of the most extraordinary pieces of legislation found in any medieval religious rule, in fact, the first such statement. While we might see in it the influence of the Fourth Lateran's call for a new Crusade to win back the Holy Land from the Muslims, we can more easily see the powerful gospel spirituality of Francis, for it resonates deeply with his profound love of the Son of God.

The Lord says: *Behold I am sending you like sheep in the midst of wolves.* Therefore, *be prudent as serpents and simple as doves* (Matt. 10:16). Let any brother, then, who desires by divine inspiration to go among the Saracens and other non-believers go with the permission of his minister and servant. Let the minister, if he sees they are fit to be sent, give them permission and not oppose them, for he will be bound to render an accounting to the Lord (cf. Luke 16:2) if he has proceeded without discernment in this and other matters.

As for the brothers who go, they can live spiritually among the Saracens and non-believers in two ways. One way is not to engage in arguments (cf. Titus 3:2) or disputes (cf. 2 Tim. 2:14) but to be subject *to every human creature for God's sake* (1 Pet. 2:13) and to acknowledge they are Christians. The other way is to announce the Word of God, when they see it pleases the Lord, in order that [unbelievers] may believe in the all-powerful God, the Father, the Son and the Holy Spirit, the Creator of all, the Son, the Redeemer and Savior, and be baptized and become Christians because *no one can enter the kingdom of God without being reborn of water and the Holy Spirit* (cf. John 3:5).

They can say to them and the others these and other things which please God because the Lord says in the Gospel: *Whoever acknowledges me before others I will acknowledge before my heavenly Father* (Matt. 10:32). *Whoever is ashamed of me and of my words, the Son of Man will be ashamed of when he comes in his glory and in the glory of the Father* (cf. Luke 9:26).

Let all my brothers, wherever they may be, remember that they have given themselves and abandoned their bodies to the Lord Jesus Christ. For love of Him, they must make themselves vulnerable to their enemies, both visible and invisible, because the Lord says: *Whoever loses his life because of me will save it* (Luke 9:24) in eternal life (Matt. 25:46). *Blessed are they who suffer persecution for the sake of justice, for theirs is the kingdom of heaven* (Matt. 5:10). *If they persecuted me, they will also persecute you* (John 15:20). *If they persecute you in one town, flee to another* (Matt. 10:23). *Blessed are you* (Matt. 5:11) *when people hate you* (Luke 6:22), *speak evil of you* (Matt. 5:11), *persecute, expel, and abuse you, denounce your name as evil* (Luke 6:22) *and utter every kind of slander against you because of me* (Matt. 5:11). *Rejoice and be glad on that day* (Luke 6:23) *because your reward is great in heaven* (cf. Matt. 5:12).

I tell you, my friends, do not be afraid of them (Luke 12:4) *and do not fear those who kill the body* (Matt. 10:28) *and afterwards have nothing more to do* (Luke 12:4). *See that you are not alarmed* (Matt. 24:6). *For by your patience, you will possess your souls* (Luke 21:19); *whoever perseveres to the end will be saved* (Matt. 10:22; 24:13).

Francis proposes three different expressions of missionary activity: witness, that is, living in minority and as sincere Christians; proclamation, that is, announcing God's Word; and, finally, martyrdom, the embrace of death after the example of Jesus. In all three instances Francis implies entering situations that are, humanly speaking, as hopeless "as sheep among wolves" and encourages us quite simply to be without guile, that is, genuine, authentic followers of Jesus, whose good news we proclaim.

"The Gospel must be proclaimed above all by witness," Paul VI maintains. "Take a Christian or a handful of Christians who, in the midst of their own community, show their capacity for understanding and acceptance, their sharing of life and destiny with other people, their solidarity with the efforts for whatever is noble and good. Let us suppose that, in addition, they radiate in an altogether simple and unaffected way their faith in values that go beyond current values, and their hope in something that is not seen and that one would not dare to imagine. Through this wordless witness these Christians stir up irresistible questions in the hearts of those who see how they live: Why are they like this? Why do they live in this way? What or who is it that inspires them? Why are they in our midst? Such a witness is already a silent proclamation of the Good News and a very powerful and effective one." The pope's words echo what Francis so succinctly suggests. Francis, however, encourages us to live this life of Christian witness in minority, by "being subject to everyone for God's sake." In his mind, this is the winning argument, for it is closest to that of Christ himself. Of course, such an attitude makes us vulnerable to the whims of others and open to suffering, but such are the inevitable consequences of identifying with Christ.

After presenting these simple guidelines for the pursuit of the Franciscan mission of proclaiming the gospel, we encounter a chapter of the Earlier Rule that suggests some strong revisional work. The first four sentences seem to have been added at a much later date as a reminder of the teachings of the Fourth Lateran Council. Thus the title that some scribe gave to the chapter, "Preachers." As we can see, however, Francis offers us more of a description of the attitudes we should develop when our gospel mission unfolds successfully.

Let no brother preach contrary to the rite and practice of the Church or without the permission of his minister. Let the minister be careful of granting it without discernment to anyone. Let all the brothers, however, preach by their deeds. No minister or preacher may make a ministry of the brothers or the office of preaching his own, but, when he is told, let him set it aside without objection.

In the love that is God (cf. 1 John 4:16), therefore, I beg all my brothers—those who preach, pray, work, cleric or lay—to strive to humble themselves in everything, not to boast or delight in themselves or inwardly exalt themselves because of the good words and deeds or, for that matter, because of any good that God says or does or at times works in and through them, in keeping with what the Lord says: *Do not rejoice because the spirits are subject to you* (Luke 10:20). We may know with certainty that nothing belongs to us except our vices and sins. We must rejoice, instead, when we fall *into various trials* (cf. James 1:2) and, in this world, suffer every kind of anguish or distress of soul and body for the sake of eternal life.

Let all the brothers, therefore, beware of all pride and vainglory. Let us guard ourselves from the wisdom of this world and the prudence of the flesh (cf. Rom. 8:6). Because the spirit of the flesh very much wants and strives to have the words but cares little for the activity; it does not seek a religion and holiness in an interior spirit, but wants and desires to have a religion and a holiness outwardly apparent to people. They are the ones of whom the Lord says: *Amen, I say to you, they have received their reward* (Matt. 6:2).

The Spirit of the Lord, however, wants the flesh to be mortified and looked down upon, considered of little worth and rejected. It strives for humility and patience, the pure, simple and true peace of the spirit. Above all, it desires the divine fear, the divine wisdom and the divine love of the Father, Son and Holy Spirit.

> Let us refer all good
> to the Lord, God Almighty and Most High,
> acknowledge that every good is His,
> and thank Him,
> "from Whom all good comes,
> for everything."
> May He,
> the Almighty and Most High,
> the only true God,
> have, be given, and receive
> all honor and respect,

all praise and blessing,
all thanks and glory,
to Whom all good belongs,
He Who alone is good.
When we see or hear evil spoken or done
or God blasphemed,
let us speak well and do well
and praise God
Who is blessed forever.

What are our attitudes when our ministry unfolds successfully? Francis would have us humble ourselves. Thomas Merton once wrote: "If we were truly humble we would not bother about ourselves at all; we'd be concerned only with God and with the objective order of things and values as they are, and not as our selfishness wants them to be" (Merton 1962, 189). These could well be the words of Francis as he teaches us that any success that we might achieve in our ministries is ultimately the work of the Lord. It is the Lord who is speaking, the Lord who is working. We are simply instruments. But then Francis calls us beyond humility to a profound inner poverty, that is, to recognize that we have nothing we can call our own except our vice and sin. As we shall see when we read Francis's *Admonitions*, this simple statement expresses the very heart of the gift of poverty and its true end. Francis asks: What can we really call our own? If everything is God's pure gift, then only the sinful side of our nature is our own. Thus material poverty becomes a means of freeing us to address the deeper issues of our lives and to abandon what we find most difficult, our vices and sins.

Yet now Francis calls us to discern what moves our hearts as we do the Lord's work, to ask the penetrating question: What is our real motivation in ministry? While he uses Paul's phraseology, "the spirit of the flesh" and "the Spirit of the Lord," it is clear that Francis points directly at many of those expressions that he had encountered in "professional" religious. He asks: Are we so desirous of being so articulate, of possessing such a powerful, persuasive way with words that we neglect our own actions? Or, on the contrary, are we so concerned about the externals of religious and spiritual life that we pay little attention to our interior lives? If so, then Francis would have us recognize that it is the spirit of the flesh that moves us. He calls us to look for manifestations of the Spirit of the Lord, mortification, acceptance of being looked down upon, considered worthless, and, therefore, rejected. In other words, are we truly humble, patient, and possessive of a spirit of peace that is true and simple? If we are, then the prayer with which Francis concludes flows quite naturally from our lips, for it expresses the fundamental attitudes that should characterize our activities: acknowledgment that all good comes from and belongs to God, thanksgiving for everything, and praise for God who is the almighty source of all good.

Some manuscripts bring that concluding prayer to an end with "Amen." Could that indicate that an edition of this Earlier Rule ended at this point? Perhaps. In fact, the following three chapters reflect the influence of the Fourth Lateran Council on Francis and his followers. (We should not forget that the primitive proposal that the first group of Francis's followers presented to Innocent III was undoubtedly expanded by the teachings of the council.) Those of us who have experienced religious life from both sides of the Second Vatican Council can readily appreciate the profundity of such an ecclesial event and be sensitive to how it has influenced our behavior, manner of expression, and patterns of thought.

The first of these chapters is a reflection of the council's twelfth decree: "In every ecclesiastical province there shall be held every three years...a general chapter of abbots and of priors having no abbots, who have not been accustomed to celebrate such chapters. In inaugurating this new arrangement, let two neighboring abbots of the Cistercian Order be invited to give them counsel and opportune assistance, since among them the celebration of such chapters is of long standing." Francis writes:

Each minister can come together with his brothers once a year, wherever they wish, on the feast of St. Michael the Archangel to treat of those things that pertain to God.

For all the ministers who are in parts beyond the sea and the Alps may come to the Chapter of Pentecost in the church of St. Mary of the Portiuncula once every three years, and the other ministers once a year, unless it has been decreed otherwise by the minister and servant of the entire fraternity.

This is another of those instances in which Francis encourages us to go beyond following the strict letter of the conciliar decree to enter deeply into its spirit. His insistence on annual chapters, however, tells us of the importance he gave to such gatherings. Spiritual chapters, he suggests, are the best means of true renewal. If nothing else, they certainly deepen the sense of unity. In the first place, Francis envisions a chapter each year in which all the brothers would come together to treat of spiritual matters, undoubtedly an echo of the directive of the council, which had spoken of "deliberations paying special attention to the reform of the order and to regular observance." Second, Francis directs that chapters be held at the Portiuncula once every three years for all the ministers beyond the Italian Peninsula, suggesting that the fraternity had grown considerably by this time. Finally, all other ministers, that is, those of the Italian Peninsula, would meet annually.

In the "Admonition and Exhortation to the Brothers and Sisters of Penance," Francis has already called us to a deeper sense of Catholicity. Now he does so by echoing the council's first decree, which spoke of "the Catholic faith"; its second, which addressed "the errors of the Abbot Joachim of Fiore"; and its third, which dealt harshly with heretics: "We excommunicate and anathematize every heresy that raises itself against the holy, orthodox and Catholic faith which we have explained above." Francis writes:

Let all the brothers be, live, and speak as Catholics.

If someone has strayed in word or in deed from Catholic faith and life and has not amended his ways, let him be expelled from our brotherhood.

Let us consider all clerics and religious as our lords in all that pertains to the salvation of our soul and does not deviate from our religion, and let us respect their order, office, and administration in the Lord.

Even in this conciliar context, Francis encourages us to a special expression of dedication to the church. After expressing his mind on those who have strayed from their Catholic principles, he calls us to show respect for the clergy and religious. It is not enough to be simply obedient to the church. That is too abstract and ethereal. No, Francis is far more challenging in wanting us to show reverence and respect for its flesh-and-blood ministers. Thomas of Celano offers us a saying of Francis that is frequently quoted in this regard: "If it should happen that I would meet at the same time some saint from heaven and any poor priest, I would first show honor to the priest and quickly go to kiss his hands. And I would say to the other: 'Wait, St. Lawrence, for the hands of this one touch the Word of Life, and have something about them that is more than human.'" This may have been an expression of Francis's deep faith, but this passage of the Earlier Rule suggests that he knew we are all tempted to look upon the human side of God's ministers. That manifestation of our Catholicity is far more demanding.

Finally, Francis reminds us of the twenty-first decree of the council, which begins: "All the faithful of both sexes, after they have reached the age of discerning, shall faithfully confess all their sins at least once a year to their own [parish] priest and perform to the best of their ability the penance imposed." He states:

Let all my blessed brothers, both clerics and lay, confess their sins to priests of our Order. If they cannot, let them confess to other discerning and Catholic priests, knowing with certainty that when they have received penance and absolution from any Catholic priest, they are without doubt absolved from their sins, provided they have humbly and faithfully fulfilled the penance imposed on them.

If they have not been able to find a priest, however, let them confess to their brother, as the Apostle James says: *Confess your sins to one another* (James 5:16). Nevertheless, because of this, let them not fail to have recourse to a priest because the power of binding and loosing (cf. Matt. 18:18) is granted only to priests.

Contrite and having confessed in this way, let them receive the Body and Blood of our Lord Jesus Christ with great humility and respect remembering what the Lord says: *Whoever eats my flesh and drinks my blood has eternal life* (cf. John 6:54), and *Do this in memory of me* (Luke 22:19).

With this directive, Francis may well have sowed the seeds for the gradual clericalization of his fraternity. His demand, echoing the church's demand that the brothers confess to one of their own, implied that more of them would have to be ordained. Were sacerdotal brothers not available, then "discerning and Catholic priests" could be approached for the sacrament. Were these not available, the brothers were encouraged to confess to one another. Why Francis's insistence? The answer lies in the qualities envisioned in a brother who approaches the Eucharist: contrition and confession. Once again, in other words, Francis encourages us to go beyond the externals to the interior dispositions that, hopefully, those external actions would instill.

At this point, we should direct our attention to an expression of those exhortations with which Francis announced his message of penance and peace. In fact, we can easily discover similarities between this model or example of exhortation and that which seems to be the form of life he offered to those first penitents.

Whenever it pleases them, all my brothers can announce this or similar exhortation and praise among all peoples with the blessing of God:

> Fear and honor,
>> praise and bless,
>> *give thanks* and adore
>>> the Lord God Almighty In Trinity and in Unity,
>>> Father, Son, and Holy Spirit,
>>>> the Creator of all.
> Do penance,
>> performing fitting fruits of penance
>> because we shall soon die.
> *Give and it will be given to you.*
> *Forgive* and you will be forgiven.
> *If you do not forgive people their sins,*
>> the Lord *will not forgive you yours.*
>> Confess all your sins.[1]
> Blessed are those who die in penance,
>> for they shall be in the kingdom of heaven.

---

1. Cf. James 5:16.

> Woe to those who do not die in penance,
> for they shall be *children of the devil*
> whose works they do
> and they shall go *into everlasting fire.*[2]
> Beware of and abstain from every evil
> and persevere till the end in good.

Why did Francis and the brothers insert this into the Earlier Rule? Perhaps it was a response to the council's third decree: "But since some, under the 'appearance of godliness, but denying the power thereof,' as the Apostle says (2 Tim. 3:5), arrogate to themselves the authority to preach, as the same Apostle says: 'How shall they preach unless they be sent?' (Rom. 10:15), all those prohibited or not sent, who, without authority of the Apostolic See or of the Catholic bishop of the locality, shall be excommunicated." We came across a trace of this in the Earlier Rule's chapter 17: "Let no brother preach contrary to the rite and practice of the Church or without the permission of his minister. Let the minister be careful of granting it without discernment to anyone." Now, however, we see a directive addressed to all, yet one allowing definite freedom of choice, "whenever it pleases them," and providing a model of exhortation to penance rather than of preaching that may or may not be followed. While we might overlook this simple formula, chapter 21 expresses the very heart of Francis's proclamation and praise of a life of penance. It reminds us quite simply of the vision he proclaimed to his followers in those first years of his conversion. In his customary manner, Francis offers us a scriptural mosaic that urges us to penance. But his reason for stressing this urgency is that same insistence so characteristic of this time of his life: the realization that we will soon die.

This brings us to one of the most spiritually rich of Francis's writings. It could stand by itself as a catechism of prayer or a summary of Francis's entire approach to gospel life. Chapter 22 of the Earlier Rule offers us a simple method for developing a gospel spirituality:

---

2. Biblical allusions: 1 Thess. 5:18; cf. Matt. 3:2; Luke 3:8; 6:38; cf. Luke 6:37; Matt. 6:14; Mark 11:25; James 5:11; cf. 1 John 8:41; Matt. 18:8; 25:41.

All my brothers: let us pay attention to what the Lord says: *Love your enemies* and *do good to those who hate you* (cf. Matt. 5:44) for our Lord Jesus Christ, Whose footprints we must follow (cf. 1 Pet. 2:21), called His betrayer a friend (cf. Matt. 26:50) and willingly offered Himself to His executioners (cf. John 10:18).

Our friends, therefore, are all those who unjustly bring us distress and anguish, shame and injury, sorrow and punishment, martyrdom and death. We must love them greatly for we will possess eternal life because of what they bring us.

Let us hate our body with its vices and sins, because by living according to the flesh (cf. Rom. 8:4), the devil wishes to take away from us the love of Jesus Christ and eternal life and to lose himself in hell with everyone else. Because, by our own fault, we are disgusting, miserable and opposed to good, yet prompt and inclined to evil, for, as the Lord says in the Gospel: *From the heart proceed* (Mark 7:21) *and come evil thoughts* (Matt. 15:19), *adultery, fornication, murder, theft, greed, malice, deceit, licentiousness, envy* (Mark 7:21–22), *false witness* (Matt. 15:19), *blasphemy, foolishness* (Mark 7:23). *All these evils come from within* (Mark 7:23), from a person's heart and *these are what defile a person* (Matt. 15:20).

Now that we have left the world, however, we have nothing else to do but to follow the will of the Lord and to please Him. Let us be careful that we are not earth along the wayside, or that which is rocky or full of thorns, in keeping with what the Lord says in the Gospel: *The word of God is a seed* (Luke 8:11).

What *fell along the wayside and was trampled under foot* (cf. Luke 8:5), *however, are those who hear* (Luke 8:12) *the word* and do not understand it (cf. Matt. 13:19). *The devil comes* (Luke 8:12) *immediately* (Mark 4:15) *and snatches* (Matt. 13:19) *what was planted in their hearts* (Mark 4:15) *and takes the word from their hearts that they may not believe and be saved* (Luke 8:12).

What *fell on rocky ground, however* (cf. Matt. 13:20), *are those who, as soon as they hear the word, receive it at once with joy* (Mark 4:16). *But when tribulation and persecution come because of the word, they immediately fall away* (Matt. 13:21). These have no roots in them; they last only for a time (cf. Mark 4:17), because *they believe only for a time and fall away in time of trial* (Luke 8:13).

What *fell among thorns, however, are those* (Luke 8:14) *who hear the word of God* (cf. Mark 4:18) *and the anxiety* (Matt. 13:22) *and worries of this world* (Mark 4:19), *the lure of riches* (Matt. 13:22), *and other inordinate desires intrude and choke the word and they remain without fruit* (cf. Mark 4:19).

But what was sown (Matt. 13:23) *in good soil* (Luke 8:15) *are those who hear the word with a good and excellent heart* (Luke 8:15), understand (cf. Matt. 13:23) *and preserve it and bear fruit in patience* (Luke 8:15).

Therefore, as the Lord says, brothers, let us let *the dead bury their own dead* (Matt. 8:22).

After repeating those biblical teachings highlighting conformity with Christ and the necessity of mortification, we read: "Now that we have left the world, however, we have nothing else to do but to follow the will of the Lord and to please Him." What a simple vision: to leave the world, which would have clearly meant to embrace a religious conversion and to embark upon a new way of life, implied only those two fundamental obligations, "following the will of God and pleasing Him." How to do that? The answer could not be more forthright: "Let us be careful that we are not earth along the wayside, or that which is rocky or full of thorns, in keeping with what the Lord says in the Gospel: *The word of God is a seed* (Luke 8:11)." What follows, then, is a program for interiorizing the Word of God.

In comparison with the Synoptic accounts of the parable of the sower and the seed, Francis is far more thorough and repeatedly accentuates the need not only of interiorizing the Word but also of checking the attitudes of our hearts. To borrow a phrase from Thomas Merton, we might see every word of God as "a seed of contemplation." Yet Francis asks us to look honestly at our hearts, the soil into which those seeds fall, that we might be far more receptive to the Word. Are we careless in hearing the Word and in working to understand it? Are we superficial in receiving and retaining it so that we easily lose it when challenged? Or do we allow it to be stifled or suffocated because of all the other concerns of our daily lives? Francis brings all of these questions to us but places them in the context of discipleship as he concludes his version of the parable of the seed with a quotation from Matthew's account of Jesus' call: "Therefore, as the Lord says, brothers, let us let *the dead bury their own dead* (Matt. 8:22)." This takes on far more significance when we consider Francis's frequent use of John 6:64 ("my words are spirit and life"), through which he reminds us that the Word is indeed life-giving. We know of a contemporary of Francis, Odo of Cheriton, who heard Francis say about the origin of the order: "He [Francis] was that woman whom the Lord impregnated by his word and thus he brought forth spiritual children." This resonates deeply with the teachings of John and Peter that the Word of God is the divine seed (*sperma*) that God infuses and through which we become children of God (cf. 1 John 3:9; 1 Pet. 1:22–23).

In light of his emphasis on interiorizing the Word of God, we can more easily understand Francis's advice to avoid any entanglements or distractions that might draw us from what is central to following the will of the Lord.

Let us beware of the malice and skill of Satan, who does not want someone to turn his mind or heart to God. As he prowls about (cf. 1 Pet. 5:8) he wants to ensnare a person's heart under the guise of some reward or assistance, to choke out the word and precepts of the Lord from our memory (cf. Mark 4:19), and, as he desires a person's heart, to blind it through worldly affairs and concerns and to live there, as the Lord says: *When an unclean spirit goes out of a person, it roams through arid and waterless regions* (Matt. 12:43; Luke 11:24) *seeking rest; and not finding any, it says: "I will return to my home from which I came* (Luke 11:24)." *Coming upon it, it finds it empty, swept, clean and tidied* (Matt. 12:44). *It goes off and brings seven other spirits more wicked than itself, who move in and dwell there, and the last state of that person is worse than the first* (Luke 11:26).

Therefore, all my brothers, let us be very much on our guard that, under the guise of some reward or assistance, we do not lose or take our mind away from God. But, in the holy love that is God (cf. 1 John 4:16), I beg all my brothers, both the ministers and the others, after overcoming every impediment and putting aside every care and anxiety, to serve, love, honor and adore the Lord God with a clean heart and a pure mind in whatever way they are best able to do so for that is what He wants above all else.

Francis repeatedly draws our attention to our hearts and reminds us how eager Satan is to prevent us from inclining our hearts to God, to ensnare, to blind, or to live in them. In a variety of ways, he asks us: Where is your heart? What is in your heart? When we see how many times he uses the phrase "under the guise of," we hear him advising us to look realistically at our motives and not to be blinded by what seems good or worthwhile.

This might make us wonder if Francis understood his calling more in terms of John 8:32 ("If you continue in my word, you are truly my disciples") or in terms of John 14:23 ("If anyone loves me, he will keep my word; and my Father will love him, and we will come to him, and we will make our home in him"). Discipleship, in John's eyes, is much more of a contemplative dwelling in the Word of God that results in the trinitarian Word ("*we* will come to him, and *we* will make our home in him") coming to live within. Was this Francis's understanding? Look at how his thought proceeds. After giving us this advice to do whatever is necessary to let the Word of God grow in our hearts, he writes: "Let us make a home and a dwelling place for Him Who is the Omnipotent Lord God, Father and Son and Holy Spirit." This is another of those passages that suggest that the words Francis heard at the beginning of his spiritual journey ("Francis, go and repair my house which, as you see, is falling into ruin") never left his mind. Thomas of Celano seems to suggest this approach when he writes of Francis: "He always made his home in the Scriptures." We should not be surprised, then, that Francis offers us a wonderful understanding of the gospel life as tremendously trinitarian, directed to the Father, animated by the Spirit that comes to us through the Word, and centered in and formed by the Son.

Let us always make a home and a dwelling-place there (cf. John 14:23) for Him Who is the Lord God Almighty, Father, Son and Holy Spirit, Who says: *Be vigilant at all times and pray that you have the strength to escape the tribulations that are imminent and to stand before the Son of Man* (Luke 21:36). *When you stand to pray* (Mark 11:25) *say* (Luke 11:2): *Our Father in heaven* (Matt. 6:9). Let us adore Him with a pure heart, *because it is necessary to pray always and not lose heart* (Luke 18:1); *for the Father seeks such* people who adore Him (John 4:23). *God is Spirit and those who adore Him must adore Him in Spirit and truth* (cf. John 4:24). Let us have recourse to Him as *to the Shepherd and Guardian of our souls* (1 Pet. 2:25), Who says: "I am the Good Shepherd Who feeds My sheep and I lay down My life for My sheep (cf. John 10:14–15)."

All of you are brothers. Do not call anyone on earth your father, you have but one Father in heaven. Do not call yourselves teachers, you have but one Teacher in heaven (cf. Matt. 23:8–10). *If you remain in me and my words remain in you, ask for whatever you want and it will be done for you* (cf. John 15:7). *Wherever two or three are gathered together in my name, there am I in the midst of them* (Matt. 18:20). *Behold I am with you until the end of the world* (Matt. 28:20). *The words I have spoken to you are spirit and life* (John 6:63). *I am the Way, the Truth and the Life* (John 14:6).

Once again Francis reminds us that we are dwellings and houses for the Word of God and encourages us to develop a prayer that is continual, attentive, and enriched by loving relationships. Our prayer, then, must be characterized by vigilance, by being continually alert to the advances of those impulses and temptations that we have rejected by turning whole-heartedly toward the stirrings of the triune God living within us. Yet this also calls us to pray unceasingly, a contemplative stance, in other words, to which Francis frequently draws our attention. It is a prayer that prompts a certain interiority, an inner dialogue with the God who is always present to us. Francis invites us to adore the Father in spirit and in truth, showing how that is more important than any other form of prayer. In one brief passage, the poet emerges in Francis as he follows John by repeating the word "adore" three times, so that it is difficult to miss his point. Mary of the Passion, foundress of the Franciscan Missionaries of Mary, beautifully defined adoration as "rendering love to love." This wonderfully summarizes the sense of Francis's words to us as we strive to allow God's Spirit to animate our prayer and Jesus to mold it.

All too frequently we overlook the biblical foundations of Francis's concept of fraternity. In addition to being formed by the gospel, it flows from it. Could that be any clearer than in those passages in which Francis defines the very foundations of a gospel life? We are all children of the same Father and students of the same divine teacher. Rooted in Christ and interiorizing his words, not only are we assured of his presence; we are also guaranteed his ever-effective intercession. How important are those words! If Francis has challenged us to look carefully at the soil of our hearts that the seed of the Word might grow and be fruitful, it is only because he realizes that God's words are the channels, the vehicles, of the Spirit and, indeed, of life itself. To listen to the words of Jesus, then, is to be in the presence of the one who is the Way, the Truth, and the Life, images that weave through Francis's writings as they do through the fabric of his life. He calls us, in other words, to transparency, that is, to allow the Spirit of gospel truth to shine through everything we do. We could hardly expect a more natural conclusion than this encouragement:

Let us, therefore, hold onto the words, the life, the teaching and the Holy Gospel of Him Who humbled Himself to beg His Father for us and to make His name known saying: *Father, glorify Your name* (John 12:28a) *and glorify Your Son that Your Son may glorify You* (John 17:1b).

   Father, I have made Your name known to those whom You have given me (John 17:6). *The words You gave to me I have given to them, and they have accepted them and truly have known that I came from You and they have believed that You sent me* (John 17:8). *I pray for them, not for the world, but for those You have given me, because they are Yours and everything of mine is Yours* (John 17:8–10). Holy Father, *keep in Your name those You have given me that they may be one as We are* (John 17:11b). *I say this while in the world that they may have joy completely. I gave them Your word, and the world hated them, because they do not belong to the world as I do not belong to the world. I do not ask you to take them out of the world but that you keep them from the evil one* (John 17:13b–15). *Glorify them in truth. Your word is truth.*

   As You sent me into the world, so I sent them into the world. And I sanctify myself for them that they also may be sanctified in truth. I ask not only for them but also for those who will believe in me through them (cf. John 17:17–20), *that they may be brought to perfection as one, and the world may know that You have sent me and loved them as You loved me* (John 17:23). *I shall make known to them Your name, that the love with which You loved me may be in them and I in them* (cf. John 17:26). *Father, I wish that those whom You have given me may be where I am that they may see Your glory* (cf. John 17:24) *in Your kingdom* (Matt. 20:21).

Francis ends his profound call to a life rooted in the inner life of God by encouraging us to "hold onto the words, the life, and the teaching of the holy Gospel of Him Who humbled Himself to ask His Father for us and to make His name known to us." Jesus the intercessor; Jesus the revelation of the name of God: an extraordinarily simple vision of the mystery of Christ. It leads us to Francis's interpretation of Jesus' prayer at the Last Supper. Yet we might wonder if Francis isn't making this prayer his own and if it isn't a prayer for us to sense the continuing revelation of God as a loving Father, an aspect of his approach that is so central to understanding his life. Twice before we have read Francis's version of this prayer, in his earlier and later exhortations to a life of penance. Now, however, we find a fuller version, one that is far more personal and expressive of a thoroughly relational spirituality.

"A Hymn of Praise and Thanksgiving," "A Canticle of the Redeemed," "A Creed of Praise": these are a few of the contemporary titles given to chapter 23 of the Earlier Rule. At the same time, many authors have suggested that it is the song of a troubadour, one who uses his musical skill to call his audience to join with him in praising the Creator, Redeemer, and Savior of us all. It is easy for us to imagine Francis joyfully singing the first section of this mysterious, captivating piece:

> All-powerful, most holy,
> Almighty and supreme God,
> *Holy* and just *Father,*
> *Lord* King *of heaven and earth*
> we thank You for Yourself
> for by Your holy will
> and by Your only Son
> with the Holy Spirit
> You have created all things spiritual and corporal

and, after making us in Your own image and likeness,
You placed us in paradise.

When we reflect upon Francis's entire relationship with God, we might easily conclude that it could be characterized as one of loving gratitude. We might even conclude that gratitude is *the* Franciscan virtue. Coventry Patmore's observation is very apropos of Francis: "What is gladness without gratitude, / And where is gratitude without a God?" Francis's life of love reads as a poem of profound joy in the goodness of God, as a heartfelt response of thanksgiving for the gifts of an ever-loving, generous God. Perhaps no other writing expresses this as poetically and as enthusiastically as this.

As we continue to read Francis's words, though, his joy even intensifies as he reminds us that our self-centered, sinful beings are the recipients of God's largesse.

Through our own fault we fell.

We thank You
for as through Your Son You created us,
so through Your holy love
with which You loved us
You brought about His birth
as true God and true man
by the glorious, ever-virgin, most blessed, holy Mary
and You willed to redeem us captives
through His cross and blood and death.

We thank You
for Your Son Himself will come again
in the glory of His majesty
to send into the everlasting fire
the wicked ones
who have not done penance
and have not known You
and to say to all those
who have known You, adored You
and served You in penance:
"Come, you blessed of my Father,

receive *the kingdom prepared for you*
from the beginning *of the world."*

Because all of us, wretches and sinners,
are not worthy to pronounce Your name,
we humbly ask
our Lord Jesus Christ,
Your *beloved Son,*
in Whom You were well pleased,
together with the Holy Spirit,
the Paraclete,
to give You thanks,
for everything
as it pleases You and Him,
Who always satisfies You in everything,
through Whom You have done so much for us.
Alleluia!

Because of Your love,
we humbly beg
the glorious Mother, the most blessed, ever-virgin Mary,
Blessed Michael, Gabriel, and Raphael
all the choirs of the blessed
seraphim, cherubim, thrones, dominations,
principalities, powers, virtues,
angels, archangels,
blessed John the Baptist,
John the Evangelist,
Peter, Paul,
the blessed patriarchs and prophets,
the Innocents, apostles, evangelists, disciples,
the martyrs, confessors and virgins
the blessed Elijah and Henoch,
all the saints who were, who will be, and who are
to give You thanks for these things,
as it pleases You,
God true and supreme,
eternal and living,
with Your most beloved Son,
our Lord Jesus Christ,
and the Holy Spirit,

the Paraclete,
world without end.
Amen.
Alleluia!

We sinned: Francis never allows us to forget that. Yet Easter person that he is, Francis invites us to luxuriate in the gift of Christ who not only shows us the incredible greatness that is ours as human beings but also brought us back from the slavery that we brought upon ourselves. Were this not enough, he does not let us lose sight of the facts that it is the Spirit that enables us to utter the praise that is pleasing to the Father and that we are caught up in a communion of angels and saints, with whom our hymn of thanksgiving takes on new meaning. Angels, archangels, apostles, evangelists, virgins, even the prophets Elijah and Enoch: Francis calls us to join with them in proclaiming the glory of God.

It is easy to imagine Francis becoming more and more excited as he not only encourages his listeners to persevere in a life of faith and penance but also invites everyone to join his company in singing a universal song of praise. G. K. Chesterton attempts to summarize the life of Francis in these words: "It is the highest and holiest of the paradoxes that the man who really knows he cannot pay his debt will be forever paying it." Francis himself expresses this paradox in these verses as he invites us to enter into his vision of God's loving goodness to us. He calls *all* of us, regardless of our state of life, of our age, of our success or lack of it, of our nationality or race. He invites us to faith and to penance because each of us has been touched by love, God's love that has created and redeemed us and that continually reaches out to us.

All of us lesser brothers, *useless servants,*
humbly ask and beg
those who wish to serve the Lord God
within the holy Catholic and Apostolic Church
and all the following orders:
priests, deacons, subdeacons,
acolytes, exorcists, lectors, porters, and all clerics,
all religious men and women,

all lay brothers and youths,
the poor and the needy,
kings and princes,
workers and farmers,
servants and masters,
all virgins, continent and married women,
all lay people, men and women,
all children, adolescents, young and old,
the healthy and the sick,
all the small and the great,
all peoples, races, tribes, and tongues,
all nations and all peoples everywhere on earth,
who are and who will be
to persevere in the true faith and in penance
for otherwise no one will be saved.

Francis's call, however, challenges us by once more reminding us of that command of love that he placed before us in his exhortations. Now he describes not only *how* we should love but why we should do so:

With our whole heart,
our whole soul,
our whole mind,
with our whole strength and fortitude
with our whole understanding
with all our powers
with every effort,
every affection,
every feeling,
every desire and wish
let us all love *the Lord God*
Who has given and gives to each one of us
our whole body, our whole soul and our whole life,
Who has created, redeemed and will save us
by His mercy alone
Who did and does everything good for us,
miserable and wretched,
rotten and foul,
ungrateful and evil ones.

"Respond with all your heart, with every fiber of your being," he encourages us, "and count everything else as nothing so that wherever you are, whatever you are doing, and whenever you are doing it, you will give praise and thanks to God!" In a sense, Francis is telling us that life should be a daring adventure of love, that is, a continuing journey of putting aside our securities to enter more profoundly into the uncharted depths of God. It is, as Bernard Lonergan writes of it, "an other-worldly falling in love." To the fivefold gospel call of giving everything in love, Francis adds an additional four. With his nine challenges to respond totally to God, he invites all of us to a total commitment of the heart and, in so doing, provides us with a key to understanding the simplicity of his life. "The only simplicity that matters is the simplicity of the heart," Chesterton maintained. He was only following the inspiration of Chaucer, who placed on the lips of the Miller: "How blessed are the simple, aye, indeed, / That only know enough to say their creed!"

In light of the call, we can more fully understand the contrasts that Francis now places before us. Three times he uses the phrase "nothing else" to focus our energies on God alone. His words remind us of the description of the ascent of Mount Carmel in which John of the Cross cries: "*Nada, nada,* and, on the mountain's summit, *nada.*"

> Therefore,
> let us desire nothing else,
> let us want nothing else
> let nothing else please us and cause us delight
> except our Creator, Redeemer and Savior,
> the only true God,
> Who is the fullness of good,
> all good, every good, the true and supreme good,
> *Who alone is good,*
> merciful, gentle, delectable, and sweet,
> Who alone is holy,
> just, true, holy, and upright
> Who alone is kind, innocent, clean,
> from Whom, through Whom and in Whom
> is all pardon, all grace, all glory

of all penitents and just ones,
of all the blessed rejoicing together in heaven.

Yet now Francis offers us another set of contrasts. His negative phrases ("let nothing hinder us, nothing separate us, nothing come between us") are balanced by positive descriptions of how we should be devoted exclusively to God ("wherever we are, in every place, at every hour, at every moment of the day..."). There are no boundaries, no self-imposed limits or contractual agreements. No, the heart knows no frontiers.

Therefore,
let nothing hinder us,
nothing separate us,
nothing come between us.
Wherever we are,
in every place,
at every hour,
at every moment of the day,
everyday and continually,
let all of us truly and humbly believe,
hold in our heart and love,
honor, adore, serve,
praise and bless,
glorify and exalt,
magnify and give thanks
to the Most High and Supreme Eternal God
Trinity and Unity,
Father, Son and Holy Spirit,
Creator of all,
Savior of all
Who believe and hope in Him,
and love Him, Who,
without beginning and end,
is unchangeable, invisible,
indescribable, ineffable,
incomprehensible, unfathomable,
blessed, praiseworthy,
glorious, exalted,
sublime, most high,

> gentle, lovable, delightful,
> and totally desirable above all else
> for ever.
> Amen.

Francis searches for adjectives and expressions that will adequately capture his admiration. Nothing seems to satisfy his poetic heart as he searches for the most fitting word or phrase to capture the love and admiration that fill his heart. He seems to be frustrated; he seems to sense that words fail. Only our experience of this all-loving, good God, Francis realizes, will fill us with praise — a praise that is in itself a gift.

Chapter 23 of the Earlier Rule is more than an expression of Francis's creed and his invitation to us to believe and respond with him; it is a poetic statement of his raison d'être, the very purpose of his gospel life. Of course, the essential themes of minority, fraternity, and loving obedience are never mentioned. That hardly matters in light of the description of the gospel life that the Earlier Rule places before us. No, in this hymn of praise, in this invitation, Francis offers us an insight into his relentless quest of gospel perfection.

Toward a Final Articulation

When we study the Earlier Rule, we can easily see how the document evolved over those first eleven years when Francis and his brothers strove to live the gospel ideals in a world that was continually challenging them. These men were not the same as those of the monastic world, who encountered different demands. Francis and his followers were struggling to be Christ's disciples without the protection of the monastic world or a fixed hour plan and were, therefore, continually recasting their understanding of the gospel way of life they had embraced. How, for example, were they to express a sense of community or fraternity when they were so frequently away from one another? What means were to be used to avoid the temptations that inevitably taxed the inner strength of those who strove to live the gospel in the secular world? How should they treat those who were unable to live up to their commitments?

The Letter to a Minister

One of the most precious of Francis's writings is a text that he wrote to a brother who was called to minister to his brothers. We should not forget that Francis never uses the word "superior" to describe those entrusted with authority. He took seriously the words of the Gospel of Matthew: "The rulers of the Gentiles lord it over them, and the great ones make their authority over them felt" (Matt. 20:26). Instead he writes of "ministers and servants" and reminds us that those entrusted with authority have simply been given a precious trust, the loving obedience of others. From this perspective, then, the minister to whom Francis writes is a symbol of all who are called to serve.

This particular brother seems to have found the burden a demanding one and expressed his desire to be relieved of the responsibility in order to pursue the life of a hermit. The first part of Francis's compassionate letter to the minister expresses how he himself understood that role:

To Brother N., minister: May the Lord bless you (cf. Num 6:24a).

I speak to you, as best I can, about the state of your soul. You must consider as grace all that impedes you from loving the Lord God and whoever has become an impediment to you, whether brothers or others, even if they lay hands on you. And may you want it to be this way and not otherwise. And let this be for you the true obedience of the Lord God and my true obedience, for I know with certitude that it is true obedience. And love those who do those things to you and do not wish anything different from them, unless it is something the Lord God shall have given you. And love them in this and do not wish that they be better Christians. And let this be more than a hermitage for you.

As he begins to encourage his brother, Francis echoes the invitation of the Earlier Rule in which he focuses on the example of the suffering Lord: "All my brothers: let us pay attention to what the Lord says: *Love your enemies* and *do good to those who hate you* (cf. Matt. 5:44), for our Lord Jesus Christ, Whose footprints we must follow (cf. 1 Pet. 2:21), called His betrayer a friend (cf. Matt. 26:50) and willingly offered Himself to His executioners (cf. John 10:18)." In light of Christ's example, his words to those called to serve others are closely aligned with those of the Earlier Rule: "Our friends, therefore, are all those who unjustly bring us distress and anguish, shame and injury, sorrow and punishment, martyrdom and death. We must love them greatly for we will possess eternal life because of what they bring us."

But we find an astounding sentiment not only in Francis's encouragement to love those brothers who make life difficult but also in his counsel: "Do not wish that they be better Christians." He directs us not to claim the right to judge or see ourselves as better than others, but always to keep in mind that, out of love for us, the Son of God entered our history and endured suffering and death. In other words, the misery and abuse we may have to endure in the fulfillment of our responsibilities offer opportunities for identifying with the Suffering Servant and are expressions of the humanity we share with all who have been redeemed by Christ's blood. In this light, then, who could deny that such indignities are "more than a hermitage"?

The second paragraph of this first section shows how profoundly Francis understands the very reason for Jesus' coming among us: to reveal the *misericordia* (see below for a discussion of the term) of God. In a certain sense, these verses form the very heart of this letter since the advice of Francis becomes more concrete and compassionate. We should consider them in light of the fifth chapter of the Earlier Rule, where we find a description of how we should react to another who has sinned: "If, after a third admonition, he refuses to improve, let them send or report him, as soon as they can, to their minister and servant; and let the minister and servant deal with him as he considers best before God." The initiative and responsibility, then, are placed in the hands of those called to serve, who are bound, in Francis's mind, to proceed *secundum Deum* (according to God):

And if you have done this, I wish to know in this way if you love the Lord and me, His servant and yours: that there is not any brother in the world who has sinned — however much he could have sinned—who, after he has looked into your eyes, would ever depart without your mercy, if he is looking for mercy. And if he were not looking for mercy, you would ask him if he wants mercy. And if he would sin a thousand times before your eyes, love him more than me so that you may draw him to the Lord; and always be merciful with brothers such as these. And you may announce this to the guardians, when you can that, for your part, you are resolved to act in this way.

As we shall see, much of Francis's attitude toward sin flows from the understanding he expresses in the second text of his *Admonitions*. After describing the sin of the first human being as eating of the tree of the knowledge of good, he proceeds to point to the result: "It becomes the apple of the knowledge of evil"; and he maintains that "it is only right that he suffer the punishment." Throughout his writings, then, Francis directs our attention to the ravages of sin. We have lost our "spiritual vision" and are, therefore, weak in perceiving the things of God. We are easily deceived and led by carnal rather than spiritual desires. It is just such a person that Francis seems to be describing in this letter to the suffering minister: not simply one who has fallen once or twice or one who has committed a grave sin, but someone whose habitual state seems to be that of sin. He might be touched by the grace of conversion, that is, looking for mercy; but he might also be so hardened that he is not. Whatever the case might be, Francis's advice is very much the same: do not allow such a person to leave your presence without your mercy.

Perhaps the greatest obstacle we face in appreciating the extraordinary advice that Francis presents is the failure of the English language to translate *misericordia* adequately. While we tend to identify *misericordia* with compassion or forgiveness, the biblical concept is more expressive of God's tender love (*cordia*) that is occasioned by our human misery (*miseria*). Thus a better translation of the word might well be: a heart sensitive to misery. In this sense, Jesus is the perfect revelation of the *misericordia* of God. It is this divine tenderness that Francis so forcefully proposes as the strongest attitude in his dealing with the sinful frailty of another. From it, we can easily detect some of the fundamental attitudes that, as we have already seen in the Earlier Rule, Francis conceives as the forces shaping the spirit of gospel fraternity: the love and care of a mother (see Earlier Rule 9.10–11); faithfulness or a commitment to remain close to one another (see Earlier Rule 4.2); readiness to pardon one another (Earlier Rule 21.5–6); and what we might call "a preferential love of the weak," which flows from identification with Christ (Earlier Rule 9.2) and is expressed *ad extra* toward the poor, oppressed, and downtrodden (ibid.) and *ad intra* to those who are sick physically (Earlier Rule 8.3, 7; 10.1–3; 15.2) or spiritually (Earlier Rule 5.8).

In these four verses, we can clearly see the heart of Francis himself and can gain an idea of his attitude toward a brother who sins. Reflective of the Earlier Rule as these verses may be, Francis seems eager to insert into it this gospel attitude toward the sinner. Thus we find him leaving the minister to consider a proposal that they will both discuss at the gathering of the brothers:

With the help of God and the advice of our brothers during the Chapter of Pentecost, we shall make one chapter such as this from all the chapters of the rule that treat of mortal sin:

If any one of the brothers, at the instigation of the enemy, shall have sinned mortally, let him be bound by obedience to have recourse to his guardian. Let all the brothers who know that he has sinned not bring shame upon him or slander him; let them, instead, show great mercy to him and keep the sin of their brother very secret because *those who are well do not need a physician, but the sick do* (Matt. 9:12; Mark 2:17; Luke 5:31). Let them be bound by obedience, likewise, to send him to his custodian with a companion. And let that custodian provide for him with a heart full of mercy as he would wish to be provided for were he in a similar position (cf. Matt. 7:12; Luke 6:31). If he falls into some venial sin, let him confess to his brother who is a priest. If there is no priest there, let him confess to his brother until he has a priest who may canonically absolve him, as it has been said (cf. James 5:16). And let them not have the power to impose any other penance on them except this: *Go and sin no more* (cf. John 8:11).

So that it may be better observed, may you have this writing with you until Pentecost, when you will be with your brothers. With the help of the Lord God, you will take care of these and everything else that is not clear in the rule.

Behind this proposal are the difficulties the brothers were having with those sections of the Earlier Rule dealing with those who sin. We see a good example of this in chapter 13, where we find this directive: "If any brother commits fornication at the instigation of the devil, let him be deprived of the habit he has lost by his wickedness, put it aside completely, and be altogether expelled from our religion. Afterwards let him do penance." As we can easily imagine, the severity of this passage may have disturbed some of Francis's first followers. While it implies his vision that the Spirit of the Lord is that which unites us to one another and that the carnal sin of fornication severs that bond of unity (notice how it follows immediately after the biblical references to the body as the dwelling place of the Spirit), it still strikes us as harsh and contrary to the otherwise compassionate Francis.

We will discuss this proposal in the context of the Later Rule. For the moment, we should look upon these verses as an indication of the problems caused by some passages of the Earlier Rule, especially those that spoke of sin, and of the need for greater precision in defining the gospel ideals in light of an ever-growing brotherhood. The charismatic presence of Francis was no longer sufficient to guide his followers. In many instances he was inaccessible. Thomas of Celano, for example, tells of two brothers who traveled a great distance simply to see Francis and to receive his blessing. Moreover, as the number of the brothers was growing somewhat dramatically, it was necessary to devise new structures to maintain a viable spirit of unity.

The Later Rule—"The Marrow of the Gospel"

It became increasingly more urgent to develop not simply new structures that would preserve the spirit of the primitive brotherhood but also formulations that would capture or define the gospel vision of Francis himself within those structures. Between the Pentecost chapters of 1221 and 1223, then, Francis and the brothers began to synthesize the Earlier Rule with its roots in that original proposal of life presented to Pope Innocent III. The result was a much shorter and far more concise document that eventually received the papal seal of approval and became incorporated into a papal brief entitled *Solet annuere*. It remains, even to this day, *the* rule of the Friars Minor, and many Franciscan commentators, following the inspiration of Thomas of Celano, consider it "the marrow of the gospel."

With one glance we can see the enormous differences between the two rules. The Earlier Rule is thoroughly biblical in its inspiration and composition. It confronts us with a high idealism while expressing at the same time the difficulties of living amid the harsh realities of the world. The Later Rule, on the other hand, reveals a more legal mind eager to define the limits to which we might go. It does not sacrifice the gospel ideals, but to grasp it fully we must be able to break through the medieval idiom in which many of those ideals are encased. Thus it is easy to understand why so many have categorized the Later Rule as the work of someone other than Francis or, as one commentator so glibly wrote of it, as "the death of the vision."

But are such judgments fair? As we have seen, the number of Francis's followers was growing dramatically with the result that it was no longer possible to guide and inspire the brothers through the power of his presence. We can also see how Cardinal Hugolino became ever more involved in guiding not only the lay penitents who followed Francis's ideals but also Clare and the Poor Ladies of St. Damian's. Without a doubt Hugolino concerned himself with the inner life of the brothers, especially those who were more educated and wanted a rule that would provide more structure, or those who simply wandered about without the knowledge or consent of their ministers, or those who traveled as missionaries and were persecuted as heretics. If he were as concerned about Francis's fledgling fraternity as the early biographers describe him, then he must have certainly been concerned about the crises and tensions that troubled it.

The second "chapters" of both documents provide good examples:

THE EARLIER RULE

If anyone, wishing by divine inspiration to accept this life, comes to our brothers, let him be received by them with kindness. If he is determined to accept our life, let the brothers be very careful not to become involved in his temporal affairs, but let them present him to their minister as quickly as possible.

THE LATER RULE

If there are any who wish to accept this life and come to our brothers, let them send them to their provincial ministers, to whom alone and to no others permission is granted to receive the brothers.

THE EARLIER RULE

On his part, let the minister receive him with kindness, encourage him and diligently explain the tenor of our life to him.

After this has been done, let the above-mentioned person — if he wishes and is capable of doing so spiritually without any difficulty — sell all his belongings and be diligent in giving everything to the poor (cf. Matt. 19:21; Luke 18:22).

Let the brothers and the minister of the brothers be careful not to interfere in any way in his temporal affairs; let them not accept money either by themselves or through an intermediary. Nevertheless, if they are in need, the brothers, like other poor people, can accept, instead of money, whatever is needed for the body.

THE LATER RULE

Let the ministers examine them carefully concerning the Catholic faith and the sacraments of the Church. If they believe all these things, will faithfully profess them, and steadfastly observe them to the end; and if they have no wives, or if they have wives who have already taken a vow of continence and are of such an age that suspicion cannot be raised about them, and who have already entered a monastery or have given their husbands permission by the authority of the bishop of the diocese, let the ministers speak to them the words of the holy Gospel that they go and sell all they have and take care to give it to the poor (cf. Matt. 19:21; Mark 10:21; Luke 18:22). If they cannot do this, let their good will suffice.

Let the brothers and the minister be careful not to interfere with their temporal goods that they may dispose of their belongings as the Lord inspires them. If, however, counsel is sought, the minister may send them to some God-fearing persons according to whose advice their goods may be distributed to the poor.

THE EARLIER RULE

When he has returned, the minister may give him the clothes of probation for a year, that is, two tunics without a hood, a cord, trousers, and a small cape reaching to the cord. When the year and term of probation has ended, let him be received into obedience.

After this it will be unlawful for him to join another Order or to 'wander outside obedience' according to the decree of the Lord Pope and the Gospel, for no one putting his hand to the plow and looking to what was left behind is fit for the kingdom of God (Luke 9:62).

If anyone comes, however, who cannot give away his belongings without difficulty and has the spiritual will to do so, let him leave them behind, and it will suffice for him.

Let no one be received contrary to the rite and practice of the Holy Church.

Let all the other brothers who have already promised obedience have one tunic with a hood and, if it is necessary, another without a hood and a cord and trousers.

THE LATER RULE

Then they may be given the clothes of probation, namely, two tunics without a hood, a cord, short trousers, and a little cape reaching to the cord, unless, at times, it seems good to these same ministers, before God, to act otherwise. When the year of probation has come to an end, let them be received to obedience promising to observe always this Rule and Life.

On no account will it be lawful for them to leave this Order, according to the decree of our Lord the Pope, for, according to the Gospel: no one who puts a hand to the plow and looks to what was left behind is fit for the kingdom of God (Luke 9:62).

Let those who have already promised obedience have one tunic with a hood and another, if they wish, without a hood.

THE EARLIER RULE	*THE LATER RULE*
	And those who are compelled by necessity may wear shoes.
Let all the brothers wear poor clothes and, with the blessing of God, they can patch them with sackcloth and other pieces, for the Lord says in the Gospel: Those who wear expensive clothing and live in luxury (Luke 7:25) and who dress in fine garments are in the houses of kings (Matt. 11:8).	Let all the brothers wear poor clothes and they may mend them with pieces of sackcloth or other material with the blessing of God.
Although they may be called hypocrites, let them nevertheless not cease from doing good and let them not seek expensive clothing in this world that they might have a garment in the kingdom of heaven (cf. Matt. 22:11)	I admonish and exhort them not to look down upon or judge those whom they see dressed in soft and fine clothes and enjoying the choicest food and drink, but rather let everyone judge and look down upon himself.

We can immediately see differences in the two documents, differences that suggest that the fraternity was becoming increasingly structured. In the Earlier Rule, for example, Francis directs the brothers to receive with kindness someone who desired to "receive life" from them. This is in sharp contrast with the Rule of Benedict 58, which states: "Do not grant newcomers to the monastic life an easy entry, but, as the Apostle says, Test the spirits to see if they are from God (1 John 4:1). Therefore, if someone comes and keeps knocking at the door, and if at the end of four or five days he has shown himself patient in bearing his harsh treatment and difficult entry, and has persisted in his request, then he should be allowed to enter." The Later Rule, while not adopting the coldness of the Benedictine approach, omits the warmth of the Earlier Rule and envisions a more conditioned acceptance in which the provincial minister must examine the candidate on his knowledge of the faith and the sacraments. Moreover, a canonical requirement concerning those who are married is added, as well as a warning that neither the minister nor the brothers should become involved in the candidate's temporal affairs. We can easily see that experience had taught the brothers to be more circumspect in their reception of those who desired to be of their number.

There is also an almost defensive tone to the Earlier Rule's teaching about wearing poor clothes, a teaching reinforced by two quotations, one from Luke's Gospel (7:25) and another from Matthew's (11:8). The Later Rule, however, suggests that the poor clothes or tunic of the earlier document had become not only acceptable but a sign of respectability. It suggests that the brothers were no longer inviting ridicule and criticism; they were now in social positions from which they could ridicule or criticize others. Thus Francis counsels avoiding arrogance by not looking down upon or judging others.

But what may have been more of a concern was inevitable conflict between the ideals of Francis's vision and the reality that daily confronted those who attempted to live them. When we look at many of those clarifying passages of the Earlier Rule, we quickly sense that activities or ministries conditioned their expressions of poverty and simplicity. There is a telling passage in the *Legend of Perugia* (114) in which the brothers go to Hugolino with the hope that he will persuade Francis to adopt the rules and teachings of St. Benedict, St. Augustine, or St. Bernard. "My brothers, my brothers," Francis replies, "God called me to walk in the way of humility and showed me the way of simplicity. I do not want to hear any mention of the rule of St. Augustine, of St. Bernard, or of St. Benedict. The Lord has told me that he wanted to make a new fool of me in the world, and God does not want to lead us by any other than that." While some authors question the authenticity of the passage, it does suggest that some of the brothers did not grasp the unique vision of Francis and appealed to those of others. The Later Rule, then, is quite straightforward in expressing the gospel way of life that Francis envisioned and does so with an economy of words.

Chapter 3 would be yet another example of discovering how the primitive fraternity had changed and needed more structure or how the liturgical practices of the postconciliar church influenced the daily life of both the clerical and lay brothers.

Let the clerical [brothers] recite the Divine Office according to the rite of the holy Roman Church excepting the Psalter, for which

reason they may have breviaries. The lay [brothers], however, may say twenty-four *Our Father's* for Matins, and five for Lauds; seven for each of the Hours of Prime, Terce, Sext, and None, twelve for Vespers, and seven for Compline. Let them pray for the dead.

Let them fast from the feast of All Saints until the Lord's Nativity. May those be blessed by the Lord who fast voluntarily during that holy Lent that begins at the Epiphany and lasts during the forty days which our Lord consecrated by His own fast (cf. Matt. 4:2; Luke 4:2); but those who do not wish to keep it will not be obliged. Let them fast, however, until the Lord's Resurrection. At other times let them not be bound to fast except on Fridays. During a time of manifest necessity, however, let not the brothers be bound by corporal fast.

I counsel, admonish and exhort my brothers in the Lord Jesus Christ not to quarrel or dispute or judge others when they go about in the world (cf. 2 Tim. 2:14); but let them be meek, peaceful, modest, gentle, and humble, speaking courteously to everyone, as is becoming. They should not ride horseback unless they are compelled by manifest necessity or infirmity. Into whatever house they enter, let them first say: "Peace be to this house!" (cf. Luke 10:5). According to the holy Gospel, let them eat whatever food is set before them (cf. Luke 10:8).

We find a much simpler directive concerning the celebration of the Liturgy of the Hours that reflects the changes that were taking place in the church after the Fourth Lateran Council. Once again, we can see the parallels between Francis's time and our own when the Second Vatican Council substantially modified the official prayer of the church. Yet what is more significant about this chapter is how clearly Francis calls us to live *in the world*. Although this is implied in the Earlier Rule, it is now clearer and challenges us to live the gospel not simply in our homes, religious houses, or designated locations but in the fields, offices, hospitals, places of controversy as well as harmony—in short, wherever we may be. This may well have been written as a reaction to those first friars who were satisfied with the rules of Benedict or Augustine, which envision a spiritual life lived in a monastery or specific community. Nevertheless, Francis highlights in a wonderfully simple way those values he would have us live intensely in the world: avoidance of arrogance and self-righteousness; the practice of meekness, modesty, humility, and courtesy; living poorly in the midst of others; being messengers of peace; and enjoying the freedom of those who thoroughly cast their care upon the Lord. These are the values of the Franciscan "civilization of love."

Chapters 4, 5, and 6, however, indicate some of the important shifts that took place in the pursuit of gospel fraternity, especially in the practice of poverty.

I strictly command all my brothers not to receive coins or money in any way, either personally or through the medium of others. Nevertheless, let the ministers and custodians alone take special care through their spiritual friends to provide for the needs of the sick and the clothing of the others according to places, seasons and cold climates, as they judge necessary, saving always that, as stated above, they do not receive coins or money.

Let those brothers to whom the Lord has given the grace of working work faithfully and devotedly that, avoiding idleness, the enemy of the soul, they do not extinguish the Spirit of holy prayer and devotion to which all temporal things must contribute.

In payment for their work they may receive whatever is necessary for the bodily support of themselves and their brothers, excepting coin or money, and let them do this humbly as is becoming for servants of God and followers of most holy poverty.

Let the brothers not make anything their own, neither house nor place nor anything at all. As pilgrims and strangers in this world (cf. 1 Pet. 2:11), serving the Lord in poverty and humility, let them go seeking alms with confidence, and they should not be ashamed because, for our sakes, our Lord made Himself poor in this world (cf. 2 Cor. 8:9). This is that sublime height of most exalted poverty that has made you, my most beloved brothers, heirs and kings of the Kingdom of Heaven, poor in temporal things but exalted in virtue (cf. James 2:5). Let this be your portion that leads into the land of the living (cf. Ps. 142:6 [V 141:6]). Giving yourselves totally to this, beloved brothers, for the name of our Lord Jesus Christ never seek anything else under heaven.

Wherever the brothers may be and meet one another, let them show that they are members of the same family. Let each one confidently make known his need to the other, for if a mother loves and cares for her son according to the flesh (cf. 1 Thess. 2:7), how much more diligently must someone love and care for his brother according to the Spirit! When any brother falls sick, the other brothers must serve him as they would wish to be served themselves (cf. Matt. 7:12).

Francis now speaks to us in much stronger language, especially in the prohibition against money; here he makes no exceptions to that prohibition as we find in the Earlier Rule. In that earlier document we do not find phrases such as "I strictly command..." or "...in any way, either personally or through the medium of others." Somehow or other the lofty idealism of the primitive fraternity suffered from the day-to-day exposure to the reality of the world. Francis speaks to us as someone more convinced of and focused on the value of poverty. If money was looked upon as security rather than a medium of exchange, then Francis is calling us to live paradoxically in a state of economic insecurity confident that our future rests in the hands of God. It is a challenge touching on the strength of our faith. Are we willing to cast our care on the Lord, to turn to the "table of the Lord" assured that God will take care of us?

In the Earlier Rule, Francis and his first followers begin with a consideration of work and continue with a prohibition against receiving money as payment. But the prohibition against receiving money takes the first place in the Later Rule while the consideration of work follows after it. Moreover, the Earlier Rule spoke of those "who know how to work": advising them to do so "provided it is not contrary to the good of their souls and can be performed honestly." The Later Rule omits all such language and, instead, speaks of "the grace of working," urging us to "work faithfully and devotedly" and placing its advice in the context of asceticism and of prayer. Work, in other words, does not define our identity. It is a grace, as is every aspect of our calling. What is most important is that it remains submissive or subservient to the primary dimension of our life, intensifying our loving relationship with God.

From this perspective, we are in a better position to read the first half of chapter 6, in which we find a clear, rich statement of Francis's vision of poverty. He now proposes its embrace for three reasons: through it, we can identify with Christ,

who "made himself poor in this world"; it can help us to reflect our inheritance and our actual sharing in the kingdom of
heaven; and, finally, it is an ascetical means of giving ourselves
more completely to Christ. In addition to being rich in content,
Francis's words are poetic in expression, beautifully crafted in
composition, and laden with a variety of meaning so that we
cannot read them without reflecting on their beauty or without
mulling over their impact.

Francis clearly links the practice of poverty and the pursuit
of brotherhood. Francis's followers have a somewhat curious
sense of fraternity. We do not consider it in the sense of community, that is, as people living together in a particular place
or region and usually linked by common interests. Neither work
nor shared vision brings us together in Francis's understanding.
It is simply the Holy Spirit. Although we might be separated by
miles from one another, we are still intimately related. Alone on
a small island in the Pacific or in the African bush, or serving
in the busy inner city, we are united to one another as brothers
or sisters. In fact, Francis proposes a spirituality that maintains:
to grow spiritually is to strengthen our fraternal bonds. Now he
proposes that our spiritual life is integrally tied with our pursuit of poverty and, in doing so, unites it with our dependence
on one another.

We may have observed this in chapter 9 of the Earlier Rule
and seen its implication in its following chapters, especially in
the directives for caring for the sick. But here we have a clear,
articulate joining of two ideas, as if Francis wanted us to be sure
of his vision that the foundation of a fraternal life is the pursuit
of a most penetrating poverty. Look at the differences between
these passages of the two rules:

THE EARLIER RULE	THE LATER RULE
Let each one confidently make known his need to another that the other might discover what is needed and minister to him.	Wherever the brothers may be and meet one another, let them show that they are members of the same family.
Let each one love and care for his brother as a mother loves and	Let each one confidently make known his need to the other, for

cares for her son in those matters in which God has given him the grace (cf. 1 Thess. 2:7).

if a mother loves and cares for her son according to the flesh (cf. 1 Thess. 2:7), how much more diligently must someone love and care for his brother according to the Spirit!

Not only is the later text more polished and grammatically correct; it is also more expressive of Francis's understanding that the glue of fraternal life is nothing other than the Spirit. It is the Spirit that makes us members of one family and that inspires us in our attitudes of care and love for one another. Once more Francis's insight highlighted by Odo of Cheriton comes to mind. Speaking of how the fraternity came to be, Francis claimed he was like a woman impregnated by the Word of God. The unusual feminine quality of the relations between brothers — "if a mother loves and cares for her son according to the flesh, how much more diligently..." — can only be understood in light of Francis's understanding that the Spirit that unites us comes through the Word that gives spirit and life. From this vantage point we can easily understand chapter 7, which touches on those who are spiritually sick, that is, sinners; chapter 8, which describes building the fraternity through chapters and choosing those whom we would have as "ministers and servants"; chapter 9, which extends the role of a chapter by entrusting some with the ministry of preaching; and the first part of chapter 10, which portrays the unique bond of a loving obedience existing between one entrusted with the responsibility of serving the other and another charged with responding to the initiatives of the other.

If any brother, at the instigation of the enemy, sin mortally in regard to those sins concerning which it has been decreed among the brothers to have recourse only to the ministers provincial, let him have recourse as quickly as possible and without delay. If these ministers are priests, with a heart full of mercy let them impose on him a penance; but, if the ministers are not priests, let them have it imposed by others who are priests of the Order, as in the sight of God appears to them more expedient. They must be careful not to be angry or disturbed at the sin of another, for anger and disturbance impede charity in themselves and in others.

Let all the brothers be bound to have always one of the brothers of this Order as minister general and servant of the whole fraternity and let them be strictly bound to obey him. When he dies, let the election of his successor be made by the ministers provincial and custodians in the Chapter of Pentecost, at which all the ministers provincial are bound to assemble in whatever place the minister general may have designated. Let them do this once in every three years, or at other longer or shorter intervals, as determined by the aforesaid minister.

If, at any time, it appears to the body of the ministers provincial and custodians that the aforesaid minister general is not qualified for the service and general welfare of the brothers, let the aforesaid brothers to whom the election is committed be bound to elect another as custodian in the name of the Lord.

Moreover, after the Chapter of Pentecost, the ministers provincial and custodians may each, if they wish and it seems expedient to them, convoke a Chapter of the brothers in their custodies once in the same year.

Let the brothers not preach in the diocese of any bishop when he has opposed their doing so. Let none of the brothers in any way dare to preach to the people unless he has been examined and approved by the minister general of this fraternity and the office of preacher has been conferred upon him.

Moreover, I admonish and exhort those brothers that when they preach their *language be well-considered and chaste* (cf. Pss. 12:7; 18:13) for the benefit and edification of the people, announcing to them vices and virtues, punishment and glory with brevity, because our Lord when on earth made "a short word" (cf. Rom. 9:28).

Let the brothers who are the ministers and servants of the others visit and admonish their brothers and humbly and charitably correct them, not commanding them anything that is against their soul and our Rule. Let the brothers who are subject, however, remember that, for God's sake, they have renounced their own wills. Therefore, I strictly command them to obey their ministers in everything they have promised the Lord to observe and which is not against their soul or our Rule.

Wherever the brothers may be who know and feel they cannot observe the Rule spiritually, they can and should have recourse to their ministers. Let the ministers, moreover, receive them charitably and kindly and have such familiarity with them that these same brothers may speak and deal with them as masters with their servants, for so it must be that the ministers are the servants of all the brothers.

In the second half of chapter 10, however, Francis synthesizes much of his understanding of the gospel life by having recourse to the Spirit:

Moreover, I admonish and exhort the brothers in the Lord Jesus Christ to beware of all pride, vainglory, envy and greed, of care and solicitude for the things of this world (cf. Matt. 13:22; Luke 12:15), of detraction and murmuring. Let those who are illiterate not be anxious to learn, but let them pay attention to what they must desire above all else: to have the Spirit of the Lord and Its holy activity, to pray always to Him with a pure heart, to have humility and patience in persecution and infirmity, and to love those who persecute, reprove and censure us, because the Lord says: *Love your enemies and pray for those who persecute and calumniate you* (cf. Matt. 5:44). *Blessed are those who suffer persecution for the sake of justice, for theirs is the kingdom of heaven* (Matt. 5:10). *But whoever perseveres to the end will be saved* (Matt. 10:22).

Thomas of Celano tells us that Francis considered the Holy Spirit the general minister of the order. Yet we should not pass over these particularly Spirit-filled passages without being sensitive to the tremendously biblical and monastic terminology in which they are expressed. This is an area in which we can perceive how the simplicity of the Later Rule belies such hidden layers of meaning and how easily we can pass over the full extent of Francis's thought. We might focus on two of these passages: "the Spirit of holy prayer and devotion" and "the Spirit of the Lord and Its holy activity."

Francis sees the primary activity of the Spirit as the prayer of a pure heart. In an earlier passage of the Later Rule's tenth chapter, Francis writes about those who cannot observe the rule *spiritually.* While he does not explain his meaning, he almost immediately proceeds to encourage us to "attend to what they must desire above all else: to have the Spirit of the Lord and

Its holy activity." In doing so, he seems to be offering his explanation of acting spiritually as well as suggesting the apogee of all spiritual observance, that is, conformity with the inner dynamic of the Holy Spirit. As Kajetan Esser maintains: "With Saint Francis it is not simply a question of an external following of the life of Christ, but rather, first of all, that the Spirit of Christ must become alive and active in the would-be follower. This doctrine of the Spirit of the Lord...may be called the very center of St. Francis's thinking and Christian behavior" (quoted in Asseldonk 1991, 106). We need only to reread those writings that we have already examined or to glance at those yet to come to see how conscious Francis was of the Spirit's presence and activity in himself and in his brothers and sisters.

Francis gives a wonderful christological nuance to the Spirit's presence. He does not write "the Spirit of God" nor even "the Holy Spirit," but "the Spirit of the Lord." This reflects the tendency of St. Paul to identify the Spirit given to the faithful with the Spirit proper to the eternal Son. "When the appointed time came," he writes to the Galatians, "God sent his Son....God sent the Spirit of his Son into hearts" (Gal. 4:4, 6). It is "the Spirit of Christ" (Rom. 8:9), "the Spirit of Jesus Christ" (Phil. 1:9), or simply "the Spirit of the Lord" (2 Cor. 3:17). The mystery of Christ cannot be dissociated from the mystery of the Spirit, and vice versa. Paul — and Francis — seem unable to write of God's Spirit without reference to the revelation of God found in Jesus. Under this Pauline influence, Francis reminds us that the desire to follow Christ's footprints is an initiative of divine inspiration, that is, the Holy Spirit, that the sign of a thorough embrace of penance is an intimacy with God characterized by the very activities of the Spirit in Christ.

From this perspective Francis writes of being "spiritual" or acting "spiritually," terms he employs in a strong sense, with clear reference to the Spirit of the Lord, not in the sense of the human spirit. Thus "to have the Spirit of the Lord and Its holy activity" means that we must allow the Spirit to work in our souls and in our conduct, that we must become transparent expressions of its presence. To keep his rule spiritually, in other words, means to observe it according to the demands of the Spirit of the Lord at work in our souls. This becomes clearer when we see how in both rules Francis contrasts the Spirit of the Lord with the spirit of the flesh, a practice that is reminiscent of Gal. 5:16–24. The spirit of the flesh expresses itself in definite "me-centered" ways, while the Spirit of the Lord does so in ways that are other-centered.

THE EARLIER RULE	THE LATER RULE
Because the spirit of the flesh very much wants and strives to have the words but cares little for the activity; it does not seek a religion and holiness in an interior spirit, but wants and desires to have a religion and a holiness outwardly apparent to people. They are the ones of whom the Lord says: *Amen, I say to you, they have received their reward* (Matt. 6:2). The Spirit of the Lord, however, wants the flesh to be mortified and looked down upon, considered of little worth and rejected. It strives for humility and patience, the pure, simple and true peace of the spirit. Above all, it desires the divine fear, the divine wisdom and the divine love of the Father, Son and Holy Spirit.	Moreover, I admonish and exhort the brothers in the Lord Jesus Christ to beware of all pride, vainglory, envy and greed, of care and solicitude for the things of this world (cf. Matt. 13:22; Luke 12:15), of detraction and murmuring. Let those who are illiterate not be anxious to learn, but let them pay attention to what they must desire above all else: to have the Spirit of the Lord and Its holy activity, to pray always to Him with a pure heart, to have humility and patience in persecution and infirmity, and to love those who persecute, reprove and censure us, because the Lord says: Love your enemies and pray for those who persecute and calumniate you (cf. Matt. 5:44). Blessed are those who suffer persecution for the sake of justice, for theirs is the kingdom of heaven (Matt. 5:10). But whoever perseveres to the end will be saved (Matt. 10:22).

We should not pass over how Francis, in describing the spirit of the flesh and the Spirit of the Lord, envisions their energies expressing themselves. Clearly the "spirit of the flesh" is in line with Paul's concern for what is the root and inner source of every sin or vice. The human spirit left to itself moves the flesh or the body to seek itself, to turn against God and neighbor, making us prisoners of the devil. In the Earlier Rule, as we have seen, Francis describes its activities in pharisaical ways (seeking a religion and holiness outwardly apparent to people) and in those that are self-aggrandizing (seeking to be glib or articulate so as to please others). In his Later Rule, he expresses these characteristics in far more pointed but nonetheless self-centered ways: pride, vainglory, envy, avarice, and activities that are destructive of the fraternity. The Spirit of the Lord, on the other hand, expresses Itself in ways that are unassuming, unpretentious, long-suffering, and single-minded. While the Earlier Rule envisions these characteristics as being mortified, looked down upon, and rejected, the Later Rule accentuates humility, patience, love, and, in the very first place, unceasing prayer with a pure heart. In both instances, however, we can see that Francis envisions the Spirit pointing beyond itself to Jesus and expressing its presence in ways that are reflective of the Incarnation.

In light of Francis's eagerness that we attend to the workings of the Spirit, we can better understand his consolidation of the Earlier Rule's frequent allusions to prayer by pointing to its primary activity, "to pray always with a pure heart." In Francis's mind, prayer was certainly one of the forms of the Spirit's presence. Thus when he attempts to articulate his conviction that everything else is secondary, Francis encourages his brothers not to "extinguish the Spirit of holy prayer and devotion to which all temporal things must contribute."

Once again we can perceive the tremendous biblical influence on Francis's thoughts on prayer. When we pray, we implicitly acknowledge the presence of the Spirit within. Prayer, adoration, praise, a liturgy that is lived, all of these are activities of the Spirit (cf. Rom. 12:1; 1 Pet. 2:5; John 4:23; Eph. 5:18ff.; Col. 3:16). St. Paul's exhortation to the Thessalonians, "Pray without ceasing" (1 Thess. 5:17), corresponds to the very nature of a life animated by the Spirit. Thomas of Celano's description of Francis as "not only praying as much as becoming a prayer" is a perfect expression of that Pauline theology. So too is Francis's own encouragement to "pray always with a pure heart," that is, to allow the Spirit's energy to be the dominant force. Moreover, the force of the Spirit tends irresistibly to unite us with the mystery of God through the person of Christ. "When we cry 'Abba,

Father!' it is the Spirit itself bearing witness with our spirit that we are children of God" (Rom. 8:15).

We can so easily pass over this simple statement concerning prayer without pausing to fathom its depths or without realizing how expressive it is of the Franciscan approach to God. Not only is this another instance of Francis's tremendous Spirit-filled approach to gospel life; it also offers us an insight into the Franciscan approach to prayer, ministry, and study. To perceive prayer as primarily an activity of the Spirit is to recognize that it is an expression of a fundamental desire. "We do not know how to pray as we ought," Paul writes to the Romans, "but the Spirit itself intercedes for us with sighs too deep for words" (Rom. 8:26). We encounter a vocabulary that reflects, then, the language of desire for the Spirit that is at the very heart of our prayer. But Francis tells us that the Spirit is also that of devotion. "Devotion" is used by Bernard of Clairvaux to describe the same reality as a gift of God that was associated with the Holy Spirit. It was an experience of fervor that was expressed in a certain enthusiasm for prayer, an enthusiasm that flowed from the desire to love God. Thus we find Francis, compelled by necessity, reducing so much of the Earlier Rule's teaching and encouragement to pray to this one simple phrase: "the Spirit of holy prayer and devotion."

Francis's teaching, however, continues as he maintains that "all temporal things must contribute" to the Spirit of holy prayer and devotion. In this he not only places the pursuit of prayer and the concerns of daily life — in this instance, work or ministry — into a proper balance; he also teaches us how to avoid a prayer that escapes reality. He envisions a prayer that also takes its expression from our day-to-day experiences and uses them as stimuli or means for discovering the presence of God. This may well be a reflection of Francis's youthful search for God that, sharpened and sensitized by long periods of solitary prayer, culminated in the decisive embrace of a leper and in a subsequent experience of God's love. It is no wonder, then, that the pulse beat of Franciscan prayer, practiced from the earliest days, has been an hour of mental prayer in the morning and a second in the evening.

The gospel life that Francis proposes dedicates us to the kingdom of God. It also implies a great sense of freedom. "Where the

Spirit of the Lord is," Paul tells us, "there is freedom." Yet this
demands authenticity. Our activities and our dealings with one
another must be reflections of God's Spirit. How can we give
ourselves to God and one another in the Spirit of freedom if
we are bound by the subtle ties of the heart? Thus Francis quite
clearly cautions us to be attentive to any dealings with those of
the opposite sex that can be misconstrued:

I strictly command all the brothers not to have any suspicious asso-
ciations or conversations with women, nor to enter the monasteries of nuns, excepting those brothers to whom special permission
has been granted by the Apostolic See; and not to be godfathers
to men or women that scandal may not arise among the brothers
or concerning them because of this.

Francis realized that to be filled with the Spirit implied being a person of love, one who easily accepted being loved and
who freely loved. The Capuchin constitutions, therefore, reflect
this by maintaining: "One of the notable characteristics of Saint
Francis is the richness of his affections and his ability to express
them. Francis, in love with God and with all people, and indeed
with all creatures, is a brother and friend of all." From this perspective, then, we might see "suspicious" as the key word in this
paragraph. Our dealings with one another, Francis tells us, must
be always genuine expressions of the Spirit within our hearts.

"Chastity without charity," William Langland declared in
Piers Plowman, "lies chained in hell, it is but an unlighted lamp."
These words resonate with a comment of Brother Giles, one of
Francis's first companions. When asked which was the better
virtue, chastity or charity, Giles responded: "What could be better than chaste charity?" Our call to live from the Spirit that is
in our heart demands a chastity that is lived not only with joyful freedom and love but also with intelligence so that the world
feels itself unmasked. Such a life of chaste charity enables love
to deepen within us and facilitates a journey from a self-centered
and possessive love to one that is self-sacrificing and capable of
giving itself to others.

Thus Francis stretches our concerns beyond our immedi-
ate worlds to those living in those difficult situations where
suffering and death are distinct possibilities:

Let those brothers who wish by divine inspiration to go among the Saracens or other non-believers ask permission to go from their ministers provincial. The ministers, however, may not grant permission except to those whom they see fit to be sent.

"The work of evangelization presupposes in the evangelizer an ever increasing love for those whom he is evangelizing," maintains Pope Paul VI. It is a love that is concerned for giving the truth and bringing people into unity; a love devoted to the proclamation of Jesus Christ, without reservation or turning back. With the echo of chapter 23 of his Earlier Rule ringing in our ears, Francis calls us to embrace these ideals. It has been the story of his followers for centuries as they set out for China within a few years of his death, joined the early Spanish explorers of Latin America, or tirelessly walked in the African bush proclaiming by their lives and words the Jesus to whom they had given their lives.

With this call to evangelization, Francis draws our attention to the church, the context in which he calls us to live the gospel life:

Finally I command the ministers through obedience to petition from our Lord the Pope for one of the Cardinals of the Holy Roman Church, who would be the governor, protector and corrector of this fraternity, so that, being always submissive and subject at the feet of the same Holy Church and steadfast in the Catholic Faith, we may observe poverty, humility and the Holy Gospel of our Lord Jesus Christ as we have firmly promised.

Although much of this final section of the Later Rule is taken up with a description of the cardinal called to be a liaison between the pope and Francis's followers, it confronts us with a call to live simply and poorly within the church. This might seem quite ordinary to our contemporary sense of spirituality, but it was somewhat uncommon in the days of Francis when such intense spiritualities were seen as more individual concerns. Francis's words call us beyond ourselves to live the mystery of the church and to enrich it by our pursuit of living poorly and humbly.

Unfortunately many read these words and limit their understanding of fidelity to the church as expressing fidelity to its magisterium. Francis would undoubtedly endorse such fidelity — many of his writings witness to his concern for the teaching church. Yet we might wonder what his response would be to the teaching of the conciliar and postconciliar church of the Second Vatican Council or to the repeated call of Pope John Paul II to involve ourselves in the pursuit of justice and peace.

For eight centuries the Later Rule has been the foundation of Franciscan life. The entire Franciscan tradition has been influenced by its vision of gospel life, manner of expression, or ecclesial consciousness. Indeed, the Rule of St. Clare, approved on her deathbed in 1253, borrows entire paragraphs and phrases, as does the Third Order Regular Rule approved by Pope John Paul II in 1982. Far from being "the death of the vision," as John Holland Smith maintains, Francis's Later Rule captures in a simple, straightforward way the essentials of his vision and does so with such clarity that it has inspired men and women since its confirmation.

Part Two

Undated Writings

At this point we must leave a chronological approach to Francis's writings to consider those that are undatable. Scholars have attempted over and again to determine when these pieces were composed but to no avail. They are in a certain sense timeless.

But this provides us, as we have suggested, a wonderful opportunity to step back from those writings that were obviously shaped by historical circumstances and to take a different approach to those that are more mysterious. In a sense, these undatable writings enable us to look more seriously into the methodology that Francis provides for approaching God. Without these considerations we might simply study these texts as the response of one medieval man living in the Umbrian Valley during a transitional period of history. His interpretations of the gospel would reflect the tension of his world not ours. Thus we could easily dismiss his call to live the gospel vision he articulates as something foreign to our own experience.

These writings prompt us to speculate about the universal attractiveness of Francis's teachings. We only have to experience a group of young people in the African bush or in a Brazilian *favela* to know that Francis's vision — and what it represents — touches the hearts of so many downtrodden human beings. The observation of the Kenyan missionary that at heart all people are Franciscan returns to us.

How do we best approach these undated writings? There are any number of ways. We could easily begin with the biblical approach suggested by chapter 22 of the Earlier Rule. Thus we would focus our attention on Francis's *Office of the Passion* and, through it, appreciate the christological underpinnings of his vision. Or we could take a more liturgical approach by reflecting upon his "Exhortation to the Praise of God" or "Praises to Be Said at All the Hours." In this way we would easily understand the biblical, liturgical, and even eschatological dimensions that permeate so many of these thoughts. But these approaches would still leave us with that unique, *historical* phenomenon, Francis of Assisi, and allow us to sidestep the method that he teaches us. Were he alive today, we might ask, would he choose the same passages from the Gospels to shape his vision? To resolve these difficulties, we begin with Francis's *Admonitions*, those twenty-eight simple texts that speak so eloquently of human nature. Through them we encounter how Francis viewed God, the human person, sin, and its undoing.

The *Admonitions*

What do we mean when speaking of "admonitions"? Our question might initially seem simplistic, but its answer might help us to understand the privileged place that Francis's work known as the *Admonitions* has in the Franciscan tradition. *Webster's New World Dictionary* defines "to admonish" as "1. to caution against specific faults; warn; 2. to reprove mildly; 3. to urge or exhort; 4. to inform or remind, by way of a warning." "Admonition" is defined as: "1. an admonishing, or warning to correct some fault; 2. a mild rebuke; reprimand." But is this the medieval meaning of *admonere* or *admonitio*, the Latin words from which our English words are derived? When we consider the *Admonitions* of Francis, are we speaking of twenty-eight warnings or cautions that he gave to his followers as the head of the order? Hardly! None of the admonitions conveys any sort of disciplinary message. Then what was the intention of the friar who first placed these twenty-eight sayings under this title? That is, what was he suggesting by gathering them together under this title?

While none of the eleven uses of "admonish" in Francis's writings tells us anything special about its meaning, its frequent appearance with "exhort" or "encourage" gives us some insight. In most of these instances, the verbs are in the first-person singular, suggesting Francis's desire to underscore some aspect of his understanding of gospel life. At first glance, we might interpret the use of "I admonish and exhort" as a means of adding emphasis. That makes sense especially when we reflect on the attitudes Francis underscores in each of these four passages. If we look more closely at them, however, we see that each passage reflects some biblical teaching. Does the phrase, then, express a pedagogical tool with which Francis presents a biblical text or allusion and encourages his brothers to follow it in their daily lives? A glance at the *Admonitions* suggests that such is the case, for they almost all begin with a biblical passage, image, or allusion. The first admonition, for example, begins with a series of scriptural quotes, the second with a passage from Genesis describing the first sin, and the third with two Synoptic passages suggesting its undoing. Throughout the remaining admonitions Francis continually brings to our attention the Beatitudes or his own version of the "Beatitudes of the Servant of God," each of which begins with a biblical reference. Only the twenty-seventh admonition fails us in this regard (although one could argue that the beginning of that admonition contains an implicit reference to 1 John 4:16). Therefore, we're left with twenty-eight pieces that follow the same pattern: a biblical quotation, allusion, or image and a practical, down-to-earth application of its thought. In all of their simplicity, these reflections reveal more clearly than Francis's other writings the contours of his biblical spirituality.

When speaking of an admonition, we should understand it as a biblical reflection or preaching. In this instance, however, we must narrow its meaning to indicate a sermon that is reminiscent or historical in nature, that is, a discourse that recalls or brings to mind some message, image, or event. Seen in this light, we can appreciate the uniqueness of this method of pedagogy employed by Francis. While contemporary translations tend to interpret the term "admonishing" as referring to an act of cautioning, advising, reproving, or warning, the more accurate way of capturing its meaning would be to accentuate the more religious characteristics of recalling the teaching of Jesus, his gracious interventions in history, or various aspects of religious observance.

The first admonition provides us a perfect introduction to these biblical reflections:

The Lord Jesus says to his disciples: *I am the way, the truth and the life; no one comes to the Father except through me. If you*

knew me, you would also know my Father; and from now on, you do know him and have seen him. Philip says to him: Lord, show us the Father and it will be enough for us. Jesus says to him: Have I been with you for so long a time and you have not known me? Philip, whoever sees me sees my *Father as well* (John 14:6–9).

The Father dwells *in inaccessible light* (cf. 1 Tim. 6:16), and *God is spirit* (John 4:24), and *no one has ever seen God* (John 1:18). He cannot be seen, therefore, except in the Spirit because *it is the Spirit that gives life; the flesh has nothing to offer* (John 6:63). But neither is the Son, inasmuch as He is equal to the Father, seen by anyone other than the Father or other than the Holy Spirit.

All those who saw the Lord Jesus according to the humanity, therefore, and did not see and believe according to the Spirit and the Divinity that He is the true Son of God were condemned. Now in the same way, all those who see the sacrament sanctified by the words of the Lord upon the altar at the hands of the priest in the form of bread and wine, and who do not see and believe according to the Spirit and the Divinity that it is truly the Body and Blood of our Lord Jesus Christ are condemned. [This] is affirmed by the Most High Himself Who says: *This is my Body and the Blood of my new covenant [which will be shed for many]* (cf. Mark 14:22, 24); and *Whoever eats my flesh and drinks my blood has eternal life* (John 6:55). It is the Spirit of the Lord, therefore, That lives in Its faithful That receives the Body and Blood of the Lord. All others who do not share in this same Spirit and presume to receive Him eat and drink *judgment on themselves* (cf. 1 Cor. 11:29).

Therefore: *children, how long will you be hard of heart?* (Ps. 4:3) Why do you not know the truth and believe *in the Son of God?* (cf. John 9:35) Behold, He humbles Himself each day (cf. Phil. 2:8) as when He came *from the royal throne* into the Virgin's womb (Wis. 18:15); each day He Himself comes to us, appearing humbly; each day He comes down *from the bosom of the Father* (cf. John 1:18) upon the altar in the hands of a priest.

As He revealed Himself to the holy apostles in true flesh, so He reveals Himself to us now in sacred bread. And as they saw only His flesh by an insight of their flesh yet believed that He was God as they contemplated Him with their spiritual eyes, let us, as we see bread and wine with our bodily eyes, see and firmly believe that they are His most holy Body and Blood living and true. In this way the Lord is always with His faithful, as He Himself says: *Behold I am with you until the end of the age* (cf. Matt. 28:20).

In the very first admonition Francis reminds us quite forcefully of the centrality of Christ in our journey to the Father. To see the Father — this is the great desire expressed by the first admonition as Francis repeatedly stresses the various levels of seeing, contemplating, and beholding the Father with the eyes of the flesh or those of the Spirit. This is undoubtedly the deep, inner struggle of every human being, to enter into the mystery of God. It is one in which we can readily identify with the apostles Thomas and Philip. Invisible and spiritual in nature, God is necessarily hidden from the eyes of every human being. We might easily imagine Francis's sympathy for or admiration of the honesty of Philip. Someone who had abandoned his father for the sake of Jesus might very well request and declare as Philip: "Lord, show us the Father and it is enough for us!" With his profound faith in Christ, Francis teaches us that foundation of the spiritual life found in the response of the Lord: "Philip, whoever sees me sees my Father."

The place of Christ, then, as the revelation of God the Father is the central issue of this first admonition and the focus of the contemplative gaze to which Francis invites us. In a remarkable way, he draws our attention to the activity of the Holy Spirit in this concentration on the mystery of Christ. Since Christ is consubstantial with the Father and of the same divine nature as the Spirit, no one can fully see or know him as he exists in the Godhead. Only the Father and the Holy Spirit have the power to penetrate fully the mystery of the Incarnation. Yet Francis seems overwhelmed at the thought that the Spirit is now within us, and, therefore, he rightly accentuates its role within us in properly seeing and believing in the mystery of the Incarnation. He goes even further in highlighting the continuing, daily revelation of Christ in his eucharistic presence. "As He revealed Himself to the holy apostles in true flesh," he writes, "so He reveals Himself to us in sacred bread in the same way." In both of these aspects of the mystery of Christ, Francis recognizes that it is only through the medium of the Holy Spirit that we can cut through the outer appearances to see and believe, as he states, "according to the Spirit and the Divinity."

Upon this foundation, composed of a remarkable trinitarian vision and strong pneumatological character, Francis reveals the fruit of his own contemplation of the Incarnate Word who remains with us in the Eucharist. He reminds us of the humility of the Son of God who empties himself so that we might see and believe in him and make our way in him to the Father. He teaches us of the all-powerful God who continues to take the initiative in coming to us in ways that speak of lowliness, poverty, and a willingness to submit to the frailty of human care. Francis proposes for our contemplation the vision of the loving and continuing revelation of God who by assuming the paradoxical state of being poor and unassuming manifests the awesome and overflowing divine might. As he describes this daily renewal of the divine presence, he provides us with a reflection of his meaning of minority. Only by identification with the Eucharist does Francis discover the way in which we human beings can undo the ravages of sin and respond to the dignity of the divine call. As he writes in the Letter to the Entire Order: only in the Body and Blood of our Lord Jesus Christ is all that "is in the heavens and on the earth brought to peace and reconciled to the all-powerful God."

At the very heart of the *Admonitions*, however, is a recognition of the relations that Francis perceives existing between the Creator and the creature. He continually reminds us of the presence of an all-good, dynamically creative, and eloquent God and calls us to struggle with our appropriate response to the divine initiatives. Yet to recognize the broad strokes of this relationship and the reasons for our struggle, we would do well to spend time with Francis's second admonition.

The Lord said to Adam: *Eat of every tree; you may not eat, however, of the tree of the knowledge of good and evil* (cf. Gen. 2:16, 17).

He was able to eat of every tree of paradise because, as long as he did not go against obedience, he did not sin. For that person eats of the tree of the knowledge of good who makes his will his own and, in this way, exalts himself over the good things the Lord says and does in him. And so, through the suggestion of the devil and the transgression of the command, it became the apple of the knowledge of evil. Therefore it is fitting that he suffer the punishment.

Francis begins in a familiar patristic, monastic, and contemplative fashion by reflecting upon the biblical description of the drama of the Garden of Eden in the book of Genesis. Early Christian writers realized that our understanding of the history of salvation is dependent on the ways in which we perceive the first three chapters of Genesis. The creative activities of Yahweh, the positions and roles of the first human beings, the presence of evil, and the effects of sin: all these fundamental concepts are shaped and colored by our reading of these narratives. The second admonition is the clearest reflection of Francis's own understanding.

How often Francis frequently draws our attention to the image of God who says and does good things! *Admonitions* alone presents seven different instances in which the dynamic power of the all-good God is mentioned and we are seen as simple beneficiaries. Our creation and formation in God's own image and likeness and our salvation are but two of these initiatives. Francis so often focuses on the good that the Lord says or does that he teaches us to believe in the ever-continuing creative and revealing God. Our calling, then, is to recognize our dependence on God's limitless, creative goodness. The very foundation of the peace and harmony of the first creation, in Francis's view, is the overwhelming generosity and goodness of God that are considered in relation to our absolute poverty and dependence.

Adam provides for Francis a rich symbol that reveals the call of each one of us. "Eat of every tree," says the Lord, inviting Adam to enjoy all the gifts of creation, to revel in the goodness of the ever-generous God, and to be, quite simply, the principal beneficiary of the largesse of the Creator. A beautiful work written within a year of Francis's death, the *Sacrum Commercium*, expresses this in poetic fashion as Lady Poverty tells her story and figuratively suggests the childlike enjoyment of the first human in the unspoiled garden:

> I was at one time in the paradise of my God, where the human person went naked; in fact I walked in man and with man in his nakedness through the whole of that most splendid paradise, fearing nothing, doubting nothing, and suspecting nothing of the adversary. I thought that I would be with him forever, for he was just, good and aware that

he was created by the Most High and placed in that most pleasant and most beautiful place. I was rejoicing exceedingly and playing before him all the while (Prov. 8:30), for, while possessing nothing, he belonged entirely to God. (no. 25)

We could not find a more idyllic and simple description of paradise. In his own reflection on this idyllic scene, however, Francis recognizes the importance of the tree and places it in a pivotal position so that it becomes a symbol of all of our possibilities as well as of our limitations. A simple command, "You may not eat of the tree of the knowledge of good," is placed upon Adam so that he would always recognize the Creator as Lord of all, as the sovereign fountain of goodness. The prohibition is not placed before the first human to torment him or to be a stumbling block before him or to tempt him to fall from the tranquillity of his state. Francis simply understands the right of the Creator, the Lord, to establish a guarantee that the first human being would always respect and not forget the generosity of his benefactor. Of course Francis is simply echoing an earlier tradition that accepted this biblical and traditional imagery to describe the foundations of the divine-human relationship that existed in the tranquil peace of Eden, a relationship that was based firmly upon a loving, attentive listening to and response to the voice of the Creator.

Yet Adam sinned. Why? Francis really does not offer any reasons, but his repeated use of "to eat" hints at what he may have had in mind. It appears four times in the opening lines of this brief writing, especially in the context of the divine command. Clearly it is taken from Gen. 2:16–17. Yet when seen in light of the nine references to the perils of knowledge throughout the *Admonitions*, Francis seems to extend the metaphor of the divine command as a warning signal concerning our dangerous, insatiable pursuit of learning. Is this what he means by his reference to the transgression as eating only "from the tree of the knowledge of good" that becomes "the apple of the knowledge of evil"? Is Francis suggesting that the apparent good of satisfying our hunger for knowledge could deceptively lead us from contemplation of the goodness of God, that is, from our true calling?

While other spiritual writers describe the sin as essentially one of disobedience, Francis portrays it as an act of appropriation of the gift of liberty and an exaltation of ourselves over the goodness that surrounds us. "For that person eats of the tree of the knowledge of good," he tells us, "who makes his will his own and...exalts himself over the good things the Lord says and does in him." Francis presents the disturbing portrait of someone who takes what is not his, claims it as his own, and uses it for his own personal advancement. Thus he describes two movements in his description of Adam's sin: one that is grasping, appropriating, or grabbing; the other that is self-exalting, self-aggrandizing, or self-elevating. He sees, in other words, actions centered on ourselves: taking things for our own purpose and lifting up ourselves over and against the Other.

In Francis's view, the first sin of the human person, then, is fundamentally one of injustice. Rather than acknowledging the rights of the Creator in setting a limit on the creature, the first human ignores these rights, takes what is not his, and attempts to establish himself as the center of the world. Rather than acknowledging the Lord as the primary initiator of all that is good, both in word and in deed, the first human makes those initiatives his own and, thereby, exalts himself. The relations between Creator and creature are radically severed and the harmonious peace of the God-given world is shattered by the self-seeking ways of Adam.

The Continuance of the Sin

Francis tells us forcefully that the imprint of the first human is stamped upon our sinful ways of acting as we take what is not truly ours, make it our own, and, consequently, exalt ourselves. He teaches us how easily we can recognize the many ways in which we continue the sin of injustice perpetrated by Adam. The translation of appropriation into our everyday lives is filled with many expressions and nuances: greed, attachment, envy, even anger; that of self-exaltation is much the same: pride, boasting, talkativeness, condescension, indignation, judgment. Francis, an intuitive observer of human nature, wisely perceives the ways in which we continue the sin of Adam. This aspect of *Admonitions* makes it uncomfortable to read. The work highlights so many of our weaknesses and does so at a time when we are lulled by an economic system that promotes not only consumerism but also a productivity-oriented culture. The accumulation of goods and the promotion of the individual, in other words, are placed as important values for our way of life.

Another characteristic of *Admonitions* that makes it so challenging is the ways in which Francis places his analysis in the context of everyday life. As we have seen, we find it difficult to determine the historical circumstances that prompted the work. That in itself attests to its value in daily life. The spectacular or dramatic element is definitely missing, leaving us with unassuming, ordinary situations with which we can easily identify. Who doesn't wince, for example, when reading the twenty-fifth admonition: "Blessed is the servant who loves and respects his brother as much when he is far away from him as when he is with him, and who would not say anything behind his back that he would not say with charity in front of him"? Or who is not challenged by Francis's reflection in the fourteenth admonition upon a poverty that highlights anger as something to which we cling? *Admonitions* has a timeless character. Although delivered in the thirteenth century, the texts are as applicable today as then. Of all Francis's writings, they best form a mirror in which we can recognize ourselves and our sinful ways.

We shouldn't overlook the wisdom of Francis in seeing that the intense life of fraternity provides the environment or the school in which the knowledge of these sinful ways is most easily learned. This is an understanding of fraternity that avoids the intellectual, abstract concept that we so easily use and with which Francis was so uncomfortable. No, this is an understanding of fraternity that is more transparent in its concentration on those who compose it than on the ideals that shape it. The very fact that Francis writes of fraternity only 10 times and of a brother or of brothers an amazing 306 tells us a great deal. In his *Admonitions*, he directs our attention to our daily life with one another and encourages us to examine the ways in which we live *today*. There is no idealized, theoretical concept of fraternity, only a focus on the day-to-day experience of life. Francis's school of fraternal life envisions a crucible in which we are challenged to undo the ravages of sin among those who are far from perfect. Those who irritate us or make us angry; who unjustly accuse or calumniate us; who take from us the credit or recognition we deserve: these are only a few of those with whom Francis imagines us sharing our lives. When we attempt to live it authentically, our fraternal life has an uncanny ability to purify us — consciously or unconsciously — through that daily rubbing of elbows, through coping with one another's flaws or idiosyncrasies. It is this realistic, challenging view of fraternity that makes the *Admonitions* so demanding. While we so easily escape into a dream of fraternity life, Francis keeps our feet on the ground and challenges us to be aware of the flaws that sin has brought to our personalities and the ways it undermines the foundations of justice and peace upon which our daily lives together should be built.

From this perspective Francis describes the person who looks enviously at the goodness that the Lord does or says in another and who wishes to receive more from another than what he or she is willing to give to God. He pities those who lead others astray by their idle and empty words, thus drawing attention to themselves and away from the Lord, and who stand in judgment of others, especially priests, thereby appropriating to themselves the right to judge another that belongs to God alone. The third admonition considers the one who suffers the persecution of others because of an inability to obey; the fourth describes the "prelate" who is upset at losing his office; the nineteenth describes the religious who clings to the office that he has been given by others. When gathered together, these references, scattered throughout *Admonitions*, demonstrate the many subtle implications of the first sin in our daily lives. Although the texts rarely move beyond the context of daily fraternal life, they clearly remind us that our brothers and sisters and the life that we live with them day after day are usually the primary recipients of our various acts of injustice. They do not let us forget that, through our clinging to what is not rightfully ours and the innumerable ways in which we exalt ourselves in acts of self-aggrandizement, we perpetuate the sin of Adam.

The thirteenth, fourteenth, and twenty-fifth admonitions further Francis's vision of the school of fraternal life. The first of these offers a variation in a more general way:

Blessed is the person who supports his neighbor in his weakness
as he would want to be supported were he in a similar situation
(cf. Gal. 6:2; Matt. 7:12).

There is a definite play on the word *sustinere* in this simple,
to-the-point admonition. Is Francis suggesting the more active
response of offering support to our neighbors in their weaknesses or the more passive attitude of enduring and patiently
suffering their weaknesses? The biblical citations support both
interpretations: "Bear one another's burdens and so fulfill the
law of Christ" (Gal. 6:2); "Do to others what you would have
them do to you. This is the law and the prophets" (Matt. 7:12).
"I used to think that being a penitential person meant performing all sorts of austerities," an old friar once said to me.
"After forty or so years of following Francis, I know it means
loving my brothers." Another seasoned friar maintained: "Anyone who praises fraternity as a great blessing has never lived
it! It's a crucifixion!" It is significant that Matthew's text is
repeated eight times in Francis's writings. That makes it one
of the most important biblical passages in understanding his
thought.

The fourteenth admonition presents a different perspective,
this time in the context of sickness:

Blessed is the servant who loves his brother as much when he is
sick and cannot repay him as when he is well and can repay him.

We've already seen in the Earlier Rule how Francis expressed
his concern for the sick. In this one brief phrase, however,
the sick provide him with one of his great insights into the
lived experience of fraternity life. Such life together challenges
us not only to generosity but also to unconditioned love. The
twenty-fifth admonition provides yet another view of fraternal life, in this instance, from the perspective of an absent
brother:

Blessed is the servant who loves and respects his brother as much
when he is far away from him as when he is with him, and who
would not say anything behind his back that he would not say
with charity in front of him.

All three admonitions contain calls to heroic charity, especially in dealing with human weakness or the sinfulness of another. They are, however, echoes of what we can find in the Earlier Rule: "Let them behave among themselves according to what the Lord says: Whatever you wish others do to you, do that to them; and what you do not wish done to you, do not do to another." This is simply another way of proposing the Golden Rule of the Beatitudes as one of the primary biblical foundations of Franciscan life.

The Human Calling

While we cannot deny that the uniqueness of all prophets' vision and leadership arises from the times in which they live and the audience they address, the intensity of Francis's prophetic message comes far more from his intimate and contemplative rapport with God than from his reactions to the vicissitudes of the rulers and people of Assisi. The opening lines of the tenth admonition, for example, wisely remind us of the natural inclination to point to another or to the circumstances in which we live as the scapegoat for our sins.

There are many people who, when they sin or are injured, frequently blame the enemy or their neighbor (cf. Gen. 3:12–13). But it is not so because each one has the enemy in his power, that is his body through which he sins.

We are, therefore, brought back to the lesson of the second admonition: it may well have been the suggestion of the devil, but it was the human person who was responsible for the Fall. In many senses the fraternal relationships described in *Admonitions* form a certain way of living that makes us more conscious of the self-centered and sinful ways in which we point to others in order to avoid confronting ourselves. We unwittingly offer one another opportunities of discovering our attitudes and actions that continue the injustices of Adam. There is, therefore, a profound and vigorous bond that exists between contemplative prayer and the prophetic witness envisioned in *Admonitions*. We can see this immediately in Francis's understanding of the sin of the first human person that shattered the amity and tranquillity of the garden; we can also perceive it in the ways he comprehends the call of the human person and the undoing of the sin.

While the second admonition suggests that Francis himself was conscious of the dignity of his call as a human being, it is the fifth admonition that best enables us to perceive the ways in which he realized it.

Consider, O human being, in what pre-eminence the Lord God has placed you, for He created and formed you *to the image* of His beloved Son according to the body and *to His likeness* according to the spirit (cf. Gen. 1:26).

All creatures under heaven serve, know and obey their Creator, each according to its own nature, better than you. Even the demons did not crucify Him, but you, together with them, have crucified Him and are still crucifying Him by delighting in vices and sins.

In what, then, can you boast? For if you were so skillful and wise that you possessed *all knowledge* (1 Cor. 13:2), knew how to interpret every *kind of language* (cf. 1 Cor. 12:28) and to scrutinize heavenly matters with skill: you cannot boast in these things. For, even though someone may have received from the Lord a special knowledge of the highest wisdom, one demon knew about heavenly matters and now knows more about those of earth than all human beings.

In the same way, even if you were more handsome and richer than everyone, and even if you worked miracles so that you put demons to flight: all these things are foreign to you; nothing belongs to you; you can boast in none of these things.

But we can boast: *in* our *weaknesses* (cf. 2 Cor. 12:5) and in carrying each day the holy cross of our Lord Jesus Christ (cf. Luke 14:27).

It is amazing how much can be read into this simple text. The opening passage seems quite straightforward, yet perhaps no passage in *Admonitions* is more difficult to understand. Although it is important to consider the nuances of this text, Francis would have us accentuate its simple principle that we have been created in the image of the Son according to his body and, therefore, should be animated in all our activities by his Spirit.

Without a doubt, Francis advocates the school of the Holy Spirit. He continually highlights the biblical understanding of the human person as composed of an energy or force that must be allowed to mold and shape the contours of our lives after the example of Christ. God breathed into the nostrils of the first human, the Old Testament tells us. St. Irenaeus reminds us of this when he teaches us that, as a result of sin, we suffered from emphysema, shortness of breath, and needed the Spirit of Pentecost to breathe anew into us. In light of those biblical reflections, Francis's words take on new meaning. To be created and formed to the image of the beloved Son implies, according to Francis's biblical wisdom, that we now live according to a much higher, divine principle, the Spirit of the Lord Jesus Christ. "The Spirit itself gives testimony with our spirit that we are children of God," Paul writes to the Romans; and again, to the Galatians: "As proof that you are children, God sent the Spirit of his Son into our hearts, crying out, 'Abba, Father!' "

Now we can better appreciate the drive of Francis's continuous reflection on the revelation of God in Christ as he struggled to understand the movements of the Holy Spirit within him. He never tires of indicating the presence of the Spirit in our lives, although he is conscious of its inconspicuous, transparent ways in always pointing beyond itself to the revelation of God in the Lord Jesus Christ. In what, then, can we boast? All of our talents or abilities are pure gifts and signs of God's presence in our lives. We cannot boast even of our natural dispositions or resources, for we did nothing to deserve them. No, Francis teaches us that we can boast only in our weaknesses and in carrying the cross of Christ each day. This is what the Spirit of the Lord impels us to do, to model our lives on that of Jesus. It is Jesus who is the form, the pattern, of our lives. It is he who teaches us our true identity and the correct conduct of our lives. This explains Francis's emphasis in *Admonitions*, as elsewhere, on conducting our lives in and according to the Spirit of the Lord. In the seventh admonition, for example, he brings to our attention the importance of following the Spirit of Sacred Scripture that gives life:

The apostle says: *The letter kills, but the spirit gives life* (2 Cor. 3:6).

Those people are put to death by the letter who only wish to know the words alone that they might be esteemed as wiser than others and be able to acquire great riches to give to their relatives and friends.

Those religious are put to death by the letter who are not willing to follow the spirit of the divine letter but, instead, wish only to know the words and to interpret them to others.

Those people are brought to life by the spirit of the divine letter who do not attribute every letter to the body but, by word and example, return them to the Most High Lord God to Whom every good belongs.

There have been any number of articles written about Francis's devotion to Sacred Scripture. A bibliographical essay published in 1976 contained 450 titles that touch on the theme, and since then innumerable studies have been published on the biblical nuances and insights that were at the basis of Thomas of Celano's observation that Francis "lived in the Scriptures." Francis presents a view of Scripture as inspiring life, as becoming the spirit of our life or the life of our spirit, and even as becoming the Spirit and the life of the Lord Jesus Christ within us. His exegesis of 2 Cor. 3:6 — "The letter kills, but the spirit gives life" — is quite explicit in describing the various ways in which we can center our lives on Scripture. In the first place, Francis teaches us that the divine Word, the letter of Sacred Scripture, can kill those who study it for only selfish reasons, such as pride or avarice, or for purely human reasons, such as knowledge or teaching. On the other hand, he reminds us that it brings life to those who point beyond themselves to the Lord and acknowledge his role not only by word but by deed. In other words, Francis makes us aware that there are some who continue the sin of the first human being by using the sacred text for their own advantage, while there are others who are brought to life or undo the sin by learning from it how to fulfill their calling. Underlying this entire approach, however, is John 6:63: "It is the spirit that gives life, the flesh is of no avail. The words I have spoken to you are spirit and life." It occurs frequently in Francis's writings and provides a key opening the riches of his entire gospel spirituality.

With this tremendously spiritual and contemplative sensitivity to the mystery of Christ, the drama of redemption becomes ever more significant in the writings of Francis. His very positive appreciation of the dignity of the human person becomes realistically tempered by his consciousness of the power of the spirit of the flesh and its effects on the body. Deceptive, myopic, and demanding as it is, the spirit of the flesh all too easily makes us its prisoners. In the tenth admonition, for example, the body becomes for Francis the instrument of sin, a thought furthered in the seventh and fourteenth admonitions, in which its grasping and extremely sensitive ways are underscored. It is no wonder that Francis frequently advises us to hate our body with its vices and sins or to hold it in contempt and scorn. Although we were recipients of God's loving, creative goodness, he reminds us, "through our own fault we fell."

Therefore we can appreciate Francis's frequent urgings to embrace a life of conversion, a life, that is, that enables us to reverse the selfish, self-centered ways of the spirit of the flesh and to reorient ourselves to the realization of our divine call. Through this "bittersweet" process, as Francis describes it, the body is necessarily transformed by knowledge of the revelation of Christ and cooperation with the prompting of his Spirit. Francis realistically and clearly sees the awesome demands placed upon the body in this continuous turning from the demands of the spirit of the flesh since, through his own conversion, he knew the implications of this Christ-centered call. Not only does it call for that penetrating purity of heart and chastity of body required by the indwelling of the Spirit; it also demands conformity to the minority of Christ. The third admonition, for example, considers the one who loses his life by "surrendering his whole body to obedience," as in the same way "A Greeting of the Virtues" praises that holy obedience that "confounds every wish of the body and of the flesh and binds its mortified body to the obedience of the Spirit and the obedience of one's brothers." The *Office of the Passion,* moreover, makes clear this emphasis on the bodily sacrifice of obedience as an integral aspect of conversion as it repeatedly counsels: "Offer your bodies and take up your cross." Continual conversion, consequently, because it is a collaborative effort uniting our spirit with that of God, turns our attention more devotedly to the Body of Christ, received in that same Spirit, so that we become totally identified with his redemptive mission.

There are many perspectives from which these daily, concrete ways may be examined. Some have seen them as a "Canticle of Inner Poverty." Others consider them as simple, down-to-earth reflections on a wide variety of Franciscan themes. We think they form a powerful "Canticle of Minority," that nebulous quality that Francis never clearly defines although he desired that it identify his brothers. Indeed, when we look closely at these twenty-eight pieces, it is possible to see that Francis was not satisfied to describe his vision of gospel life simply through the image of the servant of God. He presents as well the qualities of someone who, even among peers, is less than they, that is, a servant among others who strives daily to achieve an even lower position of subservience.

What are these qualities of the lesser servant of God, the minor among his peers? We have encountered them in the image of Christ that Francis offers in the first admonition, especially in his reflection on the Eucharist. If the Son of God daily embraces lowliness by letting go of his royal throne, humbles himself by coming to us in such a way, and allows himself to be vulnerable in the hands of humans, then Francis could propose only the same manner of condescension by means of a thoroughly "radical" poverty, humility, and patient suffering. These three qualities, woven together throughout the fabric of *Admonitions*, furnish us with the major themes of the "Canticle of Minority."

Poverty

Throughout the centuries people have sung the praises of Francis's view of poverty. The *Sacrum Commercium* maintains that it is a "special way of salvation." St. Bonaventure describes it as a unique way of making our way to God. No virtue has been so widely discussed or so controversial. What prompts all these discussions? Why is poverty so controversial? Is it simply the nature of poverty that what may be invaluable today is overlooked tomorrow? Or is it the value that we place on material things themselves so that those of more affluent countries find it more difficult to practice poverty than those of the developing countries? One thing upon which we can agree: Francis of Assisi lacked jurisprudence or legislative ability. His writings, even his rules, are filled with contradictions. On one hand, we find him insisting that a young man sell all his goods and give the proceeds to the poor before entering the fraternity; on the other hand, we are confronted with his concession that the brothers may have breviaries, an expensive proposition in the thirteenth century when books were written by hand and on parchment. At times we find him insisting that the brothers have no place or church that they can call their own; at others, we read his advice to open their houses to everyone and to decorate their churches in precious ways. Francis comes across to us — at least through his writings — as a bundle of contradictions, as an idealist who has little or no idea of practicalities.

But it is this idealism of Francis that enables us to understand the flexibility of his profound convictions. His concrete, down-to-earth belief in the Incarnate Word, Jesus Christ, made him realize the relative importance of material things. Jesus, as any human being, could not continue to be without material things. This was part of the wonder of the Incarnation: the Son of God, in whom and for whom all things were created (cf. Col 1:16), shared not only our humanity but also our dependence on things. How could Francis do or propose anything different? When, however, these material things become luxuries, comforts, or distractions preventing us from focusing our attention on our loving God and God's will, then Francis becomes upset and confrontational in his rejection of those things.

In what does this poverty consist? To answer the question we might turn to the ways in which Francis speaks of poverty. Rarely do we find him using the word "paupers." In fact, we find the word only twelve times in his writings to refer to a condition or state of life. Nowhere does he write of living *sine rebus mundi*, without the things of this world, or in destitution. Francis, however, usually writes of living *sine proprio*, without anything of one's own, without anything that is proper to one. He continually raises the question, therefore: What can I call my own? This becomes the central issue of the embrace of poverty. Material poverty is no doubt the first step in answering the question, but the more seriously and authentically it is embraced, the more it frees us to move into the uncharted depths of our lives where we discover what we really call our own.

The poverty of St. Francis, then, is "sacramental" in nature. As such, material poverty is an outward sign of a much deeper, interior poverty. It is symbolic, in other words, of an unseen, more penetrating reality. At the same time, material poverty — like the outward signs of the sacraments, water, bread, wine, the laying on of hands, and so on — leads us more effectively to that inner poverty and enables us to grapple more freely with letting go of all those things that prevent us from embracing God totally.

How then do these levels of poverty emerge in Francis's *Admonitions?* Francis does not speak of material poverty in his text. No, he emphasizes three distinct levels on which he would have us examine what we make our own. These are the areas of our inner selves, our relations with one another, and, finally, our relationships with God. On each level, Francis continues to confront us with the challenge of living *sine proprio*, without anything we can call our own, and so calls us to live as we came from the creative hand of God.

Our Inner Selves

We have already touched on the fifth admonition in our attempt to grasp Francis's understanding of the human person. We return to it now to see how he points to some of the interior riches that we make our own. While he does not use the word "appropriate," it is clear that this is his sense. We need no explanation to understand what Francis brings to our attention: our skills, wisdom, knowledge, ability with languages, our good looks, riches, and spiritual gifts. So many of the treasures that we take for granted or view as natural talents or qualities, Francis underscores as pure gift and accentuates that we cannot glory in them, for they are God's. The biblical references given by Kajetan Esser refer to the spiritual gifts highlighted by Paul in his encouragement of the Christians of Corinth. But we can easily extend the passages to include so many of the things to which we cling.

Out of all of these, we should follow the example of Francis and single out the temptation to make the gift of knowledge our own. Francis devotes the seventh admonition to this theme and points initially to those who use their knowledge of Scripture for their own self-centered goals. The context is obviously that of biblical scholars and religious who are so caught up in using their scholarship to promote their own interests that they completely overlook the obligation to live the spirit of the sacred texts. But we cannot help wondering if Francis isn't pointing beyond the biblical scholars to all those scholars and educators who use their education and skills to promote themselves and not the glory of God. Isn't it curious, for example, how many times Francis speaks of knowledge in the context of the original sin? Isn't it curious that he is suspicious of any type of study unless it contributes to "the spirit of prayer and devotion"?

In the same way, Francis points to those who cling to their empty words:

Blessed is that religious who has no happiness and joy except in the most holy words and deeds of the Lord and, with these, draws people with gladness and joy to the love of God (cf. Ps. 51:10 [V 50:10]).

Woe to that religious who delights in idle and empty words and, with these, leads people to laughter.

Laughter was generally frowned upon in the monastic world because it shattered the silence that represented the readiness of a disciple to listen. It was condemned in the sixth chapter of the Rule of Benedict and criticized by St. Ephrem, St. John Chrysostom, and others. Francis, however, directs our attention to a frivolity that provokes laughter. We don't have to stretch our imaginations to conjure up images of those who hide behind their glib or articulate tongues or who are comedians hiding behind their inability with words or their laziness in preparing their sermons. Cuthbert Hesse describes the preachers of the early Capuchin reform in a marvelous passage that echoes the thought of the twentieth admonition: "Because they were men who had learned their message in their own hard struggle against the ungodly inducements and habits of the time they lived in, their words when they spoke went true to their mark and men listened to them because they hit the truth as their hearers knew it in the hidden depths of their hearts. In the inexorable truth in which they faced their own lives, they faced their fellow men; and in the knowledge of themselves learned in their own spiritual struggles, their words rang with the compassion and humanity of the fellow sufferer." There is a great deal of practical wisdom expressed in this passage, wisdom that reflects Francis's advice to let go of our clever glibness in favor of resting in the words of God.

The sixth admonition furthers this examination of what we cling to in our inner selves by accentuating our tendency to hold on to our religious tradition rather than to be given life by it.

Let all of us, brothers, consider the Good Shepherd Who bore the suffering of the cross to save His sheep.

The Lord's sheep followed Him in tribulation and persecution, shame and hunger, in weakness and temptation, and in other ways; and for these things they received eternal life from the Lord.

Therefore, it is a great shame for us, the servants of God, that the saints have accomplished great things and we want only to receive glory and honor by recounting them.

As we have seen, there is good reason to believe that Francis may have given this admonition after receiving the news of the martyrdom in 1220 of Brother Berard and his companions, the first of the order to suffer at the hands of the nonbelievers. We can easily imagine the brothers at home boasting of the deeds of their courageous, self-sacrificing confreres and Francis's challenge to action rather than words. Isn't it always a temptation to live in the past or in the shadow of others who have blazed the way for us? All too often we hear people extol the virtues of their religious family without making a serious commitment to have their lives become transparent with its spirit. A wise Irishman highlighted the difference between traditionalism (living in days gone by) and tradition (that which we pass on to the future generations). "Traditionalism," he proposed, "is the dead spirit of the living, whereas tradition is the living spirit of the dead."

The fourteenth admonition provides one of the richest insights into Francis's understanding of poverty in relation to ourselves. In it he recalls the first beatitude — the only time he does so — and offers his own interpretation of it.

Blessed are the poor in spirit, for theirs is the kingdom of heaven (Matt. 5:3).

There are many who, while insisting upon prayers and obligations, inflict much abstinence and punishment upon their bodies. But they are immediately offended and disturbed about a single word that seems to be harmful to their bodies or about something that might be taken away from them. These people are not poor in spirit; because someone who is truly poor in spirit hates himself and loves those who strike him on the face (cf. Matt. 5:39).

Once more we encounter the intuitive wisdom of Francis and his insightful application of poverty to the subtle things to which we cling in our daily lives. Even our good name becomes matter for the embrace of a life without anything of our own as we are stripped of the reputation that we may have built for ourselves through our assiduous practice of mortification, abstinence, prayer, and good works. Francis takes the scalpel, in other words, to our self-love and preoccupation with ourselves, to what we might properly call our own, our good name, and calls us to an even deeper, more penetrating expression of poverty. There are few who would say, as one brother is quoted as joking: "I don't care what they say of me as long as they keep my name alive!" So many of us *do* care about our good name and are deeply hurt when it is dragged down. This fourteenth admonition is a difficult one to apply to ourselves not only because it touches our inner selves but also because it moves us to a most sensitive level of poverty, our relations with one another.

Our Relations with One Another

The eleventh admonition provides us a perfect example of how Francis perceives this life *sine proprio* as affecting our relationships with one another.

Nothing should upset a servant of God except sin. However another person may sin, if a servant of God becomes disturbed and angry because of this and not because of charity, he stores up a fault for himself (cf. Rom. 2:5). That servant of God who does not become angry or disturbed at anyone lives correctly without anything of his own. Blessed is the one for whom nothing remains except for him *to return to Caesar what is Caesar's and to God what is God's* (Matt. 22:21).

Francis clearly sees becoming angry or disturbed at the sin of another as assuming a prerogative of God. He reminds us to turn our attention to the sinner rather than to the sin In doing so he touches one of the most curious aspects of poverty: the ways in which we cling to our anger and upset because we self-righteously judge one who sins. When we see that "anger" in its noun and verb forms appears in eight different passages of Francis's writings and "disturbance" or "upset" in five, we can well imagine that he frequently encountered them. There is a warning in the Later Rule, the document in which every word seems to count: "[The brothers] must take care not to become angry or disturbed because of the sin of another, for anger and disturbance hinder charity in themselves and in others." Thus Francis not only places his concern about anger in his definitive Later Rule; he also enforces it by using one of his most rare obligatory verbs: "The brothers *must* take care...."

In the eleventh admonition, however, Francis goes even further: he suggests that a servant of God should avoid being angry and disturbed not simply at the sinner but *at anyone*. He sees this anger or agitation as a "possession," something to which we might cling and with which we might lord it over or manipulate another. William J. Connolly in an insightful article on spiritual direction writes of the power of anger and its effect on our relationships with God and one another. "One of the most powerful inner facts is anger," he observes.

> When prayer flattens out, or appears to be facing an iron wall, the director must always suspect the presence of unexpressed anger. However, anger is socially unacceptable in our culture and our feelings enforce the social prohibition. So it tends to come out of hiding very reluctantly. Resentment, holding a grudge, subdued rage, when they are present, are likely to be given names like hurt, indifference, and rational analysis.
>
> Not all anger, of course, will interfere with the recognition of one's spiritual identity. Hunger and thirst after justice for the Lord's people is hard to conceive of without anger, but anger which stems from love will further, not hinder, the dialogue with God. However, anger at what has happened to us, at the hurt we have sustained in our

lives, is likely to be directed at the Source of our lives or at the persons or the institutions we emotionally associate with that source. When this happens anger often will block other affectivity and until it is expressed to the Lord will reduce prayer to rational reflection (Connolly 1976, 112–21).

Francis, then, has put his finger on something that has plagued us for centuries. What a marvelous psychological insight he provides us in calling us to let go of our anger. More than that, though, he proposes a way of life in which living without anger or being upset, two seemingly natural expressions that we see as psychologically healthy to express, is to live correctly without anything of our own.

The eighth admonition contains one of the most curious blends of Scriptural passages that we will ever find in the writings of Francis, perhaps in the whole corpus of medieval writings.

The apostle says: *No one can say: Jesus is Lord, except in the Holy Spirit* (1 Cor. 12:3); and: *There is not one who does good, not even one* (Rom. 3:12).

Therefore, whoever envies his brother the good that the Lord says or does in him tends to a sin of blasphemy because he envies the Most High Who says and does every good thing (cf. Matt. 20:15).

At first the two Pauline quotations seem to be out of harmony with one another except for the somewhat oblique concept of the proclamation of Jesus as Lord as a good coming from the activity of the Holy Spirit that moves as it will. Yet Francis places both of these quotations in the context of envy and, in doing so, offers us another marvelous psychological reflection on our flawed human nature. Daniel Goleman in an article in the *New York Times* of February 27, 1991, writes of the work of the presence of envy in Harvard graduate students, seeing them as "sensitive reflections of the traits people pride themselves on and feel most vulnerable about." While experts disagree on precise definitions, Goleman observes, most see jealousy as the response to someone who threatens or is perceived to threaten a relationship, and envy as the feeling arising when someone covets what someone else has. Envy also always implies feeling sad, irritated, and insecure because of not having what the other does.

At the very core of our attachments, Francis's probing conception of a life *sine proprio* touches the deepest and most prized of our possessions: our will.

The Lord says in the Gospel: *Whoever does not renounce all that he possesses cannot be my disciple* (Luke 14:33); and: *Whoever wishes to save his life must lose it* (Luke 9:24).

That person leaves all that he possesses and loses his body who offers himself totally to obedience in the hands of his prelate. Whatever he does and says that he knows is not contrary to his will, provided that what he does is good, is true obedience.

Should a subject see that some things might be better and more useful for his soul than what a prelate commands, let him willingly offer such things to God as a sacrifice; and, instead, let him earnestly strive to fulfill the wishes of the prelate. For this is loving obedience because it pleases God and neighbor (cf. 1 Pet. 1:22).

If the prelate, however, commands something contrary to his conscience, even though he may not obey him, let him not, however, abandon him. If he then suffers persecution from some, let him love them all the more for the sake of God (cf. 1 John 3:15–16). For whoever chooses to suffer persecution rather than wish to be separated from his brothers truly remains in perfect obedience because he lays down *his life* for his brothers (cf. John 15:13). For there are many religious who, under the pretext of seeing things better than those which the prelate commands, look back (cf. Luke 9:62), and return to the vomit of their own will (cf. Prov. 26:11; 2 Pet. 2:22). These people are murderers and, because of their bad example, cause many to lose their souls.

From the perspective of the Fall, we can easily appreciate the place of loving obedience as the fundamental virtue of the third admonition. Francis sees without any difficulty that the sin of the first human being could only be undone by our loving, other-centered attentiveness. Yet this fundamental, pivotal attitude becomes a primary issue of poverty as the opening scriptural passages suggest. The two passages could not be more forthright. Jesus makes renunciation of all possessions, that is, the embrace of poverty, a primary condition of discipleship and lays down the paradoxical loss of one's life as the only way of saving it. But Francis elaborates on these two concepts: "That person leaves all that he possesses and loses his body who offers himself totally to obedience in the hands of his prelate." Obedience, in other words, becomes an expression of the embrace of poverty and of death to self. While we should note that Francis's understanding of poverty is quite broad ("Whatever he does and says that he knows is not contrary to his will, provided that what he does is good, is true obedience"), nevertheless, we should not lose sight of his vision that obedience responds to the fundamental demand of the second admonition to let go of what we have made our own, our will, and confidently entrust ourselves into the hands of another. The words "offers himself totally to obedience" are somewhat similar to those in Francis's Letter to the Entire Order: "Hold back nothing of yourselves for yourselves so that He Who gives Himself totally to you may receive you totally."

Francis sees the implication of this renunciation as, for example, he highlights the practical judgments that take place between someone placed over another and his subject. "Should a subject see that something might be better and more useful for his soul than what a prelate commands," he writes, "let him willingly offer such things to God as a sacrifice; and, instead, let him earnestly try to fulfill the wishes of the prelate." This is what Francis means when speaking of "loving obedience": the voluntary, free self-sacrifice of our judgments, even those that we know are better and more productive. Furthermore, this is the type of loving obedience, Francis realizes, that pleases both God and neighbor. "Since you have purified yourselves by obedience to the truth for sincere mutual love," Peter writes, "love one another intensely from a [pure] heart" (1 Pet. 1:22). It was this extraordinarily fraternal obedience that Francis saw as liberating us to love one another more sincerely and purely. It was an obedience of poverty that inspired letting go of what impedes or places obstacles in the way of our relationships.

Nevertheless, Francis is sensitive to that vulnerability to

which such obedience subjects us. He offers us a simple example: "If the prelate, however, commands something contrary to his conscience, even though he may not obey him, let him not, however, abandon him. If he then suffers persecution from some, let him love them all the more for the sake of God (cf. 1 John 3:15–16). For whoever chooses to suffer persecution rather than wish to be separated from his brothers truly remains in perfect obedience because he lays down *his life* for his brothers (cf. John 15:13)." There are some noteworthy insights into human nature here. In the first place, Francis draws attention to what might be a temptation of a prelate to send the brother away. We can easily imagine the scenario in which someone is told to do something that is contrary to his conscience and courageously tells the superior. "If his conscience is so sensitive," the superior might think, "better that he go elsewhere." But Francis would have the superior keep him within the fraternity. Once again Francis calls to the ministers to respect the conscience of another. His words "...and do not wish that they be better Christians" come to mind.

We should not overlook the scriptural reference that lies hidden in the last sentence of this passage. It is yet another indication of how thoroughly Francis imbibed John's writings. "Everyone who hates his brother," John writes, "is a murderer, and you know that no murderer has eternal life remaining in him" (1 John 3:15). The bond of brotherhood, the life of the gospel, demands expressions of love, expressions that foster, enhance, and deepen that life. To act contrary to those bonds, that is, to act without love, is to snuff out life or to murder. This seems exaggerated except when read in light of the mystery of Christ. "The way we came to know love," John continues, "was that he laid down his life for us; so we ought to lay down our lives for our brothers" (1 John 3:16). The foundation of fraternal life, love, prompts the embrace of vulnerability, of patient suffering, of enduring the day-to-day vicissitudes and sufferings brought on by the weakness and frailty of another.

While the third admonition focuses on the loving obedience of the subject, the fourth admonition explicitly treats of that of the prelate, the brother to whom the obedience of another is entrusted.

Let those who are placed over others glory in such a position as
much as they would if they were assigned a position of washing
the feet of their brothers. If they are more upset at having their
place over others taken away from them than at losing their position at their feet, the more they store up *a money bag* to the peril
of their soul (cf. John 12:6).

Francis is quite clear that even a prelate must be characterized by
a sense of poverty both in his willingness to let go of his office
and in his sensitivity to the needs and desires of his brothers.
The words of Jesus — "I did not come to be served but to serve"
(Matt. 20:28) — provide the foundation, the same offered in the
Earlier Rule (4.6). The thought is repeated in much the same way
in the second part of the nineteenth admonition:

Woe to that religious who has been placed in a lofty position by
others and does not want to come down by his own will.
    Blessed is that servant (Matt. 24:46) who is not placed in a
lofty position by his own will and always desires to be under the
feet of others.

In both the negative and positive assertions, Francis accentuates the will and suggests that it is something that we can use
to cling to what others have given us or to assume a position of self-emptying in the service of others. It is striking that
both admonitions refer to the feet. We all too easily pass from
the opening image of the washing of feet found in the second
verse of the fourth admonition without noting what Francis calls
the "office of the feet" or, in the nineteenth admonition, being
"under the feet of others." What is perfectly clear is Francis's
call to embrace a poverty that entails a letting go of our wills
out of love for others. Loving obedience, in other words, is an
obligation incumbent on all.
    These admonitions offer us marvelous insights into Francis's
vision of how we are best qualified to overcome the fundamental
flaw of the human personality. Not only do they touch on that
to which we most tenaciously cling: they also provide us insights
into how best we can restore the peace and justice envisioned by
God's plan. In "On Being a Bridge-Generation: Religious Men
and Women in Latin America," Segundo Galilea observes that

the vow of obedience is being seen from a new perspective in today's world. He writes:

> With the understanding of authority as service, religious obedience is being experienced as the way to resolve tensions between freedom-authority in human relations, according to the Gospel. Thus, the totalitarian exercise of authority and the individualistic concept of freedom which is at the root of injustice and dehumanization in the societies in which we live, can be denounced. Also, authority and obedience lived in this fashion, even with much tension, are part of the plan of God who asks everyone to live as a responsible child and to assume one's own mission in the church and the world by overcoming self-centeredness. (Galilea 1989, 36–37)

Francis proposes this very same vision of a loving obedience that builds rather than threatens a fraternity of love. It is this embrace of poverty in our relations with one another that searches for new expressions and frees us to probe for answers on the most profound level of what we can claim as our own.

Our Relations with God

Such a total embrace of poverty that moves ever more profoundly from material things to our inner selves and to what we cling to in our relations with one another leads us to consider its very roots, its most 'radical' expression: a life in which we stand before God without anything of our own. On this level of poverty, then, we are called to look even more deeply into the uncharted depths of our lives and ask the question: What can I truly claim as my own? The answer is unequivocally clear to Francis, as he declares in his Earlier Rule: "We may know with certainty that nothing belongs to us except our vices and sins." From a profoundly contemplative appreciation of God, Francis would have us perceive everything coming from the divine goodness so that we have no right to claim anything as our own but those two realities that we have introduced into the world, vice and sin. "We have failed through our own fault," he reminds us. "[The Lord] did and does every good for us who are miserable and wretched, rotten and foul-smelling, ungrateful and evil." The strength of his words and his extremely negative perception of the human person are understandable only in light of Francis's understanding of how contrary our ways are when compared with those of God. The Creator brought forth and offered us nothing but goodness; but we, God's creatures, introduced vice and sin and, thereby, impeded and retarded the divine initiatives.

A life without anything of our own, therefore, is one of radical conversion through which we continually strive to discover our vices and sins. "Enlighten the darkness of my heart" — we pray with Francis, who was ever-conscious of conversion — that we may accept the challenge of letting go of that to which we may unconsciously cling. In the eleventh admonition he tells us: "Blessed is the one for whom nothing remains except for him *to return to Caesar what is Caesar's and to God what is God's* (Matt. 22:21)." The sinless life, one without anything of our own, is simply a matter of giving credit where credit is due, a process of becoming transparently aware that everything comes from and reflects the goodness of God and of overcoming the temptations of taking what does not belong to us. The twenty-eighth admonition expresses this clearly:

Blessed is the servant who makes a treasure in heaven of the good the Lord reveals to him (cf. Matt. 6:20) and does not wish to show it to people under the guise of a reward, because the Most High Himself will show His deeds to whomever He wishes.

Blessed is the servant who safeguards the secrets of the Lord in his heart (cf. Luke 2:19, 51).

Repeatedly, then, Francis returns to the sin of the injustice of the first human being and our continuation of it by acts of appropriation and self-aggrandizement. The daily embrace of a life *sine proprio*, especially one without vice and sin, is the only way in which we can establish the harmony envisioned by God for our enjoyment.

Humility

If poverty is a theme of Franciscan life that has prompted so much discussion and controversy, humility is one that, in our day, has been largely overlooked. Much of the reason for this neglect seems to be rooted in the etymology of the word. "Humility" comes from the Latin word *humus*, earth, and has consistently referred to our lowliness, self-debasement, sinfulness, and feelings of worthlessness. We can easily understand its absence in contemporary spiritual literature. Ours is a day in which we tend to be far more positive in considering the human person and far more constructive in reflecting upon our strengths and weaknesses.

Nonetheless, much of our Christian spirituality is based — and rightly so — on the pursuit of humility. Benedict incorporated the practice of humility into the very structure of his rule and thus paved the way for monastic authors to develop a highly sophisticated and rich theology concerning it. Bernard of Clairvaux became one of its principal exponents, claiming that humility was the foundation of all the virtues and presenting to his readers a marvelous treatise on the seven degrees of humility. It is, in reality, a description of seven expressions of pride that is yet another proof of Bernard's penetrating insight into human nature. Bernard further developed the monastic theology of humility by associating it with the practice of charity. "There is a humility inspired and inflamed by charity," he writes in his forty-second sermon on the Canticle of Canticles, "and a humility begotten in us by truth but devoid of warmth. This latter depends on our knowledge, the former on our affections." Bernard was a forerunner, in a sense, of the humility of the Franciscan school; in fact, we could look at the writings of Francis and wonder at Bernard's influence on them: the two saints, ardent promoters of a spirituality of the heart, envisioned a humility that flowed naturally from love.

Bonaventure is most lavish in his praise of humility, especially in his descriptions of Francis. It was not only "the foundation of all virtue," as it was for Bernard; it was also "the guardian and ornament of all the virtues." In that all-important treatment of humility in the sixth chapter of the *Major Life of Saint Francis*, however, Bonaventure was building upon and refining the thought of Thomas of Celano, who described Francis as a "holy lover of complete humility," as "serene in humility," and, in his *Second Life of Saint Francis*, devoted eleven lengthy paragraphs to its practice.

For Francis himself, all this is more obvious: a life *sine proprio* brings us before God and makes us recognize that the only thing we can claim as our own is our vice and sin. Poverty, in other words, places us before God as we truly are. In Francis's view, it is the sister virtue of humility since it prompts us to recognize that all we have is gift, that all that in which we glory truly expresses the largesse of the all-good God. Humility, then, is defined not in terms of lowliness or nothingness but in light of a relationship of love: God's love for us and, from that perspective, our love for one another.

Before God

One difficulty in discussing Francis's understanding of humility is its starting point. While it is so rooted in his description of the original sin, we cannot simply begin with its external manifestation as we can with the pursuit of a life *sine proprio*. On the contrary, Francis almost suggests that humility begins when we arrive at that juncture of poverty in which we wrestle with clinging to our vices and sins, that is, when we are able to deal with all that obstructs our vision of God. Could it be a matter of achieving a clean heart? The sixteenth admonition seems to imply this:

Blessed are the clean of heart for they shall see God (Matt. 5:8). The truly clean of heart are those who look down upon the things of earth, seek those of heaven and never cease adoring and seeing the Lord God living and true with a clean heart and spirit.

Francis's appreciation of the beatitude underscores his accentuation of letting go of the material, the things of the earth that so often become obstacles and impediments to our relationship with God. Only when we are sufficiently free from the attachments of our hearts, in other words, will we be able to pursue our spiritual goals and devote ourselves to a life of adoration. Isn't it there — in adoration — that we come before the infinite majesty, recognize the divine presence as it truly is, and come to acknowledge all God's gifts? William of St. Thierry tells of St. Bernard "that he was accustomed to say, basing himself on his own experience, that the wise man was one for whom things had the taste of what they really are."

The twelfth admonition approaches humility in our relationship with God from a different perspective, that of recognizing it is a sign of the presence of the Spirit of the Lord.

A servant of God can be recognized as having the Spirit of the Lord in this way: if, when the Lord does some good through him, his flesh does not therefore exalt itself because it is always opposed to every good. Instead he regards himself the more worthless and esteems himself lesser than all others.

It is striking how frequently Francis repeats this same insight. In chapter 17 of the Earlier Rule, for example, he describes the activity of the Lord's Spirit as wanting the flesh to be "mortified and looked down upon, considered of little worth and rejected." "It strives for humility," he reiterates, leaving us little doubt that this is one of the sure signs of the Spirit's presence. Isn't the language of this twelfth admonition reminiscent of the second? The same image of self-exaltation or lifting ourselves up over what in reality the Lord has done simply echoes Francis's vision of original sin. This admonition challenges us to allow the Creator to reveal the divine goodness through us when, where, and how it pleases the almighty without the slightest shadow or taint of our self-interest. Or, to put it another way: Is humility a call to transparency? The twenty-first admonition certainly suggests as much.

Blessed is the servant who, when he speaks, does not disclose everything about himself under the guise of a reward and is not quick to speak, but who is wisely cautious about what he says and how he responds (cf. Prov. 29:20).

Woe to that religious who does not preserve in his heart the good the Lord reveals to him and does not reveal it by his behavior, but, under the guise of a reward, wishes instead to reveal it with his words (cf. Luke 2:19, 51). He receives *his reward* (cf. Matt. 6:2, 16) and his listeners carry away little fruit.

Francis repeats his thought positively and negatively in order to drive home the point, and, once again, he does not hesitate to focus on our desire for rewards and our tendency to hide behind appearances. He provides us a key that unlocks our understanding of humility as the pursuit of transparency or, to use the more monastic or biblical phrase, purity of heart. We cannot help noticing his reference to those who keep the good things the Lord reveals to them in their hearts. He unmistakably points to Mary, whom Luke describes as keeping in her heart the wonderful events of Bethlehem and Jesus' mysterious utterances after he was found by his parents teaching in the temple. No doubt, Francis had Mary as his model of the truly humble person and, as such, perceived humility as that pursuit of purity of heart or transparency that we have been highlighting.

Thomas Merton has a marvelous statement in his *New Seeds of Contemplation* that seems to echo the sentiments of Francis. "If we were truly humble," he declares, "we would not bother about ourselves at all; we'd be concerned only with God and with the objective order of things and values as they are, and not as our selfishness wants them to be" (Merton 1962, 189). Merton introduces the concept of objectivity into our consideration of humility — "the objective order of things and values," not the subjective order that we are tempted to impose on them. This objectivity echoes Francis's nineteenth admonition:

Blessed is the servant who does not consider himself any better when he is praised and exalted by people than when he is considered worthless, simple and despised, for what a person is before God that he is and no more.

Woe to that religious who has been placed in a high position by others and does not want to come down by his own will.

Blessed is that servant (Matt. 24:46) who is not placed in a high position by his own will and always desires to be under the feet of others.

We cannot help noticing how Francis draws our attention to the precariousness of positions of superiority whether we are placed there by others, desire to get there on our own, or are reluctant to leave there of our own will. He certainly underscores the tendency to jockey our way into these positions and to remain in them once we are there. How many people do we know who are convinced that they were born to be superiors, or who feel their time has come and do whatever they can to ensure that such is the case? Nevertheless, this nineteenth admonition also places us before one another and thus introduces the horizontal dimension of humility.

Before One Another

When examining Francis's concern for our growth in humility, we see that it is integrally tied to our consciousness of who we are before God and is bound to raise questions concerning reactions to the promotion of ourselves and others. We can see this by looking again at the nineteenth admonition: "Blessed is the servant who does not consider himself any better when he is praised and exalted than when he is considered worthless, simple and looked down upon." Not only does Francis touch on our attitude when others praise us; he also encourages us to remain realists: people who recognize that they might be "up" today but "down" tomorrow.

The seventeenth admonition highlights yet another perspective, that of persons who do not lift themselves or place themselves in a superior position because of appearances.

Blessed is that servant (Matt. 24:46) who no more exalts himself over the good the Lord says or does through him than over what He says or does through another.

A person sins who wants to receive from his neighbor more than what he wants to give of himself to the Lord God.

This is no more than an echo of the second admonition's description of the sin of the first human being. It continues with yet another insightful glance into our grasping ways: both verses prompt a questioning of our attitudes in the promotion of ourselves as well as our exploitation of others, and they do so by confronting us with the issues of our honesty or authenticity and our generosity or other-centeredness. "How can you be humble," Merton asks, "if you are always paying attention to yourself? True humility excludes self-consciousness, but false humility intensifies our awareness of ourselves to such a point that we are crippled, and can no longer make any movement or perform any action without putting to work a whole complex mechanism of apologies or formulas of self-accusation" (Merton 1962, 189).

This simply reiterates what we might interpret as a principle of Francis's manner of spiritual discernment. As we have seen, the twelfth admonition is quite clear in characterizing the Spirit's activities as embracing a life of humility. We can easily see Francis's incarnational spirituality, one that clearly resonates with that of St. Paul. The Spirit expresses itself by pointing beyond itself to the Other, the source of all good, while the flesh tends to draw attention to itself by exalting or lifting itself up. But Francis takes his observation a step further by suggesting that the Spirit prompts us to look upon ourselves as "more worthless" and to esteem ourselves "less than all others." Our humility before God, in other words, becomes translated or incarnated before our fellow human beings, who might be dazzled by our talents and performance but who are ignorant of the depths of our self-centered, irresponsible ways.

An incident in the life of Francis expresses perfectly the sense of these teachings. Thomas of Celano and Bonaventure describe Francis and one of his followers walking through a crowd of admirers. While Bonaventure sees Francis as wanting the brother to counterbalance the praise people were showering upon him, Thomas of Celano suggests that Francis simply wanted them to know the truth. "In obedience," Thomas quotes Francis, "revile me harshly and speak the truth against the lies of these others." In both descriptions, however, the formula recited by the brother is more or less the same: Francis, the brother unwillingly said, was *rusticus et mercenarius, imperitus et inutilis*. Each word is rich in meaning. *Rusticus* has the sense of someone who is unsophisticated, lacking in sensitivity — a rustic or "hick" — and, in this sense, someone who has little or no awareness of the wonder or gifts given by God. *Mercenarius*, however, suggests our greedy, mercenary ways when we realize the value of those gifts and our tendencies to keep them for our own benefit. From another perspective, Francis draws our attention to being *imperitus*, that is, clumsy or awkward like people in a gift shop who know the value and worth of what is before them but are irresponsible and careless so that they damage or destroy the articles. Such a person is *inutilis*, useless or inept, especially when entrusted by God with gifts and responsibilities.

Patient Suffering

Such an embrace of a humble life *sine proprio* is bound to lead to vulnerability or openness to being abused or overlooked, especially in the close confines of fraternal life. We have already reflected on Francis's frequent return to the images of the Suffering Servant and of the Lord who washes the feet of his disciples. To these we might add that of the Good Shepherd, not the one who is so concerned about the welfare of the sheep as much as the one who willingly lays down his life for the sheep:

Let all of us, brothers, consider the Good Shepherd Who endured the suffering of the cross to save His sheep.

The Lord's sheep followed Him in tribulation and persecution, in shame and hunger, in weakness and temptation and in other things; and for all these things they received eternal life from the Lord.

When these images are gathered together, we can easily perceive patient suffering as a prominent characteristic of the servant of God. What makes this painfully striking, however, is Francis's insertion of this dramatic conformity to the suffering Christ into the context of the day-to-day life of the fraternity. While Bonaventure was certainly correct in highlighting Francis's desire for martyrdom as one of the more important aspects of his life of virtue, *Admonitions* makes us wonder if Francis didn't realize that most of his brothers would suffer from one another.

The ninth admonition offers us one of the clearest examples of the patient suffering that Francis envisions:

The Lord says: Love your enemies [do good to those who hate you and pray for those who persecute you] (Matt. 5:44).

For that person truly loves his enemies who is not hurt by an injury done to him, but, because of the love of God, is disturbed by the sin of his soul. Let him show him love by his deeds.

A closer look at that frequent biblical quotation of Francis helps us understand how important this teaching of the Sermon on the Mount was to him. "Love your enemies," Jesus teaches, "do good to those who hate you and pray for those who calumniate you...that you may be children of your heavenly Father" (Matt. 5:44). It is almost as though Francis identified suffering from the abuse of his neighbor as the surest means of conforming with *the* child of God, Jesus.

But let us go further in our understanding of this principle. The twenty-second admonition confronts us with three reactions to the abuse that may be heaped upon us. The three verses form a pattern similar to that of the waves of an ocean, the third of which is the strongest:

Blessed is the servant who suffers punishment, accusation, and blame from another as patiently as he would from himself.

Blessed is the servant who, when blamed, continuously acquiesces, respectfully submits, humbly confesses, and willingly makes amends.

Blessed is the servant who is not quick to excuse himself and humbly endures shame and blame for a sin where he did not commit a fault.

In the first verse we find no mechanisms of excuse; there is the simple, straightforward acceptance of punishment, accusation, and blame. In the second verse, Francis describes the attitudes of the suffering servant — courtesy, respect, humility, and readiness to make amends — all of which are demanding qualities in themselves. Yet these pale in light of those of the third verse when the suffering endured is for some fault that the servant did not even commit. Clearly Francis has the image of the Suffering Servant of God before his eyes as he challenges his brothers to manifest these responses when enduring abuse from others.

Thus we can understand Francis's teachings on bringing peace. We find two commentaries on the beatitude of the peacemaker, "Blessed are the peacemakers for they will be called children of God" (Matt. 5:9). In the first, the thirteenth admonition, Francis focuses on our tendency to measure our possession

of patience and humility during the good times when everything goes well with us.

A servant of God cannot know how much patience and humility
he has within himself as long as he is content. When the time
comes, however, when those who should make him content do
the opposite, he has as much patience and humility as he has at
that time and no more.

How many of us do just that: we scrutinize the barometer
of our virtues during the peaceful times when things are going
smoothly for us. The wisdom of Francis, though, would have
us look more carefully at the crisis periods — those transitional
times when we are put into the crucible of life — to discover the
true strength of our virtues.

The fifteenth admonition draws our attention to our inner
peace and calm during those moments when everything goes
wrong.

Those people are truly peacemakers who, regardless of what they
suffer in this world, maintain peace of spirit and body, because of
love of our Lord Jesus Christ.

This is only another highlighting of the peace brought by
Jesus, that merited by an embrace of suffering. It is the peace
experienced and promoted by the poor, downtrodden, and oppressed of this world who have little or nothing with which
to retaliate. Francis entwines the threads of peacemaking with
those of humility, suffering, and patience. His view of the
pursuit of peace seems more centered on the acceptance of vulnerability in light of the teachings and example of Jesus than on
the adoption of programs or actions that would accentuate use
of our power, influence, or position.

The Contemplative Servant of God

Toward the end of his "Canticle of Minority," Francis presents a
simple poem or hymn, the twenty-seventh admonition:

Where there is charity and wisdom,
   there is neither fear nor ignorance.
Where there is patience and humility,
   there is neither anger nor disturbance.
Where there is poverty with joy,
   there is neither greed nor avarice.
Where there is rest and meditation,
   there is neither anxiety nor restlessness.
Where there is fear of the Lord to guard an entrance
   (cf. Luke 11:21),
   there the enemy cannot have a place to enter.
Where there is a heart full of mercy and discernment,
   there is neither excess nor hardness of heart.

This is a list of the everyday virtues that characterize a servant of God, a description of a life that is essentially harmonious, free from the self-seeking, unjust ways that impede the unfolding of God's goodness. Francis actually presents the qualities of minority that flow from charity and wisdom, that is, patience, humility, and joyful poverty, and implies that these color our life of prayer.

Charity that drives out fear and wisdom that overcomes ignorance — this is the initial set of contrasts that Francis offers us. At the very outset, he proposes a foundational virtue upon which the harmony of all our human dealings may be built. We might say the same about wisdom, the primary virtue of his "A Greeting of the Virtues": wisdom, together with simplicity, satisfies the insatiable cravings of the human person that led to the disruption of the idyllic peace of the Garden of Eden. In the majority of his references to wisdom, Francis writes of Christ, "the true wisdom of the Father," the only knowledge that is worthy of our effort. This is what quenches the frustrations of our ignorance. Patience and humility, as we have seen, are characteristics of Francis's servant of God. They are two virtues that not only prove our vulnerability to others but, at the same time, also provide antidotes for two of the more common dangers of fraternal life, anger and annoyance. All of these are helped by a poverty practiced with joy, the joy of knowing that God has provided everything for our well-being and will continue to do so while we live without anything that we claim as our own.

Francis realizes that greed and avarice have no place in such a joyous poverty since all our desires are more than satisfied in the overwhelming reality of God.

With these fundamental characteristics, Francis describes for us the contemplative activities of the lesser servant of God: resting in God, meditation, fear of God, a heart full of mercy and discernment. The contrasting qualities of these activities of prayer may strike us. Thus a contemplative life (rest or inner peace and meditation) drives out restlessness and anxiety, just as the cultivation of reverence (fear of God) safeguards and protects the inner life of grace, and a heart sensitive to suffering and discernment acts as an antidote for miserliness and hardness of heart. In each of these, Francis reminds us of the definite call to empty ourselves, to go contrary to our natural dispositions in the knowledge that these virtues will bring not only balance to our lives but also harmony and peace. In other words, Francis considers the virtues of the garden when, before sin, the human person lived without anything of his own and gloried in the all-loving goodness of the Creator. Now, however, in light of the Suffering Servant of God, Francis perceives the ways of undoing the injustice of that sinful human and, in the embrace of a minority modeled on Christ, realizes that they are the only ways of establishing justice and peace according to the divine plan.

From this contemplative stance, Francis proposes that we be more sensitive to God and to the marvels of the divine goodness. "Proud poverty, hard poverty is a dead thing that estranges us from Jesus," René Voillaume maintains. "True poverty is at the same time one of the roads to inner silence and contemplative prayer, when founded on self-dispossession and the true liberty of the soul with regard to all the created" (Voillaume 1955, 276–77). Anyone who has had the experience of living among the poor or of watching the poor as they pray knows that they approach God differently. They hear the gospel with different ears and look upon what they receive with different attitudes. In the remaining undated writings, then, Francis teaches us as a poor man, someone entirely dependent on God. He would have us approach the mysteries of revelation, redemption, and salvation as poor, humble, and vulnerable people. Perhaps it is only from this vantage point, then, that we can truly appreciate his lessons.

The *Office of the Passion*

We are now in a better position to understand Francis's devotion to Christ Crucified and his practice of reciting the *Office of the Passion*, a collection of prayers taken primarily from the Psalms but also from other passages of Scripture. Francis prayed one of these "psalms" after a corresponding hour of the Liturgy of the Hours. Thus seven times each day he focused on another aspect of the Paschal Mysteries, the Passion, Death, or Resurrection of Christ. Such a practice was not uncommon in the Middle Ages. In some monasteries, monks added a psalm in honor of the Blessed Mother and another in honor of the Passion. In fact, the rubrics we discover in some of the oldest manuscripts of the *Office of the Passion* indicate that this is precisely what Francis did.

As we have seen, this too is one of those writings that we cannot date. A Canadian friar, Laurent Gallant, maintains that Francis gradually added or modified his collection of prayers between the years 1219 and 1226, the year of his death. According to this theory, which Gallant bases on similarities between the individual psalms of Francis's collection and his other writings, we can discern the intense focus on the mystery of the Passion (psalms 1, 2, 4, 5) shifting to the wonder of the Nativity (psalm 15) at about the time of the Greccio miracle (December 1223) and to the hope of the Resurrection (psalms VI, VII, VIII, IX) after LaVerna, that is, during the last years of his stigmatized life. Whatever the case may be, daily recitation of these prayers over a period of time provides us marvelous insights into the heart of Francis and shows us how this devotion to Christ Crucified encouraged him to adopt that program of gospel life we find in *Admonitions*.

Before we examine one or two of Francis's psalms as a way of entering the others, we should point out some unique characteristics of Francis's manner of using them. In the first place, he dramatically personalizes them by frequently adding phrases such as "my most holy Father" or "most holy Father" or simply "holy Father." Thus, Francis — in a way consistent with the affective approach that we have frequently encountered — makes the less personal Lord or God far more intimate. As we pray these psalms, though, these additions prompt us to wonder who is really praying these words: Is it Jesus as he endures betrayal, abandonment, and suffering, or Francis, who struggles to identify himself ever more deeply with the suffering Son of a loving Father?

At times Francis introduces New Testament phrases into the psalms, as when he begins a verse with Ps. 96:8 ("Lift up...") but continues with phrases from Rom. 12:1 ("...your bodies," etc.) and Luke 14:27 ("...and take up his cross"). What begins with a refrain of a psalm becomes, then, an echo of Jesus' words to deny ourselves and take up the cross. This same approach shapes the pattern of yet another verse. In this case, Francis begins with Zachary's canticle ("Blessed be the Lord, the God of Israel" [Luke 1:68a]), proceeds to Ps. 34:33 ("who has redeemed the souls of his servants..."), and concludes with his own accentuation ("...with His very own most holy blood"). In both instances, we see how clearly Francis interprets the psalms from a very Christian perspective and with a definite christological focus.

We might notice a number of other curious twists in Francis's use of these psalms. For example, we find the recurrent passage of Psalm 95, "O God, come to my assistance; O Lord, make haste to help me!" Francis frequently inserts this into other psalms to underscore his absolute confidence in God. We see also the surprising way in which he reverses various verses so that in his citation of Psalm 96, he places verses 11 and 12 before verses 7 and 8. Was this because the latter verses, 11 and 12, speak of creation praising God, whereas verses 7 and 8 focus on the nations doing the same? Were this the case, Francis seems to be envisioning a hierarchy in which creation is indeed giving God praise, yet the ultimate praise comes from human beings united together. Finally, we might notice the ways in which Francis highlights kingship, the kingship of Christ, by adding the word "king" to his invocation of God or by inserting passages into various psalms to underscore this image. From this perspective, the Office becomes a key to Francis's understanding of that paradoxical minority of God revealed in Jesus, and it furthers our appreciation of his unique way of entering into that total identification with Christ that culminated in his reception of the stigmata.

Each hour of the Office, however, opens and closes by honoring the Blessed Virgin. If Francis prayed the Office throughout each day, then he would have recited this salutation fourteen times daily:

> Holy Virgin Mary,
> there is no one like you
> among the women born in the world.
> Daughter and servant
> of the most high and supreme King
> and of the Father in heaven,
> Mother of our most holy Lord Jesus Christ,
> Spouse of the Holy Spirit,
> pray for us
> with Saint Michael the Archangel,
> all the powers of heaven
> and all the saints,
> to your most holy beloved Son,
> our Lord and Master.

Francis begins his greetings in words reminiscent of those of Elizabeth, "Blessed are you among women" (Luke 1:42), or of Jesus himself, "There is no one greater born of women" (Luke 7:28). The text also shows the influence of a simple prayer used in Francis's times: "O Virgin Mary, among the women of the world, there is none like you, a flower like a rose, a fragrance like a lily, pray for us to your Son."

What follows, however, is a description of Mary's relationship with the triune God, a description that we can find in the simple Form of Life that Francis gave to Clare and the Poor Ladies of St. Damian's. When we place both writings in light of the exhortations to the Brothers and Sisters of Penance, we are better able to appreciate the role of Mary in Francis's spirituality: she is the model, the perfect expression of one filled with the Spirit of the Lord, who teaches us by her very life the essence of its activities in establishing relationships between ourselves and God. Francis, in what we have now seen is his typical, concrete, down-to-earth way, touches on fundamental relationships: spouse, mother, children, and servant — images we have seen in his earlier writings, especially the exhortations to the Brothers and Sisters of Penance. Now he reminds us — fourteen times daily — that Mary is the transparent exemplar of the Spirit. As such she is worthy to stand before her Son, our Lord and Master, and to pray to him as we strive to enter into the mysteries of his Passion, Death, and Resurrection.

But why, we may ask, does he add "with Saint Michael the Archangel, all the powers of heaven and all the saints"? Could this be an echo of the conviction we saw expressed in the Earlier Rule (23.5): "All of us, wretches and sinners, are not worthy to mention Your name"? In that passage we saw how clearly Francis saw the effects of sin in depriving us of our place in that marvelous plan God had laid out for us. As he will later sing in his "Canticle of Brother Sun": "No human is worthy to mention Your name." We can sense Francis's uncomfortableness as a sinner in standing before the Lord. He relies upon the angels, the saints, and the holy one, the Virgin Mary, to plead his cause.

With these images, that is, from this Marian perspective, we enter into Francis's psalms themselves. We must limit our attention to only two, one that will enable us to capture how each psalm may be read on a variety of levels, the other that shows us how pervasive was the thought of Christ's suffering. We begin, then, with the psalm Francis composed for the daily celebration of Prime, the first hour of the day and that which recalled Jesus' presence before Pilate's judgment seat and, at the same time, his appearance to Mary Magdalene on the morning of the Resurrection. Curiously, Francis envisioned that this psalm would be used throughout the year except for the celebration of the Christmas season.

Have mercy on me, O God, have mercy on me
    because my soul places its trust in you.
I will hope in the shadow of your wings
    until wickedness passes by.
I will cry to the Most High, *my most holy Father*,
    to the Lord who has blessed me.
[The Most High] has sent from heaven and delivered me;
    [The Most High] has disgraced those who have trampled
      upon me.
God has sent His mercy and His truth;
    the Lord has snatched my life from the strongest of my
      enemies

and from those who hated me for they were too powerful
  for me.
They prepared a trap for my feet
  and twisted my life.
They dug a pit before my face
  and fell into it themselves!
My heart is ready, O God, my heart is ready;
  I will sing and chant a psalm.
Awake, my glory, awake Psalter and harp,
  I will awaken the dawn.
I will praise you among the peoples, O Lord,
  I will chant a psalm to you among the nations.
Because your mercy is exalted even to the skies,
  and your truth even to the clouds.
Be exalted above the heavens, O God,
  and may your glory be over all the earth.[1]

The first three verses of this psalm, basically taken from
Psalm 57, are the cries of someone who is confronted by evil,
who pleads for God's mercy and protection for the simple reason that he has placed his confidence and hope in God. As
we mentioned earlier, verse 3 contains one of those personal
additions by which Francis speaks directly to his Father. The
following three verses, however, provide the Father's response.
Once again we discover Francis using Psalm 57, but in verse 5
he adds a verse of Psalm 18: "the Lord has snatched my life
from the strongest of my enemies and from those who hated
me for they were too powerful for me." While there is still a
strong emphasis on those who trampled or hated the suffering one, Francis directs our attention to the Lord's powerful
intervention. "[The Most High] sent from heaven and delivered
me, . . . has sent His mercy and His truth, . . . has snatched my life
from the strongest of my enemies." With his overriding confidence in God, a loving Father, we now find Francis — identifying
with Christ — not only accepting the sufferings that are in store
for him but even praising and rejoicing over the immeasurable

---

1. Biblical quotations and illusions, in the order referred to: Pss. 57:2a
(V 56:2a); 57:2b (V 56:2b); cf. 57:3 (V 56:3); 57:4a–b (V 56:4a–b); 57:4c–5a
(V 56:4c–5a); 18:18 (V 17:18); 57:7a–b (V 56:7a–b); 57:7c–d (V 56:7c–d); 57:8
(V 56:8); 57:9 (V 56:9); 57:10 (V 56:10); 57:11 (V 56:11); 57:12 (V 56:12).

glory that will come from the Most High. We have, then, a simple example of how Francis bases his prayer on one psalm yet adds to it — in this case, one phrase from another psalm and a personal invocation of God as Father. The prayer becomes intensely personal and a wonderful reflection of Jesus' thoughts on the mornings of Good Friday and Easter Sunday.

As we mentioned, Francis envisioned this psalm being sung throughout the year. The only exception was during the Christmas season, when this psalm would take its place:

> Exult in God our help!
>> Shout to the Lord *God living and true* with cries of
>>> gladness!
> Because the Lord, the Most High,
>> the Awesome, is the Great King over all the earth.
> *Because the Most Holy Father of heaven,* our King before all
>> ages,
>> *sent His Beloved Son from on high*
>>> *and He was born of the Blessed Virgin Holy Mary.*
> He called to me: You are my Father
>> and I will place Him, my firstborn, as the Highest,
>>> above all the kings of the earth.
> On *that* day the Lord sent His mercy
>> and at night His song.
> This is the day the Lord has made,
>> let us rejoice and be glad in it.
> *For the Most Holy Child has been given to us*
>> *and has been born for us on the way*
>>> *and placed in a manger because he did not have a place*
>>>> *in the inn.*
> Glory *to the Lord God* in the highest
>> and peace on earth to those of good will.
> Let the heavens rejoice and the earth exult,
>> let the sea and its fullness resound,
>>> let the fields and all that is in them be joyful.
> Sing a new song to the Lord,
>> sing to the Lord all the earth.
> Because the Lord is great and worthy of praise
>> He is awesome beyond all gods.
> Give to the Lord, you families of nations,

give to the Lord glory and praise,
give to the Lord the glory due His name.
Offer your bodies and take up your cross;
follow His most holy commands to the end.[2]

As we can easily see, this psalm is a collage of passages taken from both the Old and New Testaments. In its thirteen verses, we find selections from Psalms 81, 47, 74, 89, 42, 118, and 96; a reflection on a prophecy of Isaiah (9:6); three quotations from Luke's Gospel (2:7, 8; 14:27); and one from the First Letter of Peter (2:21). Here, more than in the other psalms, we must ask: Is there any pattern to Francis's thought?

The first two verses immediately express the joy that Francis feels at Christ's birth, a sense of exultation over the fact that the Most High is living, true, and our help. We stand with Francis in the presence of the transcendent God, awesome in majesty. Yet Francis now sings the praises of the Almighty Father who not only considered our lowliness but even sent His own Son to us. His hymn continues with verses from Psalms 89, 42, and 118, which dwell on the significance of this day. "A child has been given to us," he reminds us in the words of Isaiah, yet he was a pilgrim and was poor. And so, as we see Luke's Gospel blend with Psalm 96, the angels join with the heavens, the earth, and the families of nations in singing the praises of the Most High God. Nevertheless, we leave off with that frequent reminder to learn the lesson Christ left for us: "Offer your bodies and take up your cross; follow His most holy commands to the end." Thus even as Francis loses himself in singing the ecstatic praises of the Word made flesh, he does not hesitate to bring us down to earth by reminding us of our obligation to identify with the poor, suffering Christ.

The *Office of the Passion,* then, is one of the most important writings of St. Francis, for it not only expresses his spirituality but also provides an insight into how that spirituality was formed on a daily basis. Of course, Francis did not identify the biblical passages as we now have them. When he wrote them

---

2. Biblical quotations and allusions, in order referred to: Pss. 81:2a; 47:2b; 47:3; 74:12a; 89:27a; 89:28; 42:9a–b; 118:24; cf. Isa. 9:6; cf. Luke 2:7; cf. Luke 2:14; Ps. 96:11–12a; cf. Ps. 96:1; Pss. 96:4; 96:7–8a; cf. Luke 14:27; cf. 1 Pet. 2:21.

to teach to his followers, those passages undoubtedly flowed from his memory. Thomas of Celano wrote of Francis's knowledge of Scripture: "At times he would read the sacred books, and what he put into his mind once he wrote indelibly in his heart. His memory substituted for books, for he did not hear a thing once in vain, for his love meditated on it with constant devotion." What is so remarkable, though, is the portrait of Jesus that emerges from the strokes of this biblical painter and how profoundly the artist identified with his subject. As we have mentioned earlier, it is difficult to differentiate Francis from Jesus because the words of the psalmist are so personalized.

We should now look at two other writings that will enable us to learn how to read Francis's writings biblically.

"Exhortation to the Praise of God"

Fear the Lord and give Him honor.
Worthy is the Lord *to receive* praise and honor.
All you *who* fear *the Lord praise Him.*
Hail Mary, full of grace, the Lord is with you.
Heaven and earth, praise Him.
All you rivers, praise the Lord.
All you children of God, praise the Lord.
This is the day the Lord has made, let us rejoice and be glad in it!
    Alleluia, alleluia, alleluia! *The King of Israel!*
Let every spirit praise the Lord.
Praise the Lord because He is good; all you who read this,
    bless the Lord.
All you creatures, bless the Lord.
All you birds of heaven, praise the Lord.
All you *children,* praise *the Lord.*
Young men and virgins, praise the Lord.
Worthy is the Lamb Who was slain
    to receive praise, glory, and honor.
Blessed be the Holy Trinity and Undivided Unity.
Saint Michael the Archangel, defend us in battle.[3]

---

3. Biblical quotations and allusions, in the order referred to: Rev. 14:7; cf. 4:11; cf. Ps. 22:23; Luke 1:28; cf. Ps. 69:34; cf. Dan. 3:78, 82; Ps. 117:24; John

A sixteenth-century friar, Marianus of Florence, suggested that Francis composed this piece to commemorate the rededication of a small church in the Spoleto Valley dedicated to Our Lady of the Angels. He offered as his proof a wooden antependium, now lost, upon which some of these verses were carved. In any case, this very simple writing provides some insights into the very sources of Francis's inspiration.

If we spend a few moments looking at this writing, we will undoubtedly notice the Psalms. But we must look more carefully at the other biblical selections Francis presents in this text. The Book of Revelation and the Book of Daniel receive considerable attention. We also find two curious passages from the Gospels, the angel's greeting of Mary and the cry of the crowd as Jesus entered Jerusalem. Francis encourages us to praise God in fulfillment of Scripture but also to use Scripture to fulfill its purpose. Rabbinical spirituality speaks of a prayer of echoing in which we listen to God's words of praise and "echo" them back to the Almighty. This is the type of prayer that we find in these simple verses.

A second source of Francis's inspiration, however, comes from creation. He obviously chooses passages from Daniel's canticle and from the Psalms to focus on creation. According to Marianus, the antependium upon which Francis gazed had carvings of those images highlighted by the exhortation — rivers, birds, clouds, and so on. Even if this were not the case, we would expect to find a reflection of what Francis's biographers tell us: "Aroused by all things to the love of God, he rejoiced in all the works of the Lord's hands.... With a feeling of unprecedented devotion he savored in each and every creature — as in so many rivulets — that Goodness which is their fountain-source."

Finally we come to recognize inspirations that flow from his love of the liturgy. Perhaps the most obvious of these is the antiphon to the Trinity that substitutes for the more traditional doxology, Glory to the Father. This is followed by an invocation to Michael the Archangel, no doubt coming from one of the two liturgical celebrations in honor of the prince of the heavenly hosts and a favorite medieval patron. There is, however, one

---

12:13; Pss. 150:6; 147:1; cf. Ps. 103:21, 22; cf. Dan. 3:80; Ps. 148:7–10; cf. Ps. 113:1; cf. Ps. 148:12; cf. Rev. 5:12.

somewhat hidden liturgical reference: a passage from Psalm 117 ("This is the day the Lord has made") that was used in the rite of the dedication of a church. To this passage Francis adds John 12:13, the acclamation of the crowd welcoming Jesus into Jerusalem on the Sunday before his Passion, which makes it easy to imagine its composition in that context described by Marianus of Florence, that is, the rededication of that small chapel of Our Lady of the Angels.

Always known as possessing a spontaneous, poetic spirit, Francis now emerges as someone whose experiences of Scripture, liturgy, and creation elicited such creative expressions of praise. This exhortation, however, enables us to enter more profoundly into the meaning of another text that is closely associated with it, the "Praises to Be Said at All the Hours." Once again we should read the verses of this exhortation with an eye sensitive to Francis's use of Scripture and to the poetic images, for they will be most useful in determining its meaning.

"Praises to Be Said at All the Hours"

Holy, holy, holy Lord God Almighty,
  Who *is*, Who *was*, and Who is to come:
    And let us praise and glorify Him forever.
O Lord our God, You are worthy to receive
  praise and glory and honor *and blessing*.
    And let us praise and glorify Him forever.
The Lamb Who was slain is worthy to receive
  power and divinity, wisdom and strength,
    honor and glory and blessing.
      And let us praise and glorify Him forever.
Let us bless the Father and the Son with the Holy Spirit:
    And let us praise and glorify Him forever.
Bless the Lord, all you works of the Lord.
    And let us praise and glorify Him forever.
Sing praise to our God, all you His servants
  and you who fear *God,* the small and the great.
    And let us praise and glorify Him forever.
Let heaven and earth praise Him Who is *glorious.*
    And let us praise and glorify Him forever.

Every creature in heaven, on earth and *under the earth;*
and in the sea and those that *are* in it.
And let us praise and glorify Him forever.
Glory to the Father and to the Son and to the Holy Spirit.
And let us praise and glorify Him forever.
As it was in the beginning, is now, and will be forever.
And let us praise and glorify Him forever.

All-powerful, most holy, most high, supreme God: all good, supreme good, totally good, You Who alone are good, may we give
You all praise, all glory, all thanks, all honor, all blessing, and all
good. So be it! So be it! Amen.[4]

This piece may well ask us the same question as the "Exhortation to the Praise of God." Are we dealing with a piece of
poetry or the lyrics of some hymn? It would certainly seem this
is another of those exhortations that Francis has offered us before. Not only is there something invitational about this piece,
but it is even arranged with verses and refrains as if it were the
composition of someone accustomed to leading song. Therefore,
it would be better to imagine that we are reading the lyrics to a
song aimed at involving its listeners in its mood and excitement.

Francis offers us a song with three different sections divided
by two doxologies, "Let us bless the Father and the Son with the
Holy Spirit" and "Glory to the Father and to the Son and to the
Holy Spirit." While the first two sections are a collage of scriptural passages, the third is a simple prayer written with those
images of God to which we have now become so accustomed:
"most high, supreme God: all good, supreme good,... You Who
alone are good."

For the moment, let us look at the first set of biblical quotations, all of which come from the Book of Revelation. Francis
initially draws us to the assertions that these verses make about
God and, more specifically, the Lamb. To open his song, he
chooses Rev. 4:8, part of which is proclaimed each day as the
Eucharist is begun. The passage comes from a description of the
worship offered at the throne of God, Rev. 4:6–8:

---

4. Possible biblical allusions, in order: cf. Rev. 4:8, 11; 5:12; Dan. 3:57; Rev.
19:5; cf. Ps. 68:35; Rev. 5:13; cf. Mark 10:18; Luke 18:19; Rev. 4:9, 11; 5:12.

Surrounding the throne on each of its sides, were four living creatures covered with eyes in front and behind. The
first one looked like a lion; the second like a bull; the
third had a face like a man's face; and the fourth looked
like an eagle in flight.... Day and night they never stopped
singing: "holy, holy, holy is the Lord God Almighty, who
was and who is, and who is to come."

The second passage also comes from this same setting, Rev.
4:9–11:

The four living creatures sing songs of glory and honor and
thanks to the one who sits on the throne, who lives forever and ever. When they do so, the twenty-four elders fall
down before the one who sits on the throne, and worship
him who lives forever and ever. They throw their crowns
down in front of the throne and say: "Our Lord and God!
You are worthy to receive glory and honor, and power! For
you created all things, and by your will they were given
existence and life!"

The third passage, which concludes this section, uses the hymn
offered to the Lamb who was slain, Rev. 5:11–12:

Again I looked and I heard angels, thousands and millions
of them! They stood around the throne, the four living
creatures, and the elders, and sang in a loud voice: "The
Lamb Who was killed is worthy to receive power, wealth,
wisdom and strength, honor, glory, and praise!"

Each of these passages describes action that takes place around
the throne of God and of the Lamb. A variety of different beings
sing these hymns — the four living creatures, the twenty-four elders, and, finally, thousands and millions of angels. Thus Francis
reminds us of John's rather awesome description of the heavenly
liturgy that takes place before God's throne and, in doing so, sets
what has to be the highest possible standard for our worship.
By using the simple refrain, "Let us praise and glorify Him forever!" and by bringing these verses to a close with, "Let us bless
the Father and the Son with the Holy Spirit!" Francis invites us

to join our adoration to that of those heavenly worshipers in God's presence.

The second part of Francis's exhortation is far more invitational than the first. Its four stanzas encourage "all the works of the Lord" to sing songs of praise or blessing: all God's servants, all those who fear God, and all creatures. Once again he is very universal in his outreach and desire to have everyone and everything join him in praising the goodness of the Creator. And, once again, he expresses that invitational, all-embracing, first-person-plural aspect of his prayer. We are far from the God-and-I attitude of the "Prayer before the Crucifix."

He concludes quite simply, however, by accentuating the overwhelming vision of the all-good God. The words of Jesus to the rich young man seem never to leave Francis's mind as he turns repeatedly to focus on God. "Why call me good? Only one is good, the One Who is in heaven!" Thus, although Francis uses so many of those other titles that he attributes to God, "the God Who is all good" is the one that he accentuates more than the others, and, as if to remind us of what is so obvious, he does not tire in driving home the lessons of those around the throne of God that all praise, glory, thanks, honor, blessing, and good belong solely to God.

There are many nuances in this text that might tantalize us. Why, for example, does Francis change the order of "who was, who is, and who is to come"? Why does he change the adjective "powerful" in his quotation of Ps. 68:35 to "glorious"? Why does the eighth verse follow a different pattern than the three that precede it? Why does he conclude each section with a different doxology? Why does Francis end with a double "So be it" and then "Amen"? These complex questions are interesting, but it is clear that in essence the song quite simply encourages us to unite ourselves in spirit with the choir of countless angels and holy ones who stand and worship before the throne of the living God. Francis would have us, as members of the pilgrim church, join the liturgy of heaven and, together with the heavenly host, contemplate the glories of the all-good God.

Now we should turn our attention to two other types of prayer, both writings that we cannot date but that are typical of Francis's understanding that everything has its source in God. These two texts take the form of greetings or salutations.

"A Greeting of the Blessed Virgin Mary"

Hail, O Lady,
Holy Queen,
Mary, holy Mother of God!
You are the Virgin made Church,
the One chosen by the most Holy Father in heaven
whom he consecrated with His most holy beloved Son
and with the Holy Spirit the Paraclete,
in whom there was and is
all fullness of grace and all good.
Hail His Palace!
Hail His Tabernacle!
Hail His Dwelling!
Hail His Vestment!
Hail His Handmaid!
Hail His Mother!

Hail all You holy virtues
which are poured into the hearts of the faithful
through the grace and enlightenment of the Holy Spirit,
that from being faithless
You may make them faithful to God.

In his *Second Life of Saint Francis*, Thomas of Celano writes: "Toward the Mother of Jesus [Francis] was filled with an inexpressible love, because it was she who made the Lord of Majesty our brother. He sang special praises to her, poured out prayers to her, offered her his affections, so many and so great that the human tongue cannot recount them." Francis may have composed this prayer at the Portiuncula, that small chapel in which he heard the gospel that so completely changed the direction of his life. This prayer, as the antiphon found in the *Office of the Passion*, may have been a means Francis used to remind us that Mary is the paradigm of spiritual development that should always be before our eyes.

Francis describes the role Mary plays in the plan of God. She is not simply the Mother of God; she is the Virgin made Church. What an extraordinary title! It anticipated the teaching of the Second Vatican Council by centuries. Not only is she the model of one caught up in the trinitarian relations; she is also the perfect recipient of God's grace and goodness. In a litany-like greeting that is reminiscent of that of the Archangel Gabriel, Francis sings of the glories of his Lady, she who is *the* temple, *the* dwelling place of God. Then he abruptly changes his trend of thought by drawing our attention away from Mary to those virtues poured into the hearts of the faithful. Again we are left with questions that tease us and leave us wondering about his thoughts. Why this sudden shift? Was this his way of challenging us to consider Mary as our role model? Or was this a prelude or foreword to "A Greeting of the Virtues"?

"A Greeting of the Virtues"

Of all the writings of Francis, this is the one that is perhaps the most clearly influenced by chivalry or the troubadour tradition. Here Francis addresses the virtues as ladies and relates them as sisters. Here, too, he extols the glories of Christian virtue in ways that are poetic as well as theologically correct.

> Hail, Queen Wisdom!
> May the Lord protect You,
>   with Your Sister, holy pure Simplicity!
> Lady holy Poverty,
>   may the Lord protect You,
>   with Your Sister, holy Humility!
> Lady holy Charity,
>   may the Lord protect You,
>   with Your Sister, holy Obedience.
> Most holy Virtues,
>   may the Lord protect all of You
>   from Whom You come and proceed.
>
> There is certainly no one in the whole world
>   who can possess any one of You
>   unless he first dies.
> Whoever possesses one
>   and does not offend the others possesses all.

Whoever offends one
   does not possess any and offends all.
Each one confounds vice and sin.
Holy Wisdom confounds
   Satan and all his cunning.
Pure holy Simplicity confounds
   all the wisdom of this world
   and the wisdom of the body.
Holy Poverty confounds
   the desire of riches, greed,
   and the cares of this world.
Holy Humility confounds pride,
   all the people who are in the world
   and all that is in the world.
Holy Charity confounds
   every diabolical and carnal temptation
   and every carnal fear.
Holy Obedience confounds
   every corporal and carnal wish,
   binds its mortified body
   to obedience of the Spirit
   and obedience to one's brother,
   so that he is subject and submissive
   to everyone in the world,
   not only to people
   but to every beast and wild animal as well
   that they may do whatever they want with him
   insofar as it has been given to them
   from above by the Lord.

What is most interesting about this text is the way in which Francis links the virtues. Wisdom is joined with simplicity, poverty with humility, and charity with obedience. He qualifies each of these virtues and envisions their confounding activities. In many instances both the linking of the virtues as well as their activities are surprising. For example, while simplicity is the sister of wisdom, it also put the wisdom of the world and of the body into disarray. Similarly Francis describes "holy obedience," the virtue that receives the most attention, in a way that might surprise ecologists. Obedience binds us not only to the

Spirit and to one another, whether we are related or not; it even subjects us to beasts and wild animals. A recent article in the *Atlantic Monthly*, "Can Selfishness Save the Environment?" suggested that perhaps only short-term self-interest will save our universe (Ridley and Low 1993, 76–86). Francis would certainly have had difficulties with that approach.

"Prayer Based on the Our Father"

This places us in a good position to read Francis's "catechism of prayer" centered on the Our Father. We tend to overlook or neglect this writing, yet here Francis offers us a wonderful synthesis of the theology that we have noticed developing throughout his writings, a theology that accentuates God as the generous source of all good and that envisions our role in pointing beyond ourselves by acknowledging and praising that source. At the time of St. Francis, expressions of this type of prayer were somewhat frequent. Two thirteenth-century examples of this type of commentary on the Our Father confirm what we see in Francis's own: expressions of attitudes of prayer as well as strong images of the God to whom our prayer is directed. Were we to place these three contemporary expressions side-by-side without any identification, however, we would be able to distinguish immediately that of Francis because of those elements we have become accustomed to recognize in his writings.

> O *Our Father* most holy:
> Our Creator, Redeemer, Consoler and Savior;
> *Who are in heaven:*
> In the angels and the saints,
> > enlightening them to know, for You, Lord, are light;
> > inflaming them to love, for You, Lord, are love;
> > dwelling in them and filling them with happiness,
> > > for You, Lord, are Supreme Good,
> > > the Eternal Good,
> > > from Whom all good comes
> > > without Whom there is no good.

Holy be Your Name:
    May knowledge of You become clearer in us
        that we may know
            the breadth of Your blessings
                the length of Your promises,
                    the height of Your majesty
                    the depth of Your judgments.

Your kingdom come:
    That You may rule in us through Your grace
        and enable us to come to Your kingdom
            where there is clear vision of You,
                perfect love of You,
                blessed companionship with You,
                eternal enjoyment of You.

Your will be done on earth as in heaven:
    That we may love You
        with our whole heart by always thinking of You,
            with our whole soul by always desiring You,
                with our whole mind by always directing
                    all our intentions to You
                    and by seeking Your glory in everything,
            with all our whole strength by exerting
                all our energies and affections of body and soul
                in service of Your love and nothing else
        and we may love our neighbors as ourselves
            by drawing them all to Your love with our whole strength,
                by rejoicing over the good of others as over our own,
                    by suffering with others at their misfortunes,
                    and by giving offense to no one.

Give us this day:
    in remembrance, understanding, and reverence
        of that love that our Lord Jesus Christ had for us
        and of those things that He said and did and suffered
            for us.

our daily Bread:
    Your own beloved Son.

Forgive us our trespasses:
　through Your ineffable mercy
　　through the power of the passion of Your beloved Son
　　and through the merits and intercession
　　　of the ever blessed Virgin and all Your elect.

As we forgive those who trespass against us:
　And what we do not completely forgive,
　　make us, Lord, completely forgive
　　　that we may truly love our enemies because of You
　　　　and we may fervently intercede for them before You
　　　　returning no one evil for evil
　　and we may strive to help everyone in You.

And lead us not into temptation:
　hidden or seen,
　　sudden or persistent.

But deliver us from evil:
　past,
　　present,
　　　and to come.

Glory to the Father, and to the Son, and to the Holy Spirit.
　As it was in the beginning, is now, and will be forever.
　Amen.

Francis again develops his fundamental image of God as good, "the good from Whom all good comes," by expressing it in a variety of dynamic ways but always from the perspective of God as Father. "O how glorious and holy and great to have a Father in heaven!" he exclaims in both exhortations to the penitents. "Let us, therefore, hold on to the words, the life, the teaching and the Holy Gospel of Him Who humbled Himself ...to make His name known," he encourages us in the Earlier Rule. Should we be surprised, then, that he uses Jesus' own prayer to teach us the art of praying? Or can we overlook his awareness that baptism has involved us in the very inner life of God, a God who is so obviously good in giving us life, in redeeming us, and in calling us to the fullness of love?

After his typically trinitarian introduction, "O Our Father most holy: Our Creator [Father], Redeemer [Son], Consoler and

Savior [Holy Spirit]," Francis describes God's activities in the angels and the saints: enlightening them, inflaming them, and dwelling in them so that they might respond in appropriate ways. The image of God as light appears in all its splendor in Francis's words. In fact, the angels and saints can know and love God only by reason of the divine presence in them as light. From this perspective, Francis then proceeds to articulate a prayer, based on Eph. 3:18, for an increase in our knowledge of this ever-continuing goodness of God. With this awareness of God's dynamic presence within us, he sees us, like the angels and saints, responding more generously and perfectly. Thus each day becomes one of remembrance, understanding, and reverence lived in light of the revelation of God in Jesus in which we continue his forgiving, loving, intercessory presence.

We should spend more time with this prayer. It is an unusual expression of much of Francis's vision and teaches us a great deal about prayer in the Franciscan tradition. As such, it fulfills what this type of prayer attempted to achieve: to catechize, to teach in a succinct, easily memorized way an approach not simply to the Our Father but to prayer in general.

There are any number of ways in which we might read or reread these undated writings. Our approach has been to begin with *Admonitions* since it crystallizes what comes to us through those early writings, especially the Earlier and Later Rules. In light of *Admonitions*, we can better appreciate the *Office of the Passion* as one of the primary expressions of Francis's devotion to the mystery of Christ and his burning desire to conform to the Suffering Servant of God. Francis — as a poor, lowly, and suffering servant — is the one who breaks into the praises of God, who sings to and of his Lady and of the virtues that adorn her and those who emulate her. All of these writings find a beautiful synthesis in Francis's "catechism of prayer" — the "Prayer Based on the Our Father." In all of its simplicity, this prayer focuses our attention where Francis would have it: on the Father of our Lord Jesus Christ, whom Francis proclaimed before all to be his true Father. With an understanding of the "unclouded vision" for which Francis prays, we are now in a far better position to approach the works of the last years of his life, that is, those that come to us from September 1224 until the last moments of his life.

Part Three

Writings from 1224 to Francis's Death

We left our chronological reading of Francis's writings with the Later Rule, the rule that received the papal seal of approval at the Lateran, the papal palace in Rome, on November 29, 1223. On his return to Assisi, Francis spent time in Greccio, where he miraculously held the Infant Jesus in his arms during the celebration of the Christmas Midnight Mass. Although nothing in Francis's writings tells us about the miracle of Greccio, it acted as a prelude for the mystical experience of LaVerna, which was to occur within the next year.

Mystical knowledge, Bonaventure maintains, is "the raising of the mind to God through the desire of love." Love, in other words, is the motivation, the driving force behind the mystical journey, a journey that takes us beyond thoughts, images, and concepts into a world of silence. Is it surprising that we find so few writings of Francis in these last years of his life? His wisdom and knowledge came through love. It was experiential and, as such, could not be expressed in words. Any attempt to do so fell flat. Language, Francis seems to realize, leads us to an expectancy of an experience of God; it does not bring it about.

At the same time, an urgency fills these last writings, a drive to make clear the goal of the minority and fraternity Francis had discovered. That sense may have come from an awareness that his health was deteriorating. While sickness had been a frequent visitor especially since his visit to the Middle East, it was now a constant companion as Francis became weaker and his eyesight poorer. As his desire to be with the Other grew more intense, however, he nevertheless seemed to feel compelled to communicate his convictions to his brothers and sisters. We can sense that in what he writes to Leo, Clare and the Poor Ladies, and Anthony. But the brothers must have been far more aware that their spiritual father was dying, for the biographers tell us that they were frequently coming to him with questions or with requests for his insights.

These last writings, then, are characterized by two strong currents: Francis's ever-deepening mystical communion with the God to whom he had totally given his life and his brothers' awareness that he was dying.

LaVerna

Before reading the first of these writings, we should familiarize ourselves with the events that took place sometime between August 15, 1224, the feast of the Assumption, and September 29, 1224, the feast of St. Michael the Archangel. A document written in June 1274 and discovered in the archives of Chiusi tells us that Francis and his brothers received the "mountain of LaVerna" on May 8, 1213. Arnaldo Fortini maintains that Francis made six trips to this rugged Tuscan mountain before he went to prepare for the feast of Michael the Archangel in 1224. If this is the case, its ground had already become sacred to Francis prior to his ecstasy during that period.

While Thomas of Celano devotes much of his description of the LaVerna experience to the reception of the stigmata, those marks resembling the sacred wounds of Christ, Bonaventure, the perceptive mystical theologian, concentrates much of his attention on the manner of Francis's ascent to God. "There," Bonaventure writes in *The Soul's Journey into God*, "he passed over into God in ecstatic contemplation and became an example of perfect contemplation as he had previously been of action, like another Jacob and Israel, so that through him, more by example than by word, God might invite all truly spiritual men to this kind of passing over and spiritual ecstasy." Francis, however, tells us little. It is as if he were exemplifying the twenty-eighth admonition: "Blessed is that servant who stores up in heaven the good things which the Lord has revealed to him and does not desire to reveal them to others in the hope of profiting thereby, for the Most High Himself will manifest His deeds to whomever He wishes." More than likely, Bonaventure is far more perceptive when he writes: "In this passing over, if it is to be perfect, all intellectual activities must be left behind and the height of our affection must be totally transferred and transformed into God." Thus we should read with care the only writing that comes to us from LaVerna, a small piece of parchment that Francis gave to Brother Leo.

Leo himself provides the background for the parchment with the inscription that he placed on it. He writes:

> Two years before his death, in the place of LaVerna, blessed Francis kept a lent in honor of the blessed Virgin Mary, the Mother of God, and of the blessed Michael the Archangel, from the feast of the Assumption of the most holy Virgin Mary until the September feast of St. Michael. And the hand of the Lord was upon him. After the vision and words of the Seraph and the impression of the stigmata of Christ in his body, he composed those praises written on the other side of this sheet and written in his own hand, while giving thanks to God for the kindness bestowed on him.

Thomas of Celano offers another insight into its composition by telling us that Leo "longed with great desire to have something encouraging from the Lord's words written down briefly by Francis's hand. For he believed that he would escape a serious temptation that troubled him by this means." Bonaventure places Thomas's comment in the eleventh chapter of his *Major Life of Saint Francis* where, as he describes Francis's ability to read hearts, he tells us that Leo's temptation was "not of the flesh but of the spirit." What precisely was the temptation? We will never know. Leo himself is silent about it. Anyone who has spent time on the cold, windswept cliffs of LaVerna would not find it difficult to conceive that he struggled with his faith, especially as he perceived Francis becoming more thoroughly imbued with God's love. In any case, Francis responded to Leo's need by writing on one side of the small piece of parchment:

You are holy, Lord, You alone are the God Who does wonderful things.

You are strong. You are great. You are most high. You are the all-powerful king.

You are the holy Father, the king of heaven and earth.

You are the Lord God of gods three and one; You are good, all good, the sovereign good,

Lord God living and true.

You are love, charity; You are wisdom, You are humility, You are patience, You are beauty, You are meekness, You are security, You are inner peace, You are joy, You are our hope and joy, You are justice, You are moderation, You are all our riches to sufficiency.

You are beauty, You are meekness, You are a protector, You are our guardian and defender, You are strength, You are refreshment.

You are our hope, You are our faith, You are our charity, You are all our sweetness, You are our eternal life: Great and wonderful Lord, All-powerful God, Merciful Savior.

On the other side of the parchment, in addition to Leo's comment, which is written at the top of the page, we find this inscription:

May the Lord bless you and keep you.

May He show His face to you and be merciful to you.

May He turn His countenance to you and give you peace.

May the Lord bless you, Brother Leo.

After this, Leo identifies what we have just read: "With his own hand Blessed Francis wrote this blessing for me, Brother Leo." Then we find a crude drawing that Leo describes: "In a similar way he made with his own hand this sign, a Tau, together with a head."

The dictionary defines simplicity as "freedom from intricacy or complexity" or as "absence of elegance, embellishment, luxury, or the like." From both of these perspectives, the parchment given to Brother Leo is one of Francis's simplest writings. Any attempts to read intricate patterns of thought into these simple verses usually go awry: Francis's forthright statements seem to flow quite naturally from his contemplation of the living God, whose presence can be perceived in the virtues, and in whom we find our fulfillment and rest. There is no embellishment or excess of words. In fact, when we look at the original parchment, now preserved in the Basilica of St. Francis in Assisi, we have the sense that Francis carefully meditated upon his praises of God and edited and perhaps reedited them. (The original parchment, for example, shows how Francis corrected his own "Italianisms," Latin words that he wrote with Italian spellings, and added certain words and phrases.)

We might also describe simplicity as expressing oneself in the most direct and unaffected way. And from this perspective, we also have one of the simplest of all Francis's writings, for it reveals the spirit of someone overwhelmed by the experience of God, of someone of a poetic nature who finds his words fall flat in attempting to describe the reality of the divine presence. This is the writing of Francis the mystic. It is an expression — or as close as we will come to it — of ecstasy, but it leads us only to identifying the nature of the experience.

In writing of her own experience of Christ, Teresa of Avila wrote: "I used unexpectedly to experience a consciousness of the presence of God of such a kind that I could not possibly doubt that he was within me or that I was wholly engulfed in him." This is what Francis's words to Brother Leo unabashedly communicate: his awareness of the God who so powerfully moves, guides, and forms his life from within and without. We might be struck by the repetition of "You are...," a phrase Francis expresses in the very personal form, *tu es*. In itself that is somewhat surprising, for it expresses an intimacy and familiarity that we do not expect from someone who usually writes in very reverential terms. But the repetition of the phrase establishes a rhythm or pulse that suggests Francis's conviction that life itself is essentially caught up in the mystery of the living God.

We have seen many of these same characteristics throughout Francis's works. "You are *holy!*" The adjective appears more than two hundred times in the writings and, in most instances, refers to God. "You are most high! You are the all-powerful king....You are strong! You are great!" Over and over he addresses these phrases to the Creator before whom Francis stands in wonder and awe. Above all he proclaims over and again: "You are good, all good, the sovereign good." The words come so naturally to Francis's lips that we cannot help but see them as expressing his fundamental image of God. Thus his praise of God now flows from his pursuit of good, that is, his pursuit of virtue, and we see the simplicity of his understanding that God can be found in all the virtues, all the energies that we exert in our attempts to come to God. These are the praises of someone who struggles with his deficiencies and with his dependency. These are the praises of the poor one, the one who turns to the goodness and generosity of the Most High, the one who never ceases realizing that wherever he turns God is present. Is it any wonder then that he sings the praises of the God who is his "riches unto overflowing"?

But what, we may ask, is behind the other side of the parchment with its biblical blessings and the crude picture and sign of the cross? Commentators have been puzzling over the mystery for years and have proposed all sorts of interpretations. We might even wonder if Francis intended it to be that way, as a tantalizing puzzle that would draw us deeper into its mystery.

There are a few possible sources for the blessing. While its biblical inspiration is obvious, Num. 2:24–26, 27b, that biblical text was used on a variety of different occasions. For example, the Pontifical of Innocent III uses it as a blessing at the conclusion of a Holy Thursday rite of reconciliation. In a twelfth-century pontifical found in Arezzo, it is a blessing offered by the bishop during the ceremony for the giving of the tonsure. More commonly, in the monastic world the abbot uttered it at the end of Night Prayer. In this context it had a distinct trinitarian interpretation as the abbot gave the blessing of the Father ("May the Lord bless and keep you"), of the incarnate, redeeming Son ("May he turn his face to you and be merciful to you"), and of the peace-giving Holy Spirit ("May he turn his countenance to you and give you peace"). Francis may have encountered the blessing in any one of these contexts. Why did he use this particular blessing to encourage Leo in his trial? We simply do not know. But if the use of this biblical blessing is a puzzle, the drawing is even more so.

It has been most commonly described as a representation of Calvary or, more properly, Golgotha. For the medieval belief was that Christ was crucified on the place where Adam was buried. John Chrysostom, for example, wrote: "And [Christ] came to the place called the Skull. Some say that Adam had died and lay buried there, and that Jesus set up His trophy over death in the place where death had begun its rule." But all this is not as curious as is the way in which Francis wrote the final verse of the blessing. He begins with *Dñs* (the Lord) but continues with *bene*, which is continued directly below with *dicat*. Was he writing "bless you" or, as one commentator has suggested, "says well"? But we can also see that Francis intersects *f* (the initial for brother) *leo* with the sign of the tau and then continues with *te*. Some have suggested that Francis was most eager to show Leo that his very life had been filled with the Lord's blessing, signified by the very cross that had saved us. Others suggest that he wanted to be sure that Leo recognized the power of the cross. One thing is sure: Francis was most eager to accentuate the presence of the tau, that sign for which, as Thomas of Celano and Bonaventure tell us, he had a special love. Not only did Ezekiel (9:4) and John (Rev. 7:3) describe the tau as the sign of those who were saved; Innocent III also adopted it in 1213 as the special sign of the renewal embraced by the Fourth Lateran Council. So Francis was probably well aware of not only its biblical but also its contemporary significance.

Are the two sides of the parchment intertwined? All sorts of answers have been given to the question, none of which seems to satisfy. We are in the presence of the mysterious and must be content to surrender ourselves to a world that is beyond our grasp. This piece of parchment, in all its beguiling simplicity, places before us the strongest characteristic of these last writings, the mystical quality that permeated them. While we might easily be tempted to examine them within their historical contexts, they transcend that approach. Instead, they speak quite forcibly of the ubiquitous presence of God. "You are..." The words echo throughout Francis's last years and lead us to his very last breath. Sister Bodily Death, whose embrace was not far off, would be for Francis a means of liberation, a reality that would free him to come into the presence of the all-good God whom he recognized all around him.

"Canticle of the Creatures"

Thomas of Celano describes LaVerna as a profound turning point in Francis's spiritual journey. "His flesh tried to outrun his spirit," he wrote, attempting to portray how the stigmatized man was so overwhelmed by his ecstatic experience. When we read that he left LaVerna by way of a leper colony where he insisted on ministering to those who had consistently revealed God to him, we have the sense that he wanted to relive his experience of conversion, especially now that he knew to what wonders it would lead. "He was, therefore, afire with a very great desire to return to the first beginnings of humility," Thomas tells us, "and rejoicing in hope, he thought to recall his body to its former subjection, even though it had already come to such an extremity." From the ecstasy of LaVerna and his ministry to the lepers, Francis went to the hermitage of Monte Casale where he spent another long period of prayer before turning toward Assisi. Once again, we can see the pattern of his life emerging: prayer–ministry–prayer.

Between December 1224 and March 1225, Francis preached throughout the Umbrian Valley and into Le Marche of Ancona. "Now fixed with Christ to the cross in both body and spirit," Bonaventure writes, "Francis not only burned with a Seraphic love of God, but also thirsted with Christ Crucified for the salvation of souls." The theme of his preaching became not only "Let us begin, for up until now we have done little or nothing," but also the mystery of Christ Crucified, to whom he exhorted his listeners to turn and cling. What made this preaching tour so significant, however, was the severe weather during which it was conducted. The secular chronicles indicate that this was the most severe winter experienced in central Italy. Those who have felt Umbria's cold have an idea of what it must have been like.

By April, Francis had returned to Assisi and had gone to a roughly made cell outside St. Damian's. His companions tell us that his eyes had deteriorated, so that he "could not bear the light of the sun during the day or the light of the fire at night." It is difficult to determine what caused this eye condition. It may well have been a case of conjunctivitis, the so-called Egyptian Sickness, which he might have contracted while in the Near East; or it may have been brought about by malnutrition, which could have caused an enlargement of the lachrymal glands. Bonaventure suggests that Francis's excessive crying over his sins may have been the cause. Strange as this might seem to us, crying over one's sins was seen as an incentive to prayer in the Benedictine tradition ("We shall not be heard for our excessive speaking but for our purity of heart and tears of compunction" [Rule of Benedict 20]). Indeed, Walter Hilton describes Aelred of Rievaulx in just such terms: "He would hardly ever pray without tears. Tears, he would say, are the signs of perfect prayer, the ambassadors between God and men. They reveal the whole feeling of the heart and declare the will of God to the soul" (see Powicke 1950, 20). All of this led one historian to describe the thirteenth century as "a period of excessive tearfulness."

In any case, Francis had to remain in darkness because his eyes were so sensitive to the light. What little sleep he was able to enjoy was interrupted by the field mice that, his companions tell us, ran around and even over him in his cell. The companions tell us of one night in particular when Francis endured what must have been a terrible temptation of faith. Feeling sorry for himself, he said, "Lord, help me in my infirmities so that I may have the strength to bear them patiently!" He then heard: "Tell me, brother: if, in compensation for your suffering and tribulations you were given an immense and precious treasure: the whole mass of the earth changed into pure gold, pebbles into precious stones, and the water of the rivers into perfume, would you not regard the pebbles and the waters as nothing compared to such a treasure? Would you not rejoice?" "Lord," he replied, "it would be a very great, very precious, and inestimable treasure beyond all that one can love and desire!" "Well, brother," the voice said, "be glad and joyful in the midst of your infirmities and tribulations. As of now, live in peace as if you were already sharing my kingdom."

When Francis came out of that experience, he said to his companions:

If the emperor gave a kingdom to one of his servants, how joyful the servant would be! But if he gave him the whole empire, would he not rejoice all the more? I should, therefore, be full of joy in my infirmities and tribulations, seek my consolation in the Lord, and give thanks to God the Father, to his only Son our Lord Jesus Christ, and to the Holy Spirit. In fact, God has given me such a grace and blessing that he has condescended in his mercy to assure me, his poor and unworthy servant, still living on earth, that I would share his kingdom. Therefore, for his glory, for

my consolation, and the edification of my neighbor, I wish
to compose a new Praises of the Lord for his creatures.
These creatures minister to our needs every day; without
them we could not live; and through them the human race
greatly offends the Creator. Every day we fail to appreciate
so great a blessing by not praising as we should the Creator
and dispenser of all these gifts.

At this point he broke out in singing the "Canticle of the
Creatures":

Most High, all-powerful, good Lord,
> Yours are the praises, the glory, the honor, and all blessing,
To You alone, Most High, do they belong,
> and no one is worthy to mention Your name.

Praised be You, my Lord, with all Your creatures,
> especially Sir Brother Sun,
> Who is the day and through whom You give us light.
And he is beautiful and radiant with great splendor;
> and bears a likeness of You, Most High One.

Praised be You, my Lord, through Sister Moon and the stars,
> in heaven You formed them clear and precious
> and beautiful.

Praised be You, my Lord, through Brother Wind,
> and through the air, cloudy and serene, and every kind of
> weather,
> through whom You give sustenance to Your creatures.

Praised be You, my Lord, through Sister Water,
> who is very useful and humble and precious and chaste.

Praised be You, my Lord, through Brother Fire,
> through whom You light the night
> and he is beautiful and playful and robust and strong.

Praised be You, my Lord, through our Sister Mother Earth,
> who sustains and governs us,
> and who produces various fruits with colored flowers and
> herbs.

Praise and bless my Lord and give Him thanks
> and serve Him with great humility.

G. K. Chesterton once wrote that this canticle "is a supremely characteristic work and much of Saint Francis could be reconstructed from that work alone" (Chesterton 1924, 132). Some might dismiss that sweeping statement of the English editorialist on the grounds that he was not as cognizant of Francis's writings as we are now. Yet Eloi Leclerc, a contemporary French author, resonates with Chesterton's observation: "The manner in which Francis here looks at the created world is a key to his inner self, for the canticle undoubtedly has elements that reveal in a special way the personality of its author" (Leclerc 1978, 4). In order to appreciate the insights of both Chesterton and Leclerc, we must look carefully not only at the canticle's structure, the frequent practice of commentators, but also at the very words Francis uses in his praises.

Although there is no evidence to suggest that the canticle's final verse acts as a refrain for each of the previous verses or, at least, for each section, it seems almost natural that Francis would have taught it to the brothers to enable them to join in his song. If this is the case, then the refrain, "Praise and bless my Lord and give Him thanks and serve Him with great humility," clearly establishes the tenor of the rest of the work and is a reflection of the song of the servant of God who is conscious that everything comes from God. From that perspective, Francis appears to have arrived at his conviction that he was no better than any of the other pieces of creation and that he and they were members of the same family bound to reflect the goodness of their Creator. The opening verse certainly gives a sense of what *Admonitions* has shown us is a fundamental attitude of Francis — that all praise, glory, honor, and blessing belong to God. Francis emphasizes this in the following verse by accentuating that they belong to the Most High alone and, in doing so, suggests that we human beings have lost our place in the chorus that follows. We sinned; the other creatures did not. We, therefore, lost the right to pronounce God's name; creation did not. We have encountered this sentiment before, in the twenty-third chapter of the Earlier Rule, but now it is placed at the very beginning of this song of the mystic Francis who is undoubtedly far more conscious of his sinfulness than ever before. The remaining seven verses, then, are creation's hymn to their Creator.

The third verse, though, adds an even more curious note

to the canticle. Not only does Francis use the passive voice, "Praised be you, my Lord...";￼ he also tells us that God's creatures are praised as well. While we might easily pass over this all-important "with," it provides an invaluable insight into the meaning of the entire work while, at the same time, prompting us to wonder about the role of each of the creatures. Are they instruments of praise? If that were the case, then we would sing, for example, "Praised be You, my Lord, *by* Sister Moon...." Or are they occasions of gratitude? Thus, "Praised be You, my Lord, *for* Sister Moon...." We can easily translate Francis's *per* in either manner, but do they capture the full meaning of "Praised be You, My Lord, *with* all your creatures"? It would seem not, for Francis immediately gives us a sense that we can perceive God's presence or continuing activity in each of those creatures mentioned. Sir Brother Sun, for example, is not only the day but also the means through which God gives us light; Brother Wind gives sustenance; Brother Fire lights up the night. Thus it seems better to translate *per* as "through," which, in addition to expressing instrumentality, also communicates the sense of "in the midst of." This should encourage us to look more carefully at the adjectives that Francis uses to describe the creatures he identifies in the canticle, for, as we have suggested, in some way each reveals the mysterious presence of God.

First of all, we encounter the Sun, who is not only called "Brother" but is also shown greater respect than the other creatures by the addition of the title "Sir." As we have seen, Sir Brother Sun is the day, and through his activity we receive light. As we read these words, we might recall the words of the psalmist: "In your light, we see light." Thus Francis's following words have more meaning: "He is beautiful and radiant with great splendor; and bears a likeness of you, Most High One." But now we should recall Francis's own use of Scripture in the first admonition. In the context of Jesus' response to Philip ("Philip, whoever sees me sees my Father as well"), Francis places a verse from Paul's First Letter to Timothy (1 Tim. 6:16) but changes the subject of the verse from "Lord" to "Father." Thus we read: "The Father dwells *in inaccessible light.*" Do we now have an autobiographical reflection of the Francis who cannot be in the light because of his eyes yet knows that only in the mystery of God can we see things as they were meant to be seen?

That would move us to reflect upon the next light images, those regarding Sister Moon and the stars. We see the creative hand of God at work forming these heavenly lights and making them clear, precious, and beautiful. One thing that might strike us is Francis's repetition of "beautiful." We will see it again when we encounter Brother Fire and must wonder if there is some connection between the Sun, the Moon and the stars, and Fire — all of which give light — that prompts Francis to see them as beautiful. We should also pay careful attention to the adjective *chiara* (clear) and wonder if there is some connection with Sister Chiara, Clare, who was living in St. Damian's not very far away. More telling, however, might be the word "precious," which appears five times in Francis's writings and always in the context of reserving the Body and Blood of Christ, the Eucharist. From this perspective, we might see an association between *chiara* and *clarifica* or *claritas* (brightness), which Francis uses seven times, in most instances to refer to the vision of Jesus. Could this be the meaning of Sister Moon and the stars: Jesus and those who are close to him?

Brother Wind, Sister Water, and Brother Fire can obviously be seen as references to the Spirit. But we should notice the poetic way in which Francis highlights the creative activities of each or how, on a more spiritual level, they bring us into a deeper relationship with the Most High and with the Son. Each one presents a reflection in itself of the triune presence, thus pointing beyond itself to the power, wisdom, and goodness of God.

But what, then, is Sister Mother Earth? Here too we see a sign of respect, Sister *Mother* Earth, and we notice activities that are feminine and maternal in nature: sustaining, governing, and producing. Similar words can be found at the end of the Later Rule as Francis describes the role of the cardinal protector who would always remind the brothers of the church. But we might also wonder if Francis were thinking of "the Virgin made Church," Mary, the Mother of God, who epitomizes for him the Christian totally involved in the trinitarian life.

As Francis was singing this hymn to his triune Creator, however, a volatile situation was intensifying in the town of Assisi. Guido, the bishop of Assisi, had excommunicated the city's *podestà* (mayor). In return, the mayor had it announced to the sound of a trumpet in the streets of the city that every citizen was forbidden to buy from or sell anything whatsoever to the bishop or to transact any business with him. Francis said to his companions: "It is a great shame for us, the servants of God, that at a time when the *podestà* and the bishop so hate each other that no one can be found to re-establish peace between them!" So he added the following strophe to his canticle and had the brothers sing the entire canticle before the two antagonists:

> Praised be You, my Lord, through those who give pardon for
>   Your love,
>   and bear infirmity and tribulation.
> Blessed are those who endure in peace
>   for by You, Most High, shall they be crowned.

Now Francis envisions us, human beings, taking our rightful place in the hymn of praise, for we share with God that awesome power of granting pardon because of love. Yet he realizes that we are incapable of being reconcilers or peacemakers unless we assume the attitudes of the Suffering Servant of God, Jesus, who so forcefully reveals the mysterious ways of God. We find ourselves recalling the admonitions and especially those that commented on the beatitude of the peacemaker, the thirteenth and fifteenth admonitions. Or we find ourselves reflecting upon the ways of the Spirit, as Francis describes them in chapter 17 of the Earlier Rule; there he tells us that one who follows these ways "strives for humility and patience, and the pure, simple and true peace of the Spirit." Thus the "Canticle of Unity," in which we had no place, now becomes a "Canticle of Reconciliation," in which those who have identified with Jesus have their rightful place.

"Canticle of Exhortation for the Poor Ladies of St. Damian's"

Let us leave the "Canticle of the Creatures" for the moment. Not to do so would bring us to the very last hours of Francis's life when the last stanza welcoming Sister Bodily Death was composed. Now we must go to St. Damian's where Francis composed yet another song. In a way, it is a sister to the "Canticle of the Creatures," not only because it too was written to be sung in the Umbrian dialect but also because it reveals the heart of a mystic. "At the same time and in the same friary," the companions tell us, "Blessed Francis... dictated a canticle, words and music for the consolation of the Poor Ladies of the monastery of St. Damian. He was well aware of the fact that his sickness greatly grieved them. Since he could not go in person to visit and console them, he had his companions bring them what he composed for them."

> Listen, little poor ones called by the Lord,
>   who have come together from many parts and provinces.
> Live always in truth,
>   that you may die in obedience.
> Do not look at life without,
>   for that of the Spirit is better.
> I beg you out of great love,
>   to use with discernment
>   the alms the Lord gives you.
> Those weighed down by sickness
>   and the others wearied because of them,
>   all of your bear it in peace.
> For this fatigue will seem very dear
>   for each one will be crowned queen
>   with the Virgin Mary in heaven.

There is almost a sense of urgency in Francis's opening word, "Listen." As we will see, he calls us to listen or to pay attention in another writing of this period, his Letter to the Entire Order, leaving us the impression that he sensed that his sickness was grave and that he was eager for his hearers to absorb what he was telling them. His words are also reminiscent of the first word of the Rule of Benedict, which encourages its readers to observe its teaching on religious life. But it also reflects many passages of the Wisdom literature, especially Prov. 4:1, 10; 8:6, 32. Yet immediately Francis calls the Ladies by his term of endearment, *poverelle* (little poor ones), a word that Clare herself used much later in her letters to Agnes of Prague as she writes of herself and the sisters. And he further specifies them as called by the Lord from many parts and provinces, as indeed they were.

Yet what, we may ask, does Francis mean when he encourages the Poor Ladies to "live always in truth"? Is this a call to sincerity or to purity of heart, that is, to live a life that is genuine? It could well be. More than likely it is a call to live in the truth that is Christ, a call that reflects the words of John. "Consecrate them in truth," Jesus prays in John 17. "Your words are truth." In 2 John, we find John himself saying: "I rejoiced greatly to find some of your children walking in the truth just as we were commanded by the Father." And in 3 John we find: "I rejoiced greatly when some of the brothers came and testified to how truly you walk in the truth." These passages certainly resonate with Francis's exhortation in the Earlier Rule to center our lives on the Word of God.

Is this, then, why he contrasts the "life without" and "that of the Spirit"? Francis could be directing the sisters' attention either to the enclosure or to the interior life. In both instances, however, he encourages them to pay attention to the life of the Spirit within so that they are not taken up with externals or with life beyond the enclosure. In any case, Francis's advice expresses his profound wisdom for those living the enclosed life: life within the enclosure means nothing without an intense spiritual life.

While the sisters' discouragement at his illness may have inspired Francis to write this canticle, its final verses suggest that the illnesses of the sisters themselves may also have inspired it. Indeed, Clare herself became ill at this time, so much so that it was feared that she would die before Francis. It is not too difficult to imagine the causes for such illnesses. In addition to the difficulties of St. Damian's, its dampness and cold, we should remember that the sisters were dependent on alms and were continually mortifying themselves through fasting and abstinence. The sisters who testified to Clare's holiness tell us of the existence of an infirmary and of the number of those who were sick — for example, Sisters Benvenuta, Amata, Cristiana, Cecilia, Lucy, and Francesca. Among all the many virtues they attribute to Clare, four of the sisters describe her as a model infirmarian. So these words tell us a great deal about the day-to-day life within the enclosure of St. Damian's and are both an offering of encouragement and an expression of Francis's admiration for Clare and her sisters.

The Letter to the Entire Order

In the December following the events on LaVerna, Francis and the brothers received a papal document that was quite unusual for its time. On December 3, 1224, the pope permitted the brothers the privilege of celebrating the Eucharist in their residence. This was an extraordinary event in the life of the order. It provided a eucharistic focal point for Francis's followers. The first admonition certainly suggests that Francis saw God embracing poverty, humility, and patient suffering each day and, in doing so, revealing to us the way shown by Christ himself. In this letter, Francis reflects that same maturity in his understanding of the gospel life he espoused as he calls us to embrace the minority we should discover in the Eucharist. This writing is also one of the most biblical of Francis's statements and one in which he shows us the strength of his convictions, especially as he writes of celebrating the Liturgy of the Hours.

In the name of the most high Trinity and holy Unity: the Father and the Son and the Holy Spirit.

To all my reverend and dearly beloved brothers: to Brother A., the Minister General of the Order of Friars Minor, its lord, and the other ministers general who will come after him, and to the ministers, custodians, humble priests of this same brotherhood in Christ, and to all simple and obedient brothers, from the first to the last: Brother Francis, a worthless and weak man, your very little servant sends his greetings in Him Who redeemed and *washed us in His* most precious blood (Rev. 1:5). *Prostrate on the ground* (2 Ezra 8:6) with fear and reverence, adore His name, the name of that *Son of the Most High* (Luke 1:32), our Lord Jesus Christ, *Who is blessed forever* (Rom. 1:25)!

Listen, sons of the Lord and my brothers, *pay attention to my words* (Acts 2:14). *Incline the ear* (Isa. 55:3) of your heart and obey the voice of the Son of God. Observe His commands with your whole heart and fulfill His counsels with a perfect mind. *Give praise* to Him *because He is good* (Ps. 136:1 [V 135:1]); *exalt Him by your deeds* (Tob. 13:6), for He has sent you into the whole world for this reason: that in word and deed you may bear witness to His voice and bring everyone to know that there is *no one who is all-powerful* except Him (Tob. 13:4). Persevere *in discipline* and holy obedience (Heb. 12:7) and with a firm and good purpose fulfill what you have promised to Him. The Lord *God* offers *Himself* to us as to His *children* (Heb. 12:7).

The very opening verses immediately set the biblical tone to this letter as Francis uses a passage from either the Second Book of Ezra (Nehemiah) or the Book of Genesis to express his reverence for Christ. In those passages we find a reference either to the reverence of the people of God or to that of Lot before two angels. Francis, however, adds verses from the Gospel of Luke (1:32) and Paul's Letter to the Romans (1:25) to accentuate Christ's transcendence and, thus, to deepen his call to reverence. These passages set the stage for the thoroughly biblical spirituality that he presents in the following verses. He begins with "Listen," which as we saw in the "Canticle of Exhortation to the Poor Ladies" could be a reference to any number of passages from the Book of Wisdom; he then tells his readers to "pay attention to my words," a clause he borrows from the Acts of the Apostles (2:14); then he says: "Incline the ear of your heart," which refers to Isaiah's reflection on food of the poor. With these biblical texts as an introduction, Francis proceeds to provide us with a foundation for centering our lives on the Word of God. He continues by encouraging us to "persevere in discipline," a phrase from the Letter to the Hebrews, and immediately adds "and holy obedience...." His entire call is based on the biblical notion of education, *mûsar* or *paideia*, which signify "instruction through correction or discipline."

This leads Francis to direct our attention to a life centered on the Eucharist. He offers us some of his most profound teaching as he uses Paul's christological hymn in his Letter to the Colossians to underscore the role of the Body and Blood of Christ, that is, the Eucharist.

Kissing your feet, therefore, and with all that love of which I am capable, I implore all of you brothers to show all possible reverence and honor to the most holy Body and Blood of our Lord Jesus Christ in Whom that which is in heaven and on earth has been brought to peace and reconciled to the all-powerful God (cf. Col 1:20).

I also beg in the Lord all my brothers who are priests, or who will be, or who wish to be priests of the Most High that whenever they wish to celebrate Mass, being pure, they offer the true Sacrifice of the most holy Body and Blood of our Lord Jesus Christ with purity and reverence, with a holy and unblemished intention, not for any worldly reason or out of fear or love of someone, as if they were pleasing people (cf. Eph. 6:6; Col. 3:22). But let every wish, as much as grace helps, be directed to God, while desiring, thereby, to please the Most High Lord Himself alone because He alone acts there as He pleases, for He Himself says: *Do this in memory of me* (Luke 22:19; 1 Cor. 11:24); if someone acts differently, he becomes Judas the traitor and *guilty of the Body and Blood of the Lord* (cf. 1 Cor. 11:27).

Remember what is written in the law of Moses, my priest brothers: whoever committed a transgression against even externals died without mercy by a decree of the Lord (cf. Heb. 10:28). *How much greater and more severe will the punishment be of the one who tramples on the Son of God, and who treats the Blood of the Covenant as unclean in which he was sanctified and who insults the Spirit of grace* (Heb. 10:29)? For one despises, defiles and tramples upon the Lamb of God when, as the Apostle says, *not distinguishing* (cf. 1 Cor. 11:29) and discerning the holy bread of Christ from other foods or actions, he is either unworthy when he eats It or, if he is worthy, he eats It ostentatiously and unworthily since the Lord says through the prophet: The person *is cursed who* does the work of the Lord *deceitfully* (cf. Jer. 48:10). He will, in truth, condemn priests who do not wish to take this to heart, saying: *I will curse your blessings* (Mal. 2:2).

While he quotes Paul, who treats of the preexisting Christ but always considers the historical and unique person of the Son of God made man, Francis prefers to extend the presence of Christ to the Eucharist in which he finds everything reconciled. Therefore, as we can see, he presents us with a vision of the primacy of Christ in the natural order of creation and in the supernatural order of mystery. Then he reminds us of the influence of that papal document of 1219 that we encountered in our consideration of the exhortations to the clergy. To these reminders he adds quotes from the writings of Bernard of Cluny, a Carthusian monk who wrote a meditation on the priesthood that was frequently used in monastic circles. All of this acts as a prelude to some of the most beautiful lines written on the mystery of the priesthood:

Listen, my brothers: If the Blessed Virgin is so honored, as is becoming, because she carried Him in her most holy womb; if the Baptist trembled and did not dare to touch the holy head of God; if the tomb in which He lay for some time is held in veneration, how holy, just and fitting must he be who touches with his hands, receives in his heart and mouth, and offers to others to be received the One Who is not about to die but Who is to conquer and be glorified, upon Whom *the angels longed to look* (1 Pet. 1:12).

See your dignity, *brothers* [who are] priests (cf. 1 Cor. 1:26) and be holy because He is holy (cf. Lev. 19:2). As the Lord God has honored you above all others because of this ministry, for your part love, revere and honor Him above all others. It is a great misery and a miserable weakness that you are concerned with anything else in the whole world when you have Him present in this way!

> Let everyone be struck with fear,
>> the whole world tremble,
>>> and the heavens exult
>>>> when Christ, the Son of the living God,
>>>>> is present on the altar in the hands of a priest!
> O wonderful loftiness
>> and stupendous dignity!
>>> O sublime humility!
>>>> O humble sublimity!
>>>>> The Lord of the universe,
>>>>>> God and the Son of God,
>>>>>>> so humbles Himself
>>>>>>>> that He hides Himself
>>>>>>>>> for our salvation
>>>>>>>> under an ordinary piece of bread!

> See the humility of God, brothers,
>> and *pour out your hearts before Him*
>>> (Ps. 62:8 [V 61:9])!
> Humble yourselves
>> that you may be exalted by Him
>>> (cf. 1 Pet. 5:6; James 4:10)!

Hold back nothing of yourselves for yourselves,
that He Who gives Himself totally to you
may receive you totally!

In the very mystery of the Body and Blood of Christ, Francis recognizes the Most High revealing a humility and poverty that became for him a dramatic inspiration. Of course, he has told us this in his first admonition in which he teaches us that just as the Son of God revealed the Father to the apostles, so the Eucharist does for us today. Now he reminds us of the humility of God in much the same way. The Eucharist is essentially the mystery of manifestation. Each day the little things of creation become the means through which we learn of the wonder of God's love as they become the sacrament of our salvation. Only in light of it can we truly understand our gospel calling: to empty ourselves in poverty, to recognize our true place in humility, and to accept our vulnerability before one another. The Eucharist became, then, the focal point, the mirror in which Francis would have us discover our call each day.

Thus we come to the implications of this eucharistic way of life.

I admonish and exhort you in the Lord, therefore, to celebrate only one Mass a day according to the rite of the Holy Church in those places where the brothers dwell. If, however, there is more than one priest there, let the other be content, for the love of charity, at hearing the celebration of the other priest; because our Lord Jesus Christ fills those present and absent who are worthy of Him. Although He may seem to be present in many places, He remains, nevertheless, undivided and knows no loss; He acts in all places as it pleases Him, one with the Lord God the Father and the Holy Spirit the Paraclete for ever and ever. Amen.

Because *whoever belongs to God hears the words of God* (John 8:47), we who are more especially charged with divine responsibilities must not only listen to and do what the Lord says but also care for the vessels and other liturgical objects that contain His holy words in order to impress on ourselves the sublimity of our Creator and our subjection to Him. Therefore, admonish all my brothers and encourage them in Christ to venerate, as best as they can, the divine written words wherever they discover them. If they are not well kept or are carelessly left in some place, let them gather them up and arrange them, in as much as it concerns them, honoring in the words the Lord *Who spoke them* (1 Kings 2:4 [V 1 Kings 2:4]). For many things are made holy by the words of God (cf. 1 Tim. 4:5) and the sacrament of the altar is celebrated in the power of the words of Christ.

Pope John Paul II has spoken of the Eucharist as the "school of fraternal love." Francis would resonate very deeply with these words. Since the Eucharist commemorates the love of Christ, it becomes for Francis the symbol par excellence of unity and fraternal love. This prompts him, then, to underscore certain principles of gospel calling. The first of these touches on the very daily life of the fraternity and reflects the changing practice of the church in allowing a multiplicity of eucharistic celebrations. But what exactly Francis intends is puzzling, aside from his obvious desire that the entire fraternity center its daily life on the Eucharist. In that act, he implies, we will find the source of our charity and unity, for we will find these in the very mystery itself.

Then he again calls us to reverence and respect for the very instruments of worship, the "vessels and other liturgical objects that contain His holy words." His words echo those of his earlier exhortations, but now we discover a reason that was not visible in those earlier writings: we exercise this reverence and respect "in order to impress on ourselves the sublimity of our Creator." God does not need our signs of reverence and respect, Francis seems to say. We need them to remind us of God's majesty. Here, too, we find Francis broadening his concept of the words of God to those which consecrate the Eucharist.

This concentration on the words of God, however, prompts a confession of his own faults regarding the celebration of the Divine Office and leads him to his final advice concerning the Eucharist.

Moreover, I confess all my sins to the Lord God, Father, Son, and Holy Spirit, to the blessed ever Virgin Mary, all the saints in heaven and on earth, to Brother H., the Minister of our Order as my venerable lord, to the priests of our Order and all my other blessed brothers. I have offended the Lord in many ways by my serious faults especially in not observing the Rule that I have promised Him and in not saying the Office as the Rule prescribes either out of negligence or by reason of my weakness or because I am ignorant and stupid.

Why, we might ask, does Francis now unite observing the rule and reciting the Divine Office? Did he see these as the linchpins that united his followers in the pursuit of gospel life? Probably. Yet he also seems to imply that these are the food that God provides for those who embraced the poverty revealed by Jesus. He had earlier quoted that passage of Isaiah that is devoted to the food of the poor, the Word of God. Bonaventure tells us that Francis envisioned the Later Rule as a gathering of fragments of bread into one whole loaf. Taken together, the Word of God celebrated in the Office and lived in the rule is, for Francis, food for the journey. To ignore it was to ignore what God provides for the poor. Therefore he not only encourages but begs his successor:

Because of all these things, therefore, I beg, as best I can, Brother H., the Minister General, my lord, to have the Rule observed inviolably by everyone, to have the clerics say the Office with devotion before God not concentrating on the melody of the voice but on the harmony of the mind, that the voice may be in harmony with the mind, the mind truly in harmony with God, that they may be able to please God by their purity of heart and not just charm the ears of people with their sweetness of voice.

There are many twists and turns in this letter. Who, for example is the Brother A. mentioned in its very opening? Why do the manuscripts now refer to him as Brother H.? Was this a reference to Brother Helias (Elias), whose reputation was tarnished when some scribe was transcribing this letter? We'll never know. Unfortunately such questions have distracted us from the even more remarkable theological twists and turns of Francis's words — from the Word of God to the Eucharist and the priesthood, from reverence to the Liturgy of the Hours and the rule.

In a marvelous twist of phrase, Francis now takes a teaching of the Rule of Benedict and gives it his own twist. The fifth chapter of Benedict's rule calls the monk to have his

mind in harmony with his voice and tongue. For Francis, however, it is a question of a harmony between the mind, the
voice, and God. His entire approach to the Word envisions the
Word becoming part and parcel of the person, of the heart itself. Once more, then, Francis emphasizes purity of heart, that
call to transparency in which the vibrant, Spirit-filled Word
that has taken root in our hearts becomes expressed in our
actions.

After this encouragement, Francis becomes the most confrontational that we have seen him.

For my part, I firmly promise to observe these things, as God shall
give me the grace, and I pass them on to the brothers who are
with me to be observed in the Office and the other prescriptions
of the Rule.

I do not consider those brothers who do not wish to observe
these things Catholics or my brothers; I do not even wish to see
or speak with them until they have done penance. I even say
this about all those who wander about, having put aside the discipline of the Rule, for our Lord Jesus Christ gave His life that
He would not lose the obedience of His most holy Father (cf.
Phil. 2:8).

I, Brother Francis, a useless man and an unworthy creature
of the Lord God, speak through the Lord Jesus Christ to Brother
H., the Minister General of our entire Order and to all the ministers general who come after him, to the other custodians and
guardians of the brothers, who are and who will be, that they
might have this writing with them, put it into practice and eagerly
preserve it. I exhort them to guard with care what is written in it
and to have it observed more diligently according to the pleasure
of the all-powerful God, now and forever, as long as the world
lasts.

Blessed by the Lord are you who do these things and may the
Lord be with you forever. Amen.

His words are unequivocal and strong. We hardly expect to read
them in Francis's otherwise uplifting and encouraging writings.
Francis speaks to us here as nowhere else in his writings. On the
one hand, he manifests his humility, a self-deprecation that almost sounds like an insincere abdication of his human dignity;

on the other, he reveals his vivid awareness of being charged with a special mission or charism as he declares emphatically those values that he saw as essential to the gospel life. He writes this letter, then, in a binding and quasi-legislative manner, urging us not only to practice its directives but also to preserve it for future generations. In light of this, he ends as does Paul in many of his letters, promising God's blessing and presence. Yet almost as an after-thought, he then offers us a prayer that sums up better than any other Francis's approach to the trinitarian life he discovered in the Gospels:

> Almighty, eternal, just and merciful God,
> give us miserable ones
> the grace to do for you alone
> what we know you want us to do
> and to desire always what pleases you.
> Inwardly cleansed,
> interiorly enlightened
> and inflamed by the fire of the Holy Spirit,
> may we be able to follow
> in the footprints of Your beloved Son,
> our Lord Jesus Christ,
> and, by Your grace alone,
> may we make our way to You,
> Most High,
> Who live and rule
> in perfect Trinity and simple Unity,
> and are glorified
> God all-powerful,
> forever and ever.
> Amen.

Many authors write of this as *the* Franciscan prayer. Francis beautifully expresses his images of and yearning for the mystery of the triune God. He reiterates that ongoing search for knowledge of God's will that we saw at the very beginning of his journey and, most clearly, his consciousness of the Spirit's activity in that search. We might wonder if Francis is referring to the three classical ways of the spiritual life, the purgative, illuminative, and perfective, when he writes of being "inwardly cleansed, interiorly enlightened and inflamed by the fire of the Holy Spirit." The phrase is certainly reflective of the "Canticle of the Creatures" and even the "Prayer Based on the Our Father." Above all, Francis offers us a prayer with a strong pilgrimage theme expressive of an eagerness to "begin again." Thomas of Celano tells us that Francis always wanted his followers to observe "the laws of pilgrims,...namely, to be gathered under a roof of another, to go about peaceably, to thirst after their homeland." As he was coming to the end of his own journey, Francis offers us this prayer of a pilgrim, reminding us that life is quite simply a quest, a pilgrimage to the fullness of life. The one goal of Francis's vision is to lead us "with the help of grace alone" to God the Most High, who lives and reigns "in perfect Trinity and Simple unity."

The Letter to the Entire Order highlights that other underlying current flowing through the last years of Francis's life, the anxiety of his brothers at the imminent loss of their leader. His biographies are filled with examples of how crucial it was for his brothers to be in close contact with him. He had guided them more by his example than by any lengthy conferences or expositions on gospel values. When his health dramatically started to fail, therefore, a certain panic started to develop among them. They turned repeatedly to him for advice, guidance, and insights into their rule. The following three writings are all examples of this.

The Letter to Brother Anthony

The story of Anthony of Padua's entrance into the Friars Minor is well known. After hearing of the martyrdom of the five brothers in 1220, Anthony, who was educated in Coimbra in the Augustinian tradition, decided to become a follower of Francis. Anthony's early biographers maintain that he was present at the Chapter of Mats in 1221. Were this so, he may well have met Francis. In any case, sometime after the approval of the Later Rule, Anthony was asked by his brothers to use his theological and pedagogical skills. He refused unless Francis himself gave him permission. Word of Anthony's hesitation reached Francis and prompted this response:

Brother Francis sends greetings to Brother Anthony, my Bishop.
I am pleased that you teach sacred theology to the brothers as
long as you "do not extinguish the Spirit of prayer and devotion"
during study of this kind, as is contained in the Rule.

While we have already seen the key passage of this letter in
the Later Rule, "do not extinguish the Spirit of prayer and devotion," it was then presented in the context of manual labor.
Now Francis offers it in the context of the study of theology.
He would have us study theology through the prism of prayer
and devotion, that is, as those who are obviously persons in
whom the Spirit is active. The study or teaching of theology,
Francis maintains, is undoubtedly life-giving and encouraging
of spiritual growth. His words are reminiscent of his fifth admonition, in which we find many of the same sentiments. But they
also foreshadow those eloquent, poetic sentiments of Bonaventure's *Soul's Journey into God:* "I invite the reader to the groans
of prayer through Christ Crucified, through whose blood we are
cleansed from the filth of vice — so that he not believe that reading is sufficient without unction, speculation without devotion,
investigation without wonder, observation without joy, work
without piety, knowledge without love, understanding without
humility, endeavor without divine grace, reflection as a mirror
without divinely inspired wisdom." The Letter to Brother Anthony, then, offers us a precious insight into Francis's approach
to theology.

The Letter to Brother Leo

Leo brings us another perspective on that same anxiety over
Francis's death. The parchment containing the "Praises of God"
and the "Blessing" suggests how Francis responded to what may
have been a temptation of faith that Leo suffered while they
were together on LaVerna. Now we have the impression that
while they were traveling together they discussed some point
concerning the spiritual life. Whatever may have been the case,
we have this precious relic, the second of two texts that were
written by Francis's own hand. It is certainly one of the most
personal of all of the writings that we have read:

Brother Leo, health and peace from Brother Francis!

My son, I speak to you this way — as a mother would — because I put everything we said on the road in this brief message and advice. Afterwards, if you need to come to me for counsel, I advise you thus: In whatever way it seems better to you to please the Lord God and to follow His footprint and poverty, do it with the blessing of the Lord God and my obedience. And if you need and want to come to me for the sake of your soul or for some consolation, Leo, come.

Judging from the contents of this letter, Francis and Leo may well have discussed whether obedience or poverty was the more important virtue or what was the foundation for the gospel way of life that they were trying to follow. Yet for all its simplicity, the letter tells us a great deal about Francis's perceptions not only of gospel life but also of the responsible freedom that comes with maturity in struggling to live it authentically.

"My son," Francis begins in a personal, almost intimate tone, "I speak to you in this way — as a mother would...." Surely the words are reminiscent of both rules, in which Francis expresses his desire that our love and care for one another be modeled on a mother's love and care of her child. Now, however, Francis gives us a beautiful, concrete, tangible, and enduring example of that teaching. Yet he also provides another personal touch that is, unfortunately, lost in our English translation. The very first line contains what seems to be a mistake in the way Francis writes his own name, Francesco. He spells it Francessco, that is, he adds a second *s*, something that is unusual even for someone who is extremely ill. Is it a mistake or the suggestion of a nickname, "Sco"? We will probably never know, but it is certainly an interesting possibility. (In fact, some Italians named Francesco freely admit that their nickname is exactly that, "Sco.") If this is the case, is it any wonder that Leo cherished this relic?

Because of Francis's advice, "In whatever way it seems better to you... do it with the blessing of the Lord God and my obedience," some call this the "Magna Carta of Franciscan Freedom." But is that really the case? St. Augustine's famous dictum, "Love God and do as you please," immediately comes to mind. In this case, we should not overlook Francis's accent on pleasing the Lord God and following Christ's footprint and poverty.

His remarkable statement at the opening of the twenty-second chapter of the Earlier Rule gives us an indication of this: "Now that we have left the world, we have nothing else to do but to follow the will of the Lord and please Him." We have also just seen how Francis expresses a prayer for "the grace to do for you alone what we know you want us to do and to desire always what pleases you." In this advice to Leo, however, Francis accentuates what he undoubtedly discovered was the very heart of the gospel life: following the footprints of Jesus and poverty. In light of those two focal points, Francis's advice is quite straightforward: do whatever is best to follow the example of Christ, especially his poverty.

One scholar examined the handwriting in this letter in conjunction with the parchment that Leo received on LaVerna and concluded that it was written sometime after the experiences of LaVerna. That makes this piece even more remarkable. Was Leo speaking for himself or was he representing a larger group of those eager to know the basics of gospel life? This is another way of wondering if Francis was writing beyond Leo to all of us. In point of fact, that is what has occurred. This letter has become one of those landmark documents in which Francis expresses once more to those who attempt to follow him the essential values that he sees at the heart of his pursuit of the gospel.

The Testament Given at Siena

Francis's health was deteriorating quite rapidly when Brother Elias, the order's vicar, sent him to Siena for some medical treatment. While he was there he began vomiting blood. The brothers became alarmed at the thought that Francis's death was imminent and asked him not only for a blessing but also for a final expression of his will. One of the brothers, Benedict of Pioraco, immediately took down Francis's words:

Write that I bless all my brothers, those who are in the Order and those who will come until the end of the world.... Because of my weakness and the pain of my sickness I am not strong enough to speak; I make known my will to my brothers briefly in these three phrases: as a sign that they remember my blessing and

my testament, let them always love one another, always love and
be faithful to our Lady Holy Poverty, and always be faithful and
subject to the prelates and all clerics of Holy Mother Church.

Now Francis offers us another version of the essential values
that he perceives at the heart of the gospel life: a life of mutual charity, a love of and fidelity to poverty, and a fidelity and
submission to the prelates and clergy of the church. What did
Francis intend? Was this a statement or affirmation of beliefs or
convictions? Or, in a far more biblical sense, "a covenant"? In
the latter sense, the statement of the three values acts as a sort
of Ten Commandments whose observance will be a sign of the
covenant struck between God and Francis and his brothers. Was
this Francis's intention? It is extremely difficult to say.

The *Testament* — Remembrances

Francis began the journey from Siena to Assisi by way of the
Celle of Cortona, a hermitage perched precariously on the side
of a mountain overlooking an expansive Tuscan plain. It was
here that Francis began writing the first section of the work we
call the *Testament*.

The Lord gave me, Brother Francis, thus to begin doing penance in
this way: for when I was in sin, it seemed too bitter for me to see
lepers. The Lord Himself led me among them and I showed a heart
full of mercy to them. When I left them, what had seemed bitter
to me was turned into sweetness of soul and body. Afterwards I
tarried a little and left the world.

Francis begins with a retrospective in which he describes a
world that is strange to us, a world in which God is the starting
point for everything. In a sense, this represents the conclusion
of a journey begun with Francis's call to conversion. Francis "rejoiced to hear a reply of salvation and grace," Thomas of Celano
tells us. "'Francis,' God said to him in spirit, 'what you have
loved carnally and vainly you should now exchange for spiritual things, and taking the bitter for sweet, look down upon
yourself, if you wish to acknowledge me; for you will have a

taste for what I speak of even if the order is reversed.'" Now Francis writes with an order that is, indeed, reversed. He tells us not how he began to turn toward the Lord, but how the Lord enabled him to turn. This is the vision of the mystic, the one who realizes in his poverty that everything finds its source in the goodness and largess of God.

What is so striking about this vision, however, is the event to which Francis attributes the beginning of his conversion. It is not those long periods of prayer that Thomas of Celano presents in his *First Life* nor the dramatic disillusionment with the business or military worlds that all the early biographers describe. It is not a conversion that took place according to any well-tried plan or in any specific place. It is a conversion that took place in an encounter with a human being, one who was looked upon with horror, disdain, and disgust: the leper. By offering this as the starting point of his reflections, Francis presents us a key to what we might call his unique world of asceticism: if you are looking to discover God, look for the leper in your life, the person who is most troubling or abhorrent to you.

Francis continues, however, by telling us precisely what he did in that encounter. He acted with mercy, or more accurately translated, with a heart sensitive to misery. We have encountered that sentiment frequently in Francis's writings — throughout the *Office of the Passion;* the Earlier Rule; the "Exhortation to a Life of Penance," which he wrote for all his followers; and, most especially, the Letter to a Minister, in which we saw him attempting to legislate this virtue for his brothers. Once more we can see how essential acting with a heart that is sensitive to the miserable was to Francis's understanding of the spiritual life. Now, however, he reveals the wonder of the biblical *misericordia* that he has been so eager to exercise: the necessity of personally experiencing misery before being able to reach out to another. One of the lessons of LaVerna seems to have been that of the divine mercy, God assuming our misery in order to reveal the depths of divine love. Thus Francis's eagerness to begin again that he might not miss one opportunity of God's love.

The Lord gave me such faith in churches that I would pray with simplicity in this way and say: "We adore You, Lord Jesus Christ,

in all Your churches throughout the whole world and we praise
You because by Your holy cross You have redeemed the world."

Francis now introduces the Lord's gift of faith and, in particular, of faith in churches. Of course, we might see in this
progress of thought a reflection of Francis's own journey from
the embrace of the leper to his call in the Church of St. Damian
where the Lord called him to rebuild his home. But Francis's
reason for highlighting this gift seems far more focused on recognizing and worshiping God's presence in those sacred places.
How often we have encountered this theme in Francis's writings. Yet although the image of the church appears fifteen times,
Francis generally has it refer to the institutional church. Now he
writes in terms of being a sacred place, a place of prayer where
we can adore the Body and Blood of the Lord, the Lord who has
redeemed us by his cross.

Were we now to go through Francis's writings, we would be
surprised to discover how inconspicuously the concept of faith
and the activity of believing appear. It is as if Francis simply
took faith for granted. Throughout the writings, however, faith
always appears as a gift: from the "Prayer before the Crucifix,"
in which Francis prays for "a correct faith," to the *Testament*,
in which, as we have seen, he attributes his faith to the Lord's
generosity. After LaVerna, however, he describes it as a partic-
ipation in the very energy (*virtus*) of God. If we were able to
date the first admonition, we would see this most forcefully
as Francis writes of "believing according to the Spirit and the
Divinity" and of believing "with spiritual eyes." He clearly expresses the medieval concept of virtue as an energy, a force,
in which we participate in the very energy of God. Nevertheless, Francis focuses our attention on this gift that gives us the
capacity of seeing and believing in a different way, that is, according to the eyes of the Spirit. Thus Francis's understanding
of faith is that of something dynamic, a principle of life that
grows and matures or else diminishes. Was he reflecting on his
own journey of faith and the struggles that he encountered as
he entered more profoundly into the pathos of gospel life? His
Testament prompts us to pause and reflect upon this aspect of
the heritage Francis offers. Without this gift of faith, our vision
is limited.

Afterwards the Lord gave me, and gives me still, such faith in priests who live according to the rite of the holy Roman Church because of their orders that were they to persecute me, I would still want to have recourse to them. If I had as much wisdom as Solomon and found impoverished priests of this world, I would not preach in their parishes against their will. I desire to respect, love, and honor them and all others as my lords. I do not want to consider any sin in them because I discern the Son of God in them and they are my lords. I act in this way because, in this world, I see nothing corporally of the most high Son of God except His most holy Body and Blood which they receive and they alone administer to others. I want to have these most holy mysteries honored and venerated above all things and I want to reserve them in precious places. Wherever I find our Lord's most holy names and written words in unbecoming places, I want to gather them up and I beg that they be gathered up and placed in a becoming place. We must honor all theologians and those who minister the most holy divine words and respect them as those who minister to us spirit and life (cf. John 6:63).

Faith becomes all the more challenging when we read Francis's further reflections on the gift of faith in priests. What is so surprising about this declaration is the concrete expression that Francis's faith takes. He expresses his faith in priests, not the priesthood, and calls us to deal with their human weaknesses. Not only does he promise to have recourse to them; he does so despite the persecution they might inflict on him. In addition to respecting their demands concerning preaching, he also wishes to respect, love, and honor them and not to consider any sin in them. We have seen these sentiments in so many other writings, in *Admonitions*, in the exhortations to the faithful, in the "Exhortation to the Clergy," and, above all, in the Letter to the Entire Order. Now we can sense that integrity that is so eagerly sought by those close to death. In this instance, however, the reason for such reverence and respect is succinctly expressed by Francis for our benefit: "I act in this way because, in this world, I see nothing corporally of the most high Son of God except His Body and Blood which they receive and they alone administer to others." The Eucharist, the Body and Blood of the Most High, that central mystery for Francis, influences his views of priests who are so closely allied with that mystery as extensions of that sacrament and worthy of the same reverence. Yet Francis, who calls those who are priests to be pure and to act purely, to be holy, and to be identified with Christ, possesses a faith that is strong enough to see beyond their sinfulness and human frailty to the very mystery itself, Jesus, the Most High Son of God.

After the Lord gave me some brothers, no one showed me what I had to do, but the Most High Himself revealed to me that I should live according to the pattern of the Holy Gospel. I had this written down simply and in a few words and the Lord Pope confirmed it for me. Those who came to receive life gave *whatever they had* (cf. Tob. 1:3) to the poor and were content with one tunic, patched inside and out, with a cord and short trousers. We desired nothing more. We clerical brothers said the Office as other clerics did; the lay brothers said the *Our Father;* and we quite willingly remained in churches. We were simple and subject to all.

I worked with my hands and I still desire to work; and I earnestly desire all brothers to give themselves to honest work. Let those who do not know how to work learn, not from desire to receive wages, but for example and to avoid idleness. When we are not paid for our work, let us have recourse to the table of the Lord, begging alms from door to door. The Lord revealed a greeting to me that we should say: "May the Lord give you peace."

Francis reminisces about the early days of brotherhood in much the same manner as he did about his conversion, that is, as an initiative of the Lord. It was God who gave him brothers and showed him what to do. His words are even more simple and unadorned; his thought is almost naive, especially as he describes the foundations upon which this brotherhood was built. Francis gives us the impression that he is eager to spell out very clearly and succinctly the guiding principles of the brotherhood, principles that the rapidly expanding brotherhood might all too easily overlook. For the most part, he expressed these repeatedly in the Later Rule, in the Letter to the Entire Order, as well as in the Siena testament. Now, however, he does so in a far more personal context. Is he yearning for those early days when things were simpler? Hardly! More than likely he is only trying to remind us of the simple fact that the Lord had given him followers and had inspired those lofty ideals. It would be the Lord who would continue to do so in the future.

Francis now shifts his thought. No longer does he reminisce as much as he guides us in our pursuit of gospel life.

Let the brothers be careful not to receive in any way churches or poor dwellings or anything else built for them unless they are according to the holy poverty we have promised in the Rule. As pilgrims and strangers, let them always be guests there (cf. 1 Pet. 2:11).

Although the Later Rule is quite emphatic about not appropriating a house or a place, the *Testament* assumes a different position. Now there is a far more realistic approach that recognizes that we need housing. Francis's only request is that these houses be in keeping with poverty and that the brothers live in them as guests who are pilgrims and strangers. He struggles, in other words, to bring reality in accord with the ideal. While he must have found it difficult to compromise on the question of having houses, he remains firm in proposing that neither the houses nor their accessories should tempt us to settle down. This was a call not to become comfortable. No, we were meant to be restless, doomed to search for a home here on earth yet never to find one. We are to be at home only in heaven.

He continues in the same directive manner; in fact he expresses one of his rare commands:

I strictly command all the brothers through obedience, wherever they may be, not to dare to ask any letter from the Roman Curia, either personally or through an intermediary, whether for a church or another place or under the pretext of preaching or the persecution of their bodies. But, wherever they have not been received, let them flee into another country to do penance with the blessing of God.

What was behind this? It's difficult to determine. Francis's companions tell us that one day some brothers approached him with a request to ask the pope for general permission to preach. With such permission, they felt, they and their work for the salvation of souls would be better served than under the existing conditions in which they had to ask the permission of the local bishop. Francis refused. He felt that the care of souls would be more fruitful if it were exercised in union with the clergy. A lack of unity could only destroy.

Yet Francis goes much further by prohibiting *any* letters. When we examine Francis's life, we can see that he accepted privileges that advanced his ideals or helped them, but rejected such privileges decisively when they were against the spirit of poverty and humility. Here there is this definite and all-inclusive form of prohibition as a spontaneous reaction that was well known in his life, a prohibition that of itself is not protest against the curia and its system. The ways of getting such letters from the curia in the Middle Ages are well known. That is why the prohibition is directed against those who use the letters when the gospel ideals, especially those of poverty and humility, might be endangered.

In light of this, Francis calls us to be submissive to everyone and to remain in union with the church expressed through the Divine Office.

I firmly wish to obey the minister general of this fraternity and the other guardian whom it pleases him to give me. I so wish to be a captive in his hands that I cannot go anywhere or do anything beyond obedience and his will for he is my master. Although I may be simple and infirm, I nevertheless want to have a cleric always with me who will celebrate the Office for me as it is prescribed in the Rule. Let all the brothers be bound to obey their guardians and to recite the Office according to the Rule. And if some might have been found who are not reciting the Office according to the Rule and want to change it in some way or who are not Catholics, let all the brothers, wherever they may have found one of them, be bound through obedience to bring him before the custodian of that place nearest to where they found him. Let the custodian be strictly bound through obedience to keep him securely day and night as a man in chain, so that he cannot be taken from his hands until he can personally deliver him into the hands of his minister. Let the minister be bound through obedience to send him with such brothers who would guard him as a prisoner until they deliver him to the Lord of Ostia, who is the Lord, the Protector and the Corrector of this fraternity.

Once again we read a passage that clearly indicates the growth of the brotherhood, in this instance, the growth of its external organization. Moreover, we see Francis's gracious acceptance of it. Although he is its founder, principle inspiration, and guide, he asks for no exceptions. No, he quite simply expresses his desire to obey, to be subject to another, and to follow almost blindly the wishes of the other. The obedience described by this passage of Francis's *Testament* is far more strict than what we have encountered earlier in its proposition and conception of obedience.

The problem of obedience must have been a trying one during Francis's last years. In his Letter to the Entire Order we saw him issue a strong warning to follow the rule. In the same passage he also insisted on celebrating the Divine Office: "I do not consider those brothers who do not wish to observe these things Catholics or my brothers; I do not even wish to see or speak with them until they have done penance. I even say this about all those who wander about, having put aside the discipline of the Rule, for our Lord Jesus Christ gave His life that He would not lose the obedience of His most holy Father." Did Francis consider unity with the brotherhood and with the church as synonymous? It seems that he did, for he insists on celebrating the Divine Office in the same breath as staying within the bonds of obedience.

He concludes by offering us his own interpretation of this document:

Let the brothers not say: "This is another rule." Because this is a remembrance, admonition, exhortation and my testament which I, little brother Francis, make for you, my blessed brothers, that we might observe the Rule we have promised in a more Catholic manner.

Let the minister general and all the other ministers and custodians be bound through obedience not to add to or take away from these words. Let them always have this writing with them together with the Rule. In all the Chapters they hold, when they read the Rule, let them also read these words. I strictly command all my cleric and lay brothers, through obedience, not to place any gloss upon the Rule or upon these words saying: "They should be understood in this way." But as the Lord has given me simply and purely to speak and write the Rule and these words, may you understand them simply and without gloss and observe them with a holy activity until the end.

Was Francis projecting that some would consider his *Testament* a new law, in the sense of a new rule? Undoubtedly! Thus this clear, to-the-point statement that he intended this to be an admonition and exhortation, possibly similar to those twenty-eight admonitions that speak so deeply and were considered so highly. In this instance, however, Francis gives these guidelines to gospel life not in the sense of a "change" but in the sense of a necessary direction or position in reaction to some new, developing concerns. More importantly, he offers this interpretation in reaction to a permissive and perhaps legalistic casuistry. Francis reminds us once again of the Lord's role in the writing of the rule and *Testament* "simply and plainly."

What is so very clear in the *Testament* is that Francis's "last will" is, in the real sense, not the content of the *Testament* but that of the rule. It absorbed so much of his thought during these last years, even in these last few hours. How clearly we can see this concern in these final verses as he directs his brothers to read the rule together with these final thoughts when they gather together in chapter.

Finally he blesses us:

Whoever observes these things, let him be blessed in heaven with the blessing of the Most High Father and on earth with the blessing of His Beloved Son with the Most High Spirit the Paraclete and all the powers of heaven and all the saints. And, as far as I can, I, little brother Francis, your servant, confirm for you, both within and without, this most holy blessing.

His words flow even in his last moments in that trinitarian pattern to which we have become so accustomed, and he leaves us with those images of himself with which we have become so familiar, "little brother Francis, your servant."

The Final Hours

Francis dictated two letters during the last hours of his life, letters that reveal his more sentimental side. The first of these was yet another echo of his desire to return to the early days. Thomas of Celano writes of Bernard of Quintavalle: "St. Francis rejoiced with very great joy over the coming and conversion of so great a man, in that the Lord was seen to have a care for him by giving him a needed companion and a faithful friend." The two were together during the very first days of the order, traveled together to Rome to present their form of life to Pope Innocent, and later journeyed to France in 1213 and to Spain in 1215. As Francis lay dying, Bernard was living as a hermit on Monte Subasio. Francis asked him to leave his solitude and to be at his side and, once there, Francis said:

Write this just as I tell you: Brother Bernard was the first brother whom the Lord gave me, as well as the first to put into practice and fulfill most completely the perfection of the Holy Gospel by distributing all his goods to the poor. Because of this and many other prerogatives, I am bound to love him more than any other brother of the entire Order. Therefore, I desire and command, as much as I can, that whoever is the general minister, he should cherish and honor him as he would me, and, likewise, the provincial ministers and the brothers of the entire Order should esteem him in place of me.

Then he dictated a letter for Lady Jacoba da Settesoli. Lady "Brother" Jacoba was one of the prominent members of the lay penitents and frequently offered Francis hospitality during his visits to Rome. Francis had just finished dictating his final message to her when she arrived at the Portiuncula. Francis's companions tell us: "The holy woman was discovered to have brought everything for the burial of her father that the letter written just a short time before had requested. For she brought an ashen-colored cloth with which the body of the deceased would be covered, many candles, a veil for his face, a little pillow for his head, and a certain sweetmeat that the saint had desired."

The moment of his death had arrived. His companions tell

us of yet another detail: "Although St. Francis's illnesses were very grievous, he praised the Lord with great fervor of spirit and gladness within and without and said to them: 'If I am going to die soon, call Brother Angelo and Brother Leo to me that they may sing to me of Sister Death.'" Leo and Angelo were now present and heard Francis sing the final verse of the "Canticle of the Creatures," which he had composed "to the praise of God and for the comfort of his soul and those of others."

> Praise be You, my Lord, through our Sister Bodily Death,
>   from whom no one living can escape.
> Woe to those who die in mortal sin.
> Blessed are those whom death will find in Your most holy will,
>   for the second death shall do them no harm.

The death of the body is no longer something to be feared or dreaded, Francis sings. Now it is a sister, an instrument of God's presence, to be welcomed and embraced. When she finds us doing God's will, the last judgment, the second death, will not harm us. It was as if Francis knew that everything he had tasted of in this world was only a foretaste of what was to come. Thus his sorrow for those who died in mortal sin and his conviction that those whose concern is simply God's will are blessed.

Francis's last words were, then, the refrain of his "Canticle of the Creatures." As Sister Bodily Death met the Lord's servant, naked as when he entered the world, he sang ever so poignantly and left us, in all its simplicity, a reflection of his entire life.

> Praise and bless my Lord and give Him thanks
> and serve Him with great humility.

Bibliography

Works Cited

Asseldonk, Optatus Van. *See below under "Selected Secondary Sources."*

Chesterton, G. K. *Heretics.* New York: Dodd Mead & Co., 1925.

———. *Saint Francis of Assisi.* New York: George H. Doran Co., 1924.

Connolly, William J. "Noticing Key Interior Facts in the Early Stages of Spiritual Direction." *Review for Religious* 35 (1976): 112–21.

Galilea, Segundo. "On Being a Bridge-Generation: Religious Men and Women in Latin America." In *Latin American Theologians on Religious Life.* Quezon City, Philippines: Claretian Publications, 1989, 36–37.

Leclerc, Eloi. *The Canticle of Creatures: Symbols of Union.* Chicago: Franciscan Herald Press, 1978.

Lonergan, Bernard. *Method in Theology.* London: Darton, Longman & Todd, 1972.

Merton, Thomas. *New Seeds of Contemplation.* New York: New Directions, 1962.

Powicke, Maurice. "The Life of Ailred of Rievaulx by Walter Daniel." In *Nelson's Medieval Classics.* Oxford: Oxford University Press, 1950.

Ridley, Matt, and Bobbi S. Low. "Can Selfishness Save the Environment?" *Atlantic Monthly* 272, no. 3 (1993): 76–86.

Voillaume, René. *Seeds of the Desert.* London: Burns & Oates, 1955.

English Translation of Francis of Assisi's Works

Francis and Clare: The Complete Works. Edited and translated by Regis J. Armstrong and Ignatius C. Brady. New York: Paulist Press, 1982. This volume contains all the writings of Francis of Assisi, together with those of Clare of Assisi (1193–1253), and offers invaluable footnotes for understanding many nuances of the texts.

Selected Secondary Sources

Asseldonk, Optatus van. "The Spirit of the Lord and Its Holy Activity in the Writings of Francis." *Greyfriars Review* 5 (1991): 103–58. A thorough study of the theology of the Holy Spirit found in Francis's writings.

Englebert, Omer. *Saint Francis of Assisi.* Translated by Eve Marie Cooper. 2d English edition, revised and augmented by Ignatius Brady and Raphael Brown. Chicago: Franciscan Herald Press, 1965. A thorough, easy-to-read biography of Francis that, in its revised edition, offers precise footnotes.

Esser, Kajetan. "Meditations on *The Admonitions* of St. Francis of Assisi." *Greyfriars Review* 6 (1992). A meditative study of each of Francis's twenty-eight admonitions.

Fortini, Arnaldo. *Francis of Assisi.* Translated by Helen Moak. New York: Crossroad, 1981. The volume provides invaluable information concerning Francis and Assisi during his lifetime.

Green, Julian. *God's Fool: The Life and Times of Francis of Assisi.* Translated by Peter Heinegg. San Francisco: Harper and Row, 1983. A thoughtful, provocative life of Francis written in brief chapters that make it ideal for meditation.

Iriarte, Lazaro. *Franciscan Calling.* Chicago: Franciscan Herald Press, 1974.

Lehmann, Leonhard. "The Man Francis as Seen in His Letters." *Greyfriars Review* 5 (1991): 159–90.

Manselli, Raoul. "The Spirituality of St. Francis of Assisi." *Greyfriars Review* 3 (1989): 43–54.

Nguyen-Van-Khanh, Norbert. *The Teacher of His Heart: Jesus Christ in the Thought and Writings of Saint Francis.* Translated by Edward Hagman. St. Bonaventure, N.Y.: Franciscan Institute Publications, 1993. A study of the role of Christ in the writings and spirituality of Francis.

Schmucki, Oktavian. "The Passion of Christ in the Life of St. Francis of Assisi: A Comparative Study of the Sources in Light of Devotion to the Passion Practiced in His Time." *Greyfriars Review* 4 (1990).

———. "St. Francis's Letter to the Entire Order." *Greyfriars Review* 3 (1989): 1–42.

———. "The 'Way of Life according to the Gospel' as It Was Discovered by St. Francis of Assisi." *Greyfriars Review* 2 (1988): 1–56.